PHILOSOPHICAL STUDIES

Philosophical Studies

By

G. E. MOORE, Litt.D.

Hon. LL.D. (St. Andrews), F.B.A.
Lecturer in Moral Science in the University of Cambridge
Author of "Principia Ethica"

LONDON

ROUTLEDGE & KEGAN PAUL LTD

BROADWAY HOUSE: 68–74 CARTER LANE, E.C.4

First published 1922
Reprinted 1948
Reprinted 1951
Reprinted 1958
Reprinted 1960
Reprinted 1965
Reprinted 1970

ISBN 0 7100 3001 0

Printed in Great Britain
by Redwood Press Limited,
Trowbridge & London

CONTENTS

Those of the papers in this volume, which have been previously published, originally appeared as follows :—

PREFACE

ALL the papers contained in this volume, except the two ethical ones (VIII and X), have been previously published; and of those which have been previously published all, except that on "External and Internal Relations" (IX), are here re-printed without change. They were written at various dates between 1903 and 1921, and all are here printed in the order in which they were written, except that VIII on "The Conception of Intrinsic Value," which was written earlier than VI and VII, has been moved out of its proper place in order to bring it nearer to IX and X, to both of which it is closely related in subject.

All, except IV and X, were primarily intended for an audience familiar with the writings of philosophers; but I hope that they may nevertheless prove intelligible even to those who have read little or no philosophy, since I make little use of technical terms, and, where I have done so, have done my best to explain in ordinary language exactly what I mean by them. The tone of X is somewhat different from that of the rest, because it was written as a lecture for the *Leicester Philosophical Society*, with regard to which I was informed that I must not assume any previous acquaintance with philosophy in most of the audience. It accordingly bears marks throughout of the kind of audience for which it was intended.

An attentive reader will easily discover that some of the views expressed in some of the papers are inconsistent with views expressed in others. The fact is that some of the views expressed in some of the earlier ones are views with which I no longer agree ; and I feel that some apology is needed for nevertheless republishing them exactly as they stood. In all cases, except one, my excuse is that the mistaken views in question are so embedded in the form and substance of the papers in which they occur, that it would have been impossible to correct them without practically substituting new papers for the old ones ; and that, in spite of these mistakes, the old papers, as they stand, still seem to me, on the whole, to say things which are worth saying in a form which, however defective it may be, I doubt my own ability to improve upon. The only case in which I doubt whether this excuse applies is that of the first paper—" The Refutation of Idealism." This paper now appears to me to be very confused, as well as to embody a good many down-right mistakes; so I am doubtful whether I ought to have included it. But in this case I have another excuse: namely that it is a paper to which a good many allusions have been made by contemporary writers on philosophy; and I was told that, for some readers at all events, it would be a convenience that it should be reprinted along with the rest, if only for the sake of reference.

I said above that the only one of the previously published papers, in which changes have been made, is IX on "External and Internal Relations." In this case the changes are not due to any change in my views, but to the fact that, in that part of the paper in which symbols are used, I tried, when it was first published in the _Proceedings of the Aristotelian Society_, to use the symbols adopted by Whitehead and Russell in _Principia Mathematica_, and used them also without giving an explanation of their meaning which would be sufficient for readers not acquainted with that work. The symbols in question are symbols which it is difficult for printers to reproduce; and I have, therefore, thought it better, on this occasion, to use another set of symbols, which seem to me to be adequate for the limited purpose I had in view. I have tried to give an explanation of their meaning, which will enable anyone to understand them; and I have taken the opportunity of rewriting some of the parts of the paper in which they occur in a way which will, I hope, make some points clearer than they originally were.

I have to thank the Committee of the Aristotelian Society for permission to reprint the large number of papers (viz., II, III, V, VI, VII and IX), which originally appeared in the _Proceedings_ of that Society; and the Editor of the _New Quarterly_ for permission to reprint the article on Hume's Philosophy (IV), which appeared in that Journal in November, 1909.

G. E. MOORE.

CAMBRIDGE,
    January, 1922.

Philosophical Studies

—

THE REFUTATION OF IDEALISM

MODERN Idealism, if it asserts any general conclusion about the universe at all, asserts that it is
spiritual. There are two points about this assertion
to which I wish to call attention. These points are
that, whatever be its exact meaning, it is certainly
meant to assert (1) that the universe is very
different indeed from what it seems, and (2) that
it has quite a large number of properties which it
does not seem to have. Chairs and tables and
mountains *seem* to be very different from us ; but,
when the whole universe is declared to be spiritual,
it is certainly meant to assert that they are far
more like us than we think. The idealist means
to assert that they are *in some sense* neither lifeless
nor unconscious, as they certainly seem to be ; and
I do not think his language is so grossly deceptive,
but that we may assume him to believe that they
really are very different indeed from what they
seem. And secondly when he declares that they
are *spiritual,* he means to include in that term quite
a large number of different properties. When the
whole universe is declared to be spiritual, it is
meant not only that it is in some sense *conscious,*
but that it has what we recognise in ourselves as
the *higher* forms of consciousness. That it is
intelligent ; that it is purposeful ; that it is not

mechanical ; all these different things are commonly asserted of it. In general, it may be said, this phrase 'reality is spiritual' excites and expresses the belief that the *whole* universe possesses *all the qualities* the possession of which is held to make us so superior to things which seem to be inani-mate : at least, if it does not possess exactly those which we possess, it possesses not one only, but several others, which, by the same ethical standard, would be judged equal to or better than our own. When we say it is *spiritual* we mean to say that it has quite a number of excellent qualities, different from any which we commonly attribute either to stars or planets or to cups and saucers.

Now why I mention these two points is that when engaged in the intricacies of philosophic discussion, we are apt to overlook the vastness of the difference between this idealistic view and the ordinary view of the world, and to overlook the number of *different* propositions which the idealist must prove. It is, I think, owing to the vastness of this difference and owing to the number of different excellences which Idealists attribute to the universe, that it seems such an interesting and important question whether Idealism be true or not. But, when we begin to argue about it, I think we are apt to forget what a vast number of arguments this interesting question must involve : we are apt to assume, that if one or two points be made on either side, the whole case is won. I say this lest it should be thought that any of the arguments which will be advanced in this paper would be sufficient to disprove, or any refutation of them sufficient to prove, the truly interesting and im-portant proposition that reality is spiritual. For my own part I wish it to be clearly understood that I do not suppose that anything I shall say has the smallest tendency to prove that reality is not spiritual : I do not believe it possible to refute a single one of the many important propositions contained in the assertion that it is so. Reality may be spiritual, for all I know ; and I devoutly hope it is. But I take 'Idealism' to be a wide term and to include not only this interesting conclusion but a number of arguments which are supposed to be, if not sufficient, at least *necessary*, to prove it. Indeed I take it that modern Idealists are chiefly distinguished by certain arguments which they have in common. That reality is spiritual has, I believe, been the tenet of many theologians ; and yet, for believing that alone, they should hardly be called Idealists. There are besides, I believe, many persons, not improperly called Idealists, who hold certain characteristic propositions, without venturing to think them quite sufficient to prove so grand a conclusion. It is, therefore, only with Idealistic *arguments* that I am concerned ; and if any Idealist holds that *no* argument is necessary to prove that reality is spiritual, I shall certainly not have refuted him. I shall, however, attack at least one argument, which, to the best of my belief, is considered necessary to their position by *all* Idealists. And I wish to point out a certain advantage which this procedure gives me—an advantage which justifies the assertion that, if my arguments are sound, they will have refuted Idealism. If I can refute a single proposition which is a necessary and essential step in all Idealistic arguments, then, no matter how good the rest of these arguments may be, I shall have proved that Idealists have *no reason whatever* for their conclusion.

Suppose we have a chain of argument which takes the form : Since A is B, and B is C, and C is D, it follows A is D. In such an argument, though 'B is C' and 'C is D' may both be perfectly true, yet if ' A is B ' be false, we have no more reason for asserting A is D than if all three were false.   It does not, indeed, follow that A is D is false ; nor does it follow that no other arguments would prove it to be true.   But it does follow that, so far as this argument goes, it is the barest supposition, without the least bit of evidence.   I propose to attack a proposition which seems to me to stand in this relation to the conclusion ' Reality is spiritual.'   I do not propose to dispute that ' Reality is spiritual ; ' I do not deny that there may be reasons for thinking that it is : but I do propose to show that one reason upon which, to the best of my judgment, all other arguments ever used by Idealists depend is *false.* These other arguments may, for all I shall say, be eminently ingenious and true ; they are very many and various, and different Idealists use the most different arguments to prove the same most important conclusions.   Some of these *may* be sufficient to prove that B is C and C is D ; but if, as I shall try to show, their ' A is B ' is false the conclusion A is D remains a pleasant supposition. I do not deny that to suggest pleasant and plaus- ible suppositions may be the proper function of philosophy : but I am assuming that the name Idealism can only be properly applied where there is a certain amount of argument, intended to be cogent.

The subject of this paper is, therefore, quite uninteresting.   Even if I prove my point, I shall have proved nothing about the Universe in general. Upon the important question whether Reality is or is not spiritual my argument will not have the remotest bearing.   I shall only attempt to arrive at the truth about a matter, which is in itself quite trivial and insignificant, and from which, so far as I can see and certainly so far as I shall say, no con- clusions can be drawn about any of the subjects about which we most want to know. The only importance I can claim for the subject I shall investigate is that it seems to me to be a matter upon which not Idealists only, but all philosophers and psychologists also, have been in error, and from their erroneous view of which they have inferred (validly or invalidly) their most striking and interesting conclusions. And that it has even this importance I cannot hope to prove. If it has this importance, it will indeed follow that all the most striking results of philosophy — Sensationalism. Agnosticism and Idealism alike—have, for all that has hitherto been urged in their favour, no more foundation than the supposition that a chimera lives in the moon. It will follow that, unless new reasons never urged hitherto can be found, all the most important philosophic doctrines have as little claim to assent as the most superstitious beliefs of the lowest savages. Upon the question what we have *reason* to believe in the most interesting matters, I do therefore think that my results will have an important bearing ; but I cannot too clearly insist that upon the question whether these beliefs are true they will have none whatever.

The trivial proposition which I propose to dispute is this : that *esse* is *percipi*. This is a very ambiguous proposition, but, in some sense or other, it has been very widely held. That it is, in some sense, essential to Idealism, I must for the present merely assume. What I propose to show is that, in all the senses ever given to it, it is false.

But, first of all, it may be useful to point out briefly in what relation I conceive it to stand to Idealistic arguments. That wherever you can truly predicate *esse* you can truly predicate *percipi*, in some sense or other, is, I take it, a necessary step in all arguments, properly to be called Idealistic, and, what is more, in all arguments hitherto offered for the Idealistic conclusion. If *esse* is *percipi*, this is at once equivalent to saying that whatever is, is experienced; and this, again, is equivalent, in a sense, to saying that whatever is, is something mental. But this is not the sense in which the Idealist *conclusion* must maintain that Reality is *mental*. The Idealist *conclusion* is that *esse* is *percipere*; and hence, whether *esse* be *percipi* or not, a further and different discussion is needed to show whether or not it is also *percipere*. And again, even if *esse* be *percipere*, we need a vast quantity of further argument to show that what has *esse* has also those higher mental qualities which are denoted by spiritual. This is why I said that the question I should discuss, namely, whether or not *esse* is *percipi*, must be utterly insufficient either to prove or to disprove that reality is spiritual. But, on the other hand, I believe that every argument ever used to show that reality is spiritual has inferred this (validly or invalidly) from '*esse* is *percipere*' as one of its premisses; and that this again has never been pretended to be proved except by use of the premiss that *esse* is *percipi*. The type of argument used for the latter purpose is familiar enough. It is said that since whatever is, is experienced, and since some things are which are not experienced by the individual, these must at least form part of some experience. Or again that, since an object necessarily implies a subject, and since the whole world must be an object, we must conceive it to belong to some subject or subjects, in the same sense in which whatever is the object of our experience belongs to us. Or again, that, since thought enters into the essence of all reality, we must conceive behind it, in it, or as its essence, a spirit akin to ours, who think: that 'spirit greets spirit' in its object. Into the validity of these inferences I do not propose to enter: they obviously require a great deal of discussion. I only desire to point out that, however correct they may be, yet if *esse* is not *percipi*, they leave us as far from a proof that reality is spiritual, as if they were all false too.

But now : Is *esse percipi* ?   There are three very ambiguous terms in this proposition, and I must begin by distinguishing the different things that may be meant by some of them.

And first with regard to *percipi*.   This term need not trouble us long at present.   It was, perhaps, originally used to mean 'sensation' only ; but I am not going to be so unfair to modern Idealists—the only Idealists to whom the term should now be applied without qualification—as to hold that, if they say *esse* is *percipi*, they mean by *percipi* sensation only.   On the contrary I quite agree with them that, if *esse* be *percipi* at all, *percipi* must be understood to include not sensation only, but that other type of mental fact, which is called 'thought'; and, whether *esse* be *percipi* or not, I consider it to be the main service of the philosophic school, to which modern Idealists belong, that they have insisted on distinguishing 'sensation' and 'thought' and on emphasising the importance of the latter.   Against Sensationalism and Empiricism they have maintained the true view.   But the distinction between sensation and thought need not detain us here.   For, in whatever respects they differ, they have at least this in common, that they are both forms of consciousness or, to use a term that seems to be more in fashion just now, they are both ways of experiencing.   Accordingly, whatever *esse* is *percipi* may mean, it does *at least* assert that whatever is, is *experienced*.   And since what I wish to maintain is, that even this is untrue, the question whether it be experienced by way of sensation or thought or both is for my purpose quite irrelevant.   If it be not experienced at all, it

cannot be either an object of thought or an object
of sense.   It is only if being involves 'experience'
that the question, whether it involves sensation or
thought or both, becomes important.   I beg,
therefore, that *percipi* may be understood, in what
follows, to refer merely to what is *common* to
sensation and thought.   A very recent article
states the meaning of *esse* is *percipi* with all desirable clearness in so far as *percipi* is concerned.
'I will undertake to show,' says Mr. Taylor, [1] 'that
what makes [any piece of fact] real can be nothing
but its presence as an inseparable aspect of *a
sentient experience.*'   I am glad to think that Mr.
Taylor has been in time to supply me with so
definite a statement that this is the ultimate premiss
of Idealism.   My paper will at least refute Mr.
Taylor's Idealism, if it refutes anything at all: for I
shall undertake to show that what makes a thing
real cannot possibly be its presence as an inseparable
aspect of a senient experience.

But Mr. Taylor's statement though clear, I think,
with regard to the meaning of *percipi* is highly
ambiguous in other respects.   I will leave it for
the present to consider the next ambiguity in the
statement: *Esse* is *percipi.*   What does the copula
mean?   What can be meant by saying that Esse
is percipi?   There are just three meanings, one or
other of which such a statement *must* have, if it
is to be true; and of these there is only one which
it can have, if it is to be important.   (1) The
statement may be meant to assert that the word
'esse' is used to signify nothing either more or less
than the word 'percipi': that the two words are
precise synonyms: that they are merely different
names for one and the same thing: that what is
meant by *esse* is absolutely identical with what is

meant by *percipi*. I think I need not prove that the principle *esse* is *percipi* is *not* thus intended merely to define a word ; nor yet that, if it were, it would be an extremely bad definition. But if it does *not* mean this, only two alternatives remain. The second is (2) that what is meant by *esse*, though not absolutely identical with what is meant by *percipi*, yet *includes* the latter as a *part* of its meaning. If this were the meaning of 'esse is percipi,' then to say that a thing was real would not be the same thing as to say that it was experienced. That it was *real* would mean that it was experienced and *something else besides*: 'being experienced' would be *analytically essential* to reality, but would not be the whole meaning of the term. From the fact that a thing was real we should be able to infer, by the law of contradiction, that it was experienced ; since the latter would be *part* of what is meant by the former. But, on the other hand, from the fact a thing was experienced we should *not* be able to infer that it was real ; since it would not follow from the fact that it had one of the attributes essential to reality, that it *also* had the other or others. Now, if we understand *esse* is *percipi* in this second sense, we must distinguish *three* different things which it asserts. First of all, it gives a definition of the word 'reality,' asserting that word stands for a complex whole, of which what is meant by 'percipi' forms a part. And secondly it asserts that 'being experienced' forms a part of a certain whole. Both these propositions may be true, and at all events I do not wish to dispute them. I do not, indeed, think that the word 'reality' is commonly used to include 'percipi': but I do not wish to argue about the meaning of words. And that many things which are experienced are also something else—that to be experienced forms part of certain wholes, is, of course, indisputable.   But what I wish to point out is, that neither of these propositions is of any importance, unless we add to them a *third*.   That 'real' is a convenient name for a union of attributes which *sometimes* occurs, it could not be worth any one's while to assert: no inferences of any importance could be drawn from such an assertion. Our principle could only mean that when a thing happens to have *percipi* as well as the other qualities included under *esse*, it has *percipi* : and we should never be able to *infer* that it was experienced, except from a proposition which already asserted that it was both experienced and something else. Accordingly, if the assertion that *percipi* forms part of the whole meant by reality is to have any importance, it must mean that the whole is organic, at least in this sense, that the other constituent or constituents of it *cannot* occur without percipi, even if percipi can occur without them.   Let us call these other constituents x.   The proposition that *esse* includes *percipi*, and that therefore from *esse percipi* can be inferred, can only be important if it is meant to assert that *percipi* can be inferred from x. The only importance of the question whether the whole *esse* includes the part *percipi* rests therefore on the question whether the part x is necessarily connected with the part *percipi*.   And this is (3) the third possible meaning of the assertion *esse is percipi* : and, as we now see, the only important one.   *Esse* is *percipi* asserts that wherever you have x you also have *percipi* that whatever has the property x also has the property that it is *experienced*.   And this being so, it will be convenient if, for the future, I may be allowed to use the term '*esse*' to denote x *alone*.   I do not wish thereby to beg the question whether what we commonly mean by the word 'real' does or does not include *percipi* as well as x.   I am quite content that my definition of 'esse' to denote x, should be regarded merely as an arbitrary verbal definition. Whether it is so or not, the only question of interest is whether from x *percipi* can be inferred, and I should prefer to be able to express this in the form : can *percipi* be inferred from *esse* ?   Only let it be understood that when I say *esse*, that term will not for the future *include percipi* : it denotes only that x, which Idealists, perhaps rightly, include *along with percipi* under *their* term *esse*.   That there is such an x they must admit on pain of making the proposition an *absolute* tautology ; and that from this x *percipi* can be inferred they must admit, on pain of making it a perfectly barren analytic proposition.   Whether x alone should or should not be called *esse* is not worth a dispute : what is worth dispute is whether *percipi* is necessarily connected with x.

We have therefore discovered the ambiguity of the copula in *esse* is *percipi*, so far as to see that this principle asserts two distinct terms to be so related, that whatever has the *one*, which I call *esse*, has *also* the property that it is experienced.   It asserts a necessary connexion between *esse* on the one hand and *percipi* on the other ; these two words denoting each a distinct term, and *esse* denoting a term in which that denoted by *percipi* is not included.   We have, then in *esse* is *percipi*, a *necessary synthetic* proposition which I have undertaken to refute.   And I may say at once that, understood as such, it cannot be refuted.   If the Idealist chooses to assert that it is merely a self-evident truth, I have only to say that it does not appear to me to be so.   But I believe that no Idealist ever has maintained it to be so.   Although this—that two distinct terms are necessarily related—is the only sense which 'esse is percipi' can have if it is to be true and important, it *can* have another sense, if it is to be an important falsehood. I believe that Idealists all hold this important falsehood. They do not perceive that *Esse* is *percipi* must, if true, be *merely* a self-evident synthetic truth : they either identify with it or give as a reason for it another proposition which must be false because it is self-contradictory. Unless they did so, they would have to admit that it was a perfectly unfounded assumption ; and if they recognised that it was *unfounded*, I do not think they would maintain its truth to be evident. *Esse* is *percipi*, in the sense I have found for it, *may* indeed be true ; I cannot refute it : but if this sense were clearly apprehended, no one, I think, would *believe* that it was true.

Idealists, we have seen, must assert that whatever is experienced, is *necessarily* so. And this doctrine they commonly express by saying that 'the object of experience is inconceivable apart from the subject.' I have hitherto been concerned with pointing out what meaning this assertion must have, if it is to be an important truth. I now propose to show that it may have an important meaning, which must be false, because it is self-contradictory.

It is a well-known fact in the history of philosophy that *necessary* truths in general, but especially those of which it is said that the opposite is inconceivable, have been commonly supposed to be *analytic*, in the sense that the proposition denying them was self-contradictory. It was in this way, commonly supposed, before Kant, that many truths could be proved by the law of contradiction alone. This is, therefore, a mistake which it is plainly easy for the best philosophers to make. Even since Kant many have continued to assert it ; but I am aware that among those Idealists, who most properly deserve the name, it has become more fashionable to assert that truths are *both* analytic and synthetic. Now

with many of their reasons for asserting this I am
not concerned : it is possible that in some connexions the assertion may bear a useful and true
sense. But if we understand 'analytic' in the
sense just defined, namely, what is proved by the
law of contradiction *alone*, it is plain that, if
'synthetic' means what is *not* proved by this alone,
no truth can be both analytic and synthetic. Now
it seems to me that those who do maintain truths
to be both, do nevertheless maintain that they are
so in this as well as in other senses. It is, indeed,
extremely unlikely that so essential a part of the
historical meaning of 'analytic' and 'synthetic'
should have been entirely discarded, especially
since we find no express recognition that it is discarded. In that case it is fair to suppose that
modern Idealists have been influenced by the view
that certain truths can be proved by the law of
contradiction alone. I admit they also expressly
declare that they can *not :* but this is by no means
sufficient to prove that they do not also think they
are ; since it is very easy to hold two mutually
contradictory opinions. What I suggest then is
that Idealists hold the particular doctrine in
question, concerning the relation of subject and
object in experience, because they think it is an
analytic truth in this restricted sense that it is
proved by the law of contradiction alone.

I am suggesting that the Idealist maintains that
object and subject are necessarily connected, mainly
because he fails to see that they are *distinct*, that
they are *two*, at all. When he thinks of 'yellow'
and when he thinks of the 'sensation of yellow,'
he fails to see that there is anything whatever in
the latter which is not in the former. This being
so, to deny that yellow can ever *be* apart from the
sensation of yellow is merely to deny that yellow
can ever be other than it is ; since yellow and the

sensation of yellow are absolutely identical. To assert that yellow is necessarily an object of experience is to assert that yellow is necessarily yellow—a purely identical proposition, and therefore proved by the law of contradiction alone. Of course, the proposition also implies that experience is, after all, something distinct from yellow—else there would be no reason for insisting that yellow is a sensation : and that the argument thus both affirms and denies that yellow and sensation of yellow are distinct, is what sufficiently refutes it. But this contradiction can easily be overlooked, because though we are convinced, in other connexions, that 'experience' does mean something and something most important, yet we are never distinctly aware *what* it means, and thus in every particular case we do not notice its presence. The facts present themselves as a kind of antinomy : (1) Experience *is* something unique and different from anything else ; (2) Experience of green is entirely indistinguishable from green ; two propositions which cannot both be true. Idealists, holding both, can only take refuge in arguing from the one in some connexions and from the other in others.

But I am well aware that there are many Idealists who would repel it as an utterly unfounded charge that they fail to distinguish between a sensation or idea and what I will call its object. And there are, I admit, many who not only imply, as we all do, that green is distinct from the sensation of green, but expressly insist upon the distinction as an important part of their system. They would perhaps only assert that the two form an inseparable unity. But I wish to point out that many, who use this phrase, and who do admit the distinction, are not thereby absolved from the charge that they deny it. For there is a certain doctrine, very

prevalent among philosophers nowadays, which by
a very simple reduction may be seen to assert that
two distinct things both are and are not distinct.
A distinction is asserted ; but it is *also* asserted that
the things distinguished form an 'organic unity,'
But, forming such a unity, it is held, each would
not be what it is *apart from its relation to the other.*
Hence to consider either by itself is to make an
illegitimate abstraction. The recognition that there
are 'organic unities' and 'illegitimate abstractions'
in this sense is regarded as one of the chief con-
quests of modern philosophy. But what is the
sense attached to these terms? An abstraction is
illegitimate, when and only when we attempt to
assert of *a part*—of something abstracted—that
which is true only of the *whole* to which it belongs :
and it may perhaps be useful to point out that this
should not be done. But the application actually
made of this principle, and what perhaps would be
expressly acknowledged as its meaning, is something much the reverse of useful. The principle is
used to assert that certain abstractions are *in all
cases* illegitimate ; that whenever you try to assert
anything whatever of that which is *part* of an
organic whole, what you assert can only be true of
the whole. And this principle, so far from being a
useful truth, is necessarily false. For if the whole
can, nay *must*, be substituted for the part in all
propositions and for all purposes, this can only be
because the whole is absolutely identical with the
part. When, therefore, we are told that green and
the sensation of green are certainly distinct but
yet are not separable, or that it is an illegitimate
abstraction to consider the one apart from the other,
what these provisos are used to assert is, that
though the two things are distinct yet you not only
can but must treat them as if they were not. Many
philosophers, therefore, when they admit a dis-

tinction, yet (following the lead of Hegel) boldly assert their right, in a slightly more obscure form of words, *also* to deny it. The principle of organic unities, like that of combined analysis and synthesis, is mainly used to defend the practice of holding *both* of two contradictory propositions, wherever this may seem convenient. In this, as in other matters, Hegel's main service to philosophy has consisted in giving a name to and erecting into a principle, a type of fallacy to which experience had shown philosophers, along with the rest of mankind, to be addicted. No wonder that he has followers and admirers.

I have shown then, so far, that when the Idealist asserts the important principle '*Esse* is *percipi*' he must, if it is to be true, mean by this that : Whatever is experienced also *must* be experienced. And I have also shown that he *may* identify with, or give as a reason for, this proposition, one which must be false, because it is self contradictory. But at this point I propose to make a complete break in my argument. '*Esse* is *percipi*,' we have seen, asserts of two terms, as distinct from one another as 'green' and 'sweet,' that whatever has the one has also the other : it asserts that 'being' and 'being experienced' are necessarily connected : that whatever *is* is *also* experienced. And this, I admit, cannot be directly refuted. But I believe it to be false ; and I have asserted that anybody who saw that '*esse* and *percipi*' *were* as distinct as 'green' and 'sweet' would be no more ready to believe that whatever *is* is *also* experienced, than to believe that whatever is green is also sweet. I have asserted that no one would believe that '*esse* is *percipi*' if they saw how different *esse* is from *percipi* : but *this* I shall not try to prove. I have asserted that all who do believe that '*esse* is *percipi*' identify with it or take as a reason for it a self-contradictory proposition: but this I shall not try to prove. I shall only try to show that certain propositions which I assert to be believed, are false. That they are believed, and that without this belief '*esse* is *percipi*' would not be believed either, I must leave without a proof.

I pass, then, from the uninteresting question 'Is '*esse percipi*?' to the still more uninteresting and apparently irrelevant question 'What is a sensation or idea?'

We all know that the sensation of blue differs from that of green. But it is plain that if both are *sensations* they also have some point in common. What is it that they have in common? And how is this common element related to the points in which they differ?

I will call the common element 'consciousness' without yet attempting to say what the thing I so call *is*. We have then in every sensation two distinct terms, (1) 'consciousness,' in respect of which all sensations are alike; and (2) something else, in respect of which one sensation differs from another. It will be convenient if I may be allowed to call this second term the 'object' of a sensation: this also without yet attempting to say what I mean by the word.

We have then in every sensation two distinct elements, one which I call consciousness, and another which I call the object of consciousness. This must be so if the sensation of blue and the sensation of green, though different in one respect, are alike in another: blue is one object of sensation and green is another, and consciousness, which both sensations have in common, is different from either.

But, further, sometimes the sensation of blue exists in my mind and sometimes it does not; and knowing, as we now do, that the sensation of blue includes two different elements, namely consciousness and blue, the question arises whether, when the sensation of blue exists, it is the consciousness which exists, or the blue which exists, or both. And one point at least is plain : namely that these three alternatives are all different from one another. So that, if any one tells us that to say ' Blue exists ' is the *same* thing as to say that ' Both blue and consciousness exist,' he makes a mistake and a self-contradictory mistake.

But another point is also plain, namely, that when the sensation exists, the consciousness, at least, certainly does exist; for when I say that the sensations of blue and of green both exist, I certainly mean that what is common to both and in virtue of which both are called sensations, exists in each case.   The only alternative left, then, is that *either* both exist or the consciousness exists alone. If, therefore, any one tells us that the existence of blue is the same thing as the existence of the sensation of blue he makes a mistake and a self-contradictory mistake, for he asserts *either* that blue is the same thing as blue together with consciousness, *or* that it is the same thing as consciousness alone.

Accordingly to identify either " blue " or any other of what I have called "*objects*" of sensation, with the corresponding sensation is in every case, a self-contradictory error.   It is to identify a part either with the whole of which it is a part or else with the other part of the same whole.   If we are told that the assertion " Blue exists " is *meaningless* unless we mean by it that " The sensation of blue exists," we are told what is certainly false and self-contradictory. If we are told that the existence of blue is inconceivable apart from the existence of the sensation, the speaker *probably* means to convey to us, by this ambiguous expression, what is a self-contradictory error.   For we can and must conceive the existence of blue as something quite distinct from the existence of the sensation. We can and must conceive that blue might exist and yet the sensation of blue not exist. For my own part I not only conceive this, but conceive it to be true. Either therefore this terrific assertion of inconceivability means what is false and self-contradictory or else it means only that *as a matter of fact* blue never can exist unless the sensation of it exists also.

And at this point I need not conceal my opinion that no philosopher has ever yet succeeded in avoiding this self-contradictory error: that the most striking results both of Idealism and of Agnosticism are only obtained by identifying blue with the sensation of blue: that *esse* is held to be *percipi*, solely because *what is experienced* is held to be identical with *the experience of it*. That Berkeley and Mill committed this error will, perhaps, be granted: that modern Idealists make it will, I hope, appear more probable later. But that my opinion is plausible, I will now offer two pieces of evidence. The first is that language offers us no means of referring to such objects as "blue" and "green" and "sweet," except by calling them sensations: it is an obvious violation of language to call them "things" or "objects" or "terms." And similarly we have no natural means of referring to such objects as "causality" or "likeness" or "identity," except by calling them "ideas" or "notions" or "conceptions." But it is hardly likely that if philosophers had clearly distinguished in the past between a sensation or idea and what I have called its object, there should have been no separate name for the latter. They have always used the same name for these two different "things" (if I may call them so) : and hence there is some probability that they have supposed these "things"

not to be two and different, but one and the same.
And, secondly, there is a very good reason why
they should have supposed so, in the fact that when
we refer to introspection and try to discover what
the sensation of blue is, it is very easy to suppose
that we have before us only a single term.   The
term " blue " is easy enough to distinguish, but the
other element which I have called "consciousness "
—that which sensation of blue has in common with
sensation of green—is extremely difficult to fix.
That many people fail to distinguish it at all is
sufficiently shown by the fact that there are
materialists.   And, in general, that which makes
the sensation of blue a mental fact seems to escape
us :   it seems, if I may use a metaphor, to be
transparent—we look through it and see nothing
but the blue ;   we may be convinced that there *is*
something but *what* it is no philosopher, I think, has
yet clearly recognised.

But this was a digression.   The point I had
established so far was that in every sensation or idea
we must distinguish two elements, (1) the "object,"
or that in which one differs from another ;   and
(2) "consciousness," or that which all have in
common—that which makes them sensations or
mental facts.   This being so, it followed that when
a sensation or idea exists, we have to choose
between the alternatives that either object alone, or
consciousness alone, or both, exist ;   and I showed
that of these alternatives one, namely that the
object only exists, is excluded by the fact that what
we mean to assert is certainly the existence of a
mental fact.   There remains the question : Do both
exist ?   Or does the consciousness alone ?   And to
this question one answer has hitherto been given
universally :   That both exist.

This answer follows from the analysis hitherto
accepted of the relation of what I have called

THE REFUTATION OF IDEALISM   21

"object" to "consciousness" in any sensation or idea. It is held that what I call the object is merely the "content" of a sensation or idea. It is held that in each case we can distinguish two elements and two only, (1) the fact that there is feeling or experience, and (2) *what* is felt or experienced ; the sensation or idea, it is said, forms a whole, in which we must distinguish two "inseparable aspects," "content" and "existence." I shall try to show that this analysis is false ; and for that purpose I must ask what may seem an extraordinary question : namely what is meant by saying that one thing is "content" of another? It is not usual to ask this question ; the term is used as if everybody must understand it. But since I am going to maintain that "blue" is *not* the content of the sensation of blue, and what is more important, that, even if it were this analysis would leave out the most important element in the sensation of blue, it is necessary that I should try to explain precisely what it is that I shall deny.

What then is meant by saying that one thing is the "content" of another? First of all I wish to point out that "blue" is rightly and properly said to be part of the content of a blue flower. If, therefore, we also assert that it is part of the content of the sensation of blue, we assert that it has to the other parts (if any) of this whole the same relation which it has to the other parts of a blue flower—and we assert only this : we cannot mean to assert that it has to the sensation of blue any relation which it does not have to the blue flower. And we have seen that the sensation of blue contains at least one other element beside blue—namely, what I call "consciousness," which makes it a sensation. So far then as we assert that blue is the content of the sensation, we assert that it has to this "consciousness" the same relation which it has to the other parts of a blue flower : we do assert this, and we assert no more than this.   Into the question what exactly the relation is between blue and a blue flower in virtue of which we call the former part of its "content" I do not propose to enter.   It is sufficient for my purpose to point out that it is the general relation most commonly meant when we talk of a thing and its qualities ; and that this relation is such that to say the thing exists implies that the qualities also exist.   The *content* of the thing is *what* we assert to exist, when we assert *that* the thing exists.

When, therefore, blue is said to be part of the content of the "sensation of blue," the latter is treated as if it were a whole constituted in exactly the same way as any other "thing."   The "sensation of blue," on this view, differs from a blue bead or a blue beard, in exactly the same way in which the two latter differ from one another : the blue bead differs from the blue beard, in that while the former contains glass, the latter contains hair ; and the "sensation of blue" differs from both in that, instead of glass or hair, it contains consciousness. The relation of the blue to the consciousness is conceived to be exactly the same as that of the blue to the glass or hair : it is in all three cases the *quality* of a *thing*.

But I said just now that the sensation of blue was analysed into "content" and "existence," and that blue was said to be *the* content of the idea of blue. There is an ambiguity in this and a possible error, which I must note in passing.   The term "content" may be used in two senses.   If we use "content" as equivalent to what Mr. Bradley calls the "*what*"— if we mean by it the *whole* of what is said to exist, when the thing is said to exist, then blue is certainly not *the* content of the sensation of blue : part of the *content* of the sensation is, in this sense of the term, that other element which I have called consciousness.   The analysis of this sensation into the " content" " blue," on the one hand, and mere existence on the other, is therefore certainly false ; in it we have again the self-contradictory identification of " Blue exists " with " The sensation of blue exists,"   But there is another sense in which " blue " might properly be said to be *the* content of the sensation—namely, the sense in which " content," like εἶδος, is opposed to " substance " or " matter.' For the element " consciousness," being common to all sensations, may be and certainly is regarded as in some sense their " substance," and by the " content " of each is only meant that in respect of which one differs from another.   In this sense then " blue " might be said to be *the* content of the sensation ;   but, in that case, the analysis into " content " and " existence " is, at least, misleading, since under " existence " must be included " *what* exists " in the sensation other than blue.

We have it, then, as a universally received opinion that blue is related to the sensation or idea of blue, as its *content*, and that this view, if it is to be true, must mean that blue is part of *what* is said to exist when we say that the sensation exists. To say that the sensation exists is to say both that blue exists and that " consciousness," whether we call it the substance of which blue is *the* content or call it another part of the content, exists too.   Any sensation or idea is a " *thing*," and what I have called its object is the quality of this thing.   Such a " thing " is what we think of when we think of a *mental image*.   A mental image is conceived as if it were related to that of which it is the image (if there be any such thing) in exactly the same way as the image in a looking-glass is related to that of which it is the reflection ; in both cases there is identity of content, and the image in the looking-glass differs from that in the mind solely in respect of the fact that in the one case the other constituent of the image is "glass" and in the other case it is consciousness.   If the image is of blue, it is not conceived that this "content" has any relation to the consciousness but what it has to the glass : it is conceived *merely* to be its *content*.   And owing to the fact that sensations and ideas are all considered to be *wholes* of this description—things in the mind— the question :   What do we know ? is considered to be identical with the question : What reason have we for supposing that there are things outside the mind *corrseponding* to these that are inside it ?

What I wish to point out is (1) that we have no reason for supposing that there are such things as mental images at all—for supposing that blue *is* part of the content of the sensation of blue, and (2) that even if there are mental images, no mental image and no sensation or idea is *merely* a thing of this kind : that 'blue,' even if it is part of the content of the image or sensation or idea of blue, is always *also* related to it in quite another way, and that this other relation, omitted in the traditional analysis, is the *only* one which makes the sensation of blue a mental fact at all.

The true analysis of a sensation or idea is as follows.   The element that is common to them all, and which I have called 'consciousness," really *is* consciousness.   A sensation is, in reality, a case of 'knowing' or 'being aware of' or 'experiencing' something.   When we know that the sensation of blue exists, the fact we know is that there exists an awareness of blue.   And this awareness is not merely, as we have hitherto seen it must be, itself something distinct and unique, utterly different from blue : it also has a perfectly distinct and unique relation to blue, a relation which is *not* that of thing or substance to content, nor of one part of content

to another part of content. This relation is just
that which we mean in every case by 'knowing.'
To have in your mind 'knowledge' of blue, is *not*
to have in your mind a 'thing' or 'image' of which
blue is the content. To be aware of the sensation
of blue is *not* to be aware of a mental image—of a
"thing," of which 'blue' and some other element
are constituent parts in the same sense in which
blue and glass are constituents of a blue bead. It
is to be aware of an awareness of blue ; awareness
being used, in both cases, in exactly the same sense.
This element, we have seen, is certainly neglected
by the 'content' theory : that theory entirely fails to
express the fact that there is, in the sensation of
blue, this unique relation between blue and the
other constituent. And what I contend is that this
omission is *not* mere negligence of expression, but
is due to the fact that though philosophers have
recognised that *something* distinct is meant by
consciousness, they have never yet had a clear
conception of *what* that something is. They have
not been able to hold *it* and *blue* before their minds
and to compare them, in the same way in which
they can compare *blue* and *green*. And this for the
reason I gave above : namely that the moment we
try to fix our attention upon consciousness and to
see *what*, distinctly, it is, it seems to vanish : it
seems as if we had before us a mere emptiness.
When we try to introspect the sensation of blue, all
we can see is the blue : the other element is as if it
were diaphanous. Yet it *can* be distinguished if we
look attentively enough, and if we know that there
is something to look for. My main object in this
paragraph has been to try to make the reader *see*
it ; but I fear I shall have succeeded very ill.

It being the case, then, that the sensation of blue
includes in its analysis, beside blue, *both* a unique
element 'awareness' *and* a unique relation of this

element to blue, I can make plain what I meant by asserting, as two distinct propositions, (1) that blue is probably not part of the content of the sensation at all, and (2) that, even it were, the sensation would nevertheless not be the sensation *of* blue, if blue had only this relation to it.   The first hypothesis may now be expressed by saying that, if it were true, then, when the sensation of blue exists, there exists a *blue awareness* : offence may be taken at the expression, but yet it expresses just what should be and is meant by saying that blue is, in this case, a *content* of consciousness or experience. Whether or not, when I have the sensation of blue, my consciousness or awareness is thus blue, my introspection does not enable me to decide with certainty : I only see no reason for thinking that it is.   But whether it is or not, the point is un-important, for introspection *does* enable me to decide that something else is also true : namely that I am aware *of* blue, and by this I mean, that my aware-ness has to blue a quite different and distinct relation.   It is possible, I admit, that my awareness is blue *as well* as being *of* blue : but what I am quite sure of is that it is *of* blue ; that it has to blue the simple and unique relation the existence of which alone justifies us in distinguishing knowledge of a thing from the thing known, indeed in distinguishing mind from matter.   And this result I may express by saying that what is called the *content* of a sensation is in very truth what I originally called it —the sensation's *object*.

But, if all this be true, what follows ?

Idealists admit that some things really exist of which they are not aware : there are some things, they hold, which are not inseparable aspects of *their* experience, even if they be inseparable aspects of some experience.   They further hold that some of the things of which they are sometimes aware do really exist, even when they are not aware of them : they hold for instance that they are sometimes aware of other minds, which continue to exist even when they are not aware of them. They are, therefore, sometimes aware of something which is *not* an inseparable aspect of their own experience. They do *know some* things which are *not* a mere part or content of their experience. And what my analysis of sensation has been designed to show is, that whenever I have a mere sensation or idea, the fact is that I am then aware of something which is equally and in the same sense *not* an inseparable aspect of my experience. The awareness which I have maintained to be included in sensation is the very same unique fact which constitutes every kind of knowledge : "blue" is as much an object, and as little a mere content, of my experience, when I experience it, as the most exalted and independent real thing of which I am ever aware. There is, therefore, no question of how we are to "get outside the circle of our own ideas and sensations." Merely to have a sensation is already to *be* outside that circle. It is to know something which is as truly and really *not* a part of *my* experience, as anything which I can ever know.

Now I think I am not mistaken in asserting that the reason why Idealists suppose that everything which *is* must be an inseparable aspect of some experience, is that they suppose some things, at least, to be inseparable aspects of *their* experience. And there is certainly nothing which they are so firmly convinced to be an inseparable aspect of their experience as what they call the *content* of their ideas and sensations. If, therefore, *this* turns out in every case, whether it be also the content or not, to be at least *not* an inseparable aspect of the experience of it, it will be readily admitted that nothing else which *we* experience ever is such an inseparable aspect.   But if we never experience anything but what is *not* an inseparable aspect of *that* experience, how can we infer that anything whatever, let alone *everything*, is an inseparable aspect of *any* experience?   How utterly unfounded is the assumption that "*esse* is *percipi*" appears in the clearest light.

But further I think it may be seen that if the object of an Idealist's sensation were, as he supposes, *not* the object but merely the content of that sensation, if, that is to say, it really were an inseparable aspect of his experience, each Idealist could never be aware either of himself or of any other real thing.   For the relation of a sensation to its object is certainly the same as that of any other instance of experience to its object ; and this, I think, is generally admitted even by Idealists : they state as readily that *what* is judged or thought or perceived is the *content* of that judgment or thought or perception, as that blue is the content of the sensation of blue.   But, if so, then when any Idealist thinks he is *aware* of himself or of any one else, this cannot really be the case.   The fact is, on his own theory, that himself and that other person are in reality mere *contents* of an awareness, which is aware *of* nothing whatever.   All that can be said is that there is an awareness in him, *with* a certain content : it can never be true that there is in him a consciousness *of* anything.   And similarly he is never aware either of the fact that he exists or that reality is spiritual.   The real fact, which he describes in those terms, is that his existence and the spirituality of reality are *contents* of an awareness, which is aware of nothing—certainly not, then, of it own content.

And further if everything, of which he thinks he is aware, is in reality merely a content of his own experience he has certainly no *reason* for holding

that anything does exist except himself: it will, of
course, be possible that other persons do exist;
solipsism will not be necessarily true; but he cannot possibly infer from anything he holds that it
is not true.   That he himself exists will of course
follow from his premiss that many things are
contents of *his* experience.   But since everything,
of which he thinks himself aware, is in reality
merely an inseparable aspect of that awareness;
this premiss allows no inference that any of these
contents, far less any other consciousness, exists at
all except as an inseparable aspect of his awareness,
that is, as part of himself.

Such, and not those which he takes to follow
from it, are the consequences which *do* follow from
the Idealist's supposition that the object of an
experience is in reality merely a content or inseparable aspect of that experience.   If, on the
other hand, we clearly recognise the nature of that
peculiar relation which I have called "awareness
of anything"; if we see that *this* is involved
equally in the analysis of *every* experience—from
the merest sensation to the most developed perception or reflexion, and that *this* is in fact the only
essential element in an experience—the only thing
that is both common and peculiar to all experiences—
the only thing which gives us reason to call any
fact mental; if, further, we recognise that this
awareness is and must be in all cases of such a
nature that its object, when we are aware of it, is
precisely what it would be, if we were not aware:
then it becomes plain that the existence of a table
in space is related to my experience of *it* in precisely the same way as the existence of my own
experience is related to my experience of *that*.   Of
both we are merely aware : if we are aware that
the one exists, we are aware in precisely the same
sense that the other exists ; and if it is true that my

experience can exist, even when I do not happen to be aware of its existence, we have exactly the same reason for supposing that the table can do so also.   When, therefore, Berkeley, supposed that the only thing of which I am directly aware is my own sensations and ideas, he supposed what was false ; and when Kant supposed that the objectivity of things in space *consisted* in the fact that they were " Vorstellungen " having to one another different relations from those which the same " Vorstellungen " have to one another in subjective experience, he supposed what was equally false.   I am as directly aware of the existence of material things in space as of my own sensations ; and *what* I am aware of with regard to each is exactly the same—namely that in one case the material thing, and in the other case my sensation does really exist.   The question requiring to be asked about material things is thus not : What reason have we for supposing that anything exists *corresponding* to our sensations ? but : What reason have we for supposing that material things do *not* exist, since *their* existence has precisely the same evidence as that of our sensations ?   That either exist *may* be false ; but if it is a reason for doubting the existence of matter, that it is an inseparable aspect of our experience, the same reasoning will prove con-clusively that our experience does not exist either, since that must also be an inseparable aspect of our experience of *it*.   The only *reasonable* alternative to the admission that matter exists *as well as* spirit, is absolute Scepticism—that, as likely as not *nothing* exists at all.   All other suppositions—the Agnostic's, that something, at all events, does exist, as much as the Idealist's, that spirit does—are, if we have no reason for believing in matter, as baseless as the grossest superstitions.

THE NATURE AND REALITY OF OBJECTS OF PERCEPTION

THERE are two beliefs in which almost all philosophers, and almost all ordinary people are agreed. Almost everyone believes that he himself and what he directly perceives do not constitute the whole of reality : he believes that *something* other than himself and what he directly perceives *exists* or is *real*. I do not mean to say that almost everyone believes that what he directly perceives is real : I only mean that he does believe that, whether what he directly perceives is real or not, something other than it and other than himself certainly is so. And not only does each of us thus agree in believing that *something* other than himself and what he directly perceives is real : almost everyone also believes that *among* the real things, other than himself and what he directly perceives, are other persons who have thoughts and perceptions in some respects similar to his own. That most people believe this I think I need scarcely try to show. But since a good many philosophers may appear to have held views contradictory of this one, I will briefly point out my reason for asserting that most philosophers, even among those (if any) who have believed the contradictory of this, have yet held this as well. Almost all philosophers tell us something about the nature of *human* knowledge and *human* perception. They tell us that *we* perceive so and so; that the nature or origin of *our* perceptions is such and such; or (as I have just been telling you) that men in general have such and such beliefs. It might, indeed, be said that we are not to interpret such language too strictly: that, though a philosopher talks about *human* knowledge and *our* perceptions, he only means to talk about his own. But in many cases a philosopher will leave no doubt upon this point, by expressly assuming that there are other perceptions, which differ in some respects from his own: such, for instance, is the case when (as is so common nowadays) a philosopher introduces psycho-genetic considerations into his arguments —considerations concerning the nature of the perceptions of men who existed before and at a much lower stage of culture than himself. Any philosopher, who uses such arguments, obviously assumes that perceptions other than his own have existed or been real. And even those philosophers who think themselves justified in the conclusion that neither their own perceptions nor any perceptions like theirs are *ultimately* real, would, I think admit, that *phenomenally*, at least, they *are* real, and are certainly *more* real than some other things.

Almost everyone, then, does believe that some perceptions other than his own, and which he himself does not directly perceive, are real; and believing this, he believes that something other than himself and what he directly perceives is real. But how do we know that anything exists except our own perceptions, and what we directly perceive? How do we know that there are any other people, who have perceptions in some respects similar to our own?

I believe that these two questions express very exactly the nature of the problem which it is my chief object, in this paper, to discuss. When I say these words to you, they will at once suggest to your minds the very question, to which I desire to find an answer; they will convey to you the very same meaning which I have before my mind, when I use the words. You will understand at once what question it is that I mean to ask. But, for all that, the words which I have used are highly ambiguous. If you begin to ask yourselves what I do mean by them, you will find that there are several quite different things which I might mean. And there is, I think, great danger of confusing these different meanings with one another. I think that philosophers, when they have asked this question in one sense, have often answered it in quite a different sense; and yet have supposed that the answer which they have given is an answer to the very same question which they originally asked. It is precisely because there is this ambiguity—this danger of confusion, in the words which I have used, that I have chosen to use them. I wish to point out as clearly as I can, not only what I do mean by them, but also some things which I do *not* mean; and I wish to make it clear that the questions which I do *not* mean to ask, are different questions from that which I do mean to ask.

I will take the second of my two questions, since there is in the other an additional ambiguity to which I do not now wish to call attention. My second question was : How do we know that there exist any other people who have perceptions in some respects similar to our own? What does this question mean?

Now I think you may have noticed that when you make a statement to another person, and he answers " How do you know that that is so? " he very often means to suggest that you do *not* know it. And yet, though he means to suggest that you do not *know* it, he may not for a moment wish to suggest that you do not *believe* it, nor even that you have not that degree or kind of conviction, which goes beyond mere belief, and which may be taken to be essential to anything which can properly be called knowledge. He does not mean to suggest for a moment that you are saying something which you do not believe to be true, or even that you are not thoroughly convinced of its truth. What he does mean to suggest is that what you asserted was not *true*, even though you may not only have believed it but felt sure that it was true. He suggests that you don't *know* it, in the sense that what you believe or feel sure of is not true.

Now I point this out, not because I myself mean to suggest that we don't know the existence of other persons, but merely in order to show that the word "know" is sometimes used in a sense in which it is not merely equivalent to "believe" or "feel sure of." When the question "How do you *know* that?" is asked, the questioner does not merely mean to ask "how do you come to believe that, or to be convinced of it?" He sometimes, and I think generally, means to ask a question with regard to the *truth*, and not with regard to the *existence* of your belief. And similarly when I ask the question "How do we know that other people exist?" I do *not* mean to ask "How do we come to believe in or be convinced of their existence?" I do not intend to discuss this question *at all*. I shall not ask what *suggests* to us our belief in the existence of other persons or of an external world; I shall not ask whether we arrive at it by inference or by "instinct" or in any other manner, which ever has been or may be suggested: I shall discuss no question of any kind whatever with regard to its origin, or cause, or the way in which it arises. These psychological questions are *not* what I propose to discuss. When I ask the question "How do we know that other people exist?" I do *not* mean:

" How does our belief in their existence arise ? "

But if I do not mean this what do I mean? I have said that I mean to ask a question with regard to the *truth* of that belief; and the particular question which I mean to ask might be expressed in the words : *What reason have* we for our belief in the existence of other persons? But these are words which themselves need some explanation, and I will try to give it.

In the first place, then, when I talk of "a reason," I mean *only* a good reason and *not* a bad one. A bad reason is, no doubt, a reason, in one sense of the word; but I mean to use the word "reason" exclusively in the sense in which it is equivalent to "good reason." But what, then, is meant by a good reason for a belief? I think I can express sufficiently accurately what I mean by it in this connection, as follows :—A good reason for a belief is a proposition which is true, and which would not be true unless the belief were also true. We should, I think, commonly say that when a man knows such a proposition, he has a good reason for his belief; and, when he knows no such proposition, we should say that he has no reason for it. When he knows such a proposition, we should say he knows something which is a reason for thinking his belief to be true—something from which it *could* be validly inferred. And if, in answer to the question " How do you know so and so?" he were to state such a proposition, we should, I think, feel that he had answered the question which we meant to ask. Suppose, for instance, in answer to the question " How do you know that?" he were to say " I saw it in the *Times*." Then, if we believed that he had seen it in the *Times*, and also believed that it would not have been in the *Times*, unless it had been true, we should admit that he had answered our question.

We should no longer doubt that he did *know* what he asserted, we should no longer doubt that his belief was true.   But if, on the other hand, we believed that he had not seen it in the *Times*—if, for instance, we had reason to believe that what he saw was not the statement which he made, but some other statement which he mistook for it ; or if we believed that the kind of statement in question was one with regard to which there was no presumption that, being in the *Times*, it would be true : in *either* of these cases we should, I think, feel that he had *not* answered our question.   We should still doubt whether what he had said was true.   We should still doubt whether he *knew* what he asserted ; and since a man cannot tell you how he *knows* a thing unless he does know that thing, we should think that, though he might have told us truly how he *came to believe it*, he had certainly not told us how he *knew* it.   But though we should thus hold that he had *not* told us *how he knew* what he had asserted, and that he had given us no reason for believing it to be true ; we must yet admit that he had given us a reason in a sense—a *bad* reason, a reason which was no reason because it had no tendency to show that what he believed was true ; and we might also be perfectly convinced that he had given us *the reason* why he believed it—the proposition by believing which he was induced also to believe his original assertion.

I mean, then, by my question, " How do we know that other people exist ? " what, I believe, is ordinarily meant, namely, " What reason have we for believing that they exist ? " and by this again I mean, what I also believe is ordinarily meant, namely, " What proposition do we believe, which is both true itself and is also such that it would not be true, unless other people existed ? "   And I hope it is plain that this question, thus explained, is quite a different question from the psychological question, which I said I did *not* mean to ask—from the question, " How does our belief in the existence of other people arise ? " My illustration, I hope, has made this plain. For I have pointed out that we may quite well hold that a man has told us how a belief of his arises, and even what was the reason which made him adopt that belief, and yet may have failed to give us any *good reason* for his belief—any proposition which is both true itself, and also such that the truth of his belief follows from it. And, indeed, it is plain that if any one ever believes what is false, he is believing something for which there *is* no good reason, in the sense which I have explained, and for which, therefore, he cannot possibly have a good reason ; and yet it plainly does not follow that his belief did not arise in anyway whatever, nor even that he had no reason for it—no bad reason. It is plain that false beliefs do arise in some way or other—they have origins and causes : and many people who hold them *have* bad reasons for holding them—their belief does arise (by inference or otherwise) from their belief in some other proposition, which is not itself true, or else is not a *good* reason for holding that, which they infer from it, or which, in some other way, it induces them to believe. I submit, therefore, that the question, " What good reason have we for believing in the existence of other people ? " is different from the question, " How does that belief arise ? " But when I say this, I must not be misunderstood ; I must not be understood to affirm that the answer to both questions *may* not, in a sense, be the same. I fully admit that the very same fact, which suggests to us the belief in the existence of other people, *may* also be a good reason for believing that they do exist. All that I maintain is that the question whether it is a good reason for that belief is a different question from the question whether it suggests that belief : if we assert that a certain fact *both* suggests our belief in the existence of other persons and is *also* a good reason for holding that belief, we are asserting two different things and not one only. And hence, when I assert, as I shall assert, that we *have* a good reason for our belief in the existence of other persons, I must not be understood also to assert either that we infer the existence of other persons from this good reason, or that our belief in that good reason suggests our belief in the existence of other persons in any other way.   It is plain, I think, that a man may believe two true propositions, of which the one would not be true, unless the other were true too, without, in any sense whatever, having arrived at his belief in the one *from* his belief in the other ; and it is plain, at all events, that the question whether his belief in the one *did* arise from his belief in the other, is a different question from the question whether the truth of the one belief follows from the truth of the other.

I hope, then, that I have made it a little clearer what I mean by the question : "What reason have we for believing in the existence of other people?" and that what I mean by it is at all events different from what is meant by the question : "How does our belief in the existence of other people arise?"

But I am sorry to say that I have not yet reached the end of my explanations as to what my meaning is.   I am afraid that the subject may seem very tedious.   I can assure you that I have found it excessively tedious to try to make my meaning clear to myself.   I have constantly found that I was confusing one question with another, and that, where I had thought I had a good reason for some assertion, I had in reality no good reason.   But I may perhaps remind you that this question, "How do we know so and so?"   "What reason have we for believing it ? " is one of which philosophy is full ; and one to which the most various answers have been given. Philosophy largely consists in giving reasons ; and the question what are good reasons for a particular conclusion and what are bad, is one upon which philosophers have disagreed as much as on any other question. For one and the same conclusion different philosophers have given not only different, but incompatible, reasons ; and conversely different philosophers have maintained that one and the same fact is a reason for incompatible conclusions. We are apt, I think, sometimes to pay too little attention to this fact. When we have taken, perhaps, no little pains to assure ourselves that our own reasoning is correct, and especially when we know that a great many other philosophers agree with us, we are apt to assume that the arguments of those philosophers, who have come to a contradictory conclusion, are scarcely worthy of serious consideration. And yet, I think, there is scarcely a single reasoned conclusion in philosophy, as to which we shall not find that some other philosopher, who has, so far as we know, bestowed equal pains on his reasoning, and with equal ability, has reached a conclusion incompatible with ours. We may be satisfied that we are right, and we may, in fact, be so ; but it is certain that *both* cannot be right : either our opponent or we must have mistaken bad reasons for good. And this being so, however satisfied we may be that it is not we who have done so, I think we should at least draw the conclusion that it is by no means easy to avoid mistaking bad reasons for good ; and that no process, however laborious, which is in the least likely to help us in avoiding this should be evaded. But it is at least possible that one source of error lies in mistaking one kind of reason for another—in supposing that, because there is, in one

sense, a reason for a given conclusion, there is also
a reason in another, or that because there is, in one
sense, no reason for a given conclusion, there is,
therefore, no reason at all.   I believe myself that
this *is* a very frequent source of error : but it is at
least a possible one.   And where, as disagreements
show, there certainly is error on one side or the
other, and reason, too, to suppose that the error is
not easy to detect, I think we should spare no pains
in investigating any source, from which it is even
possible that the error may arise.   For these reasons
I think I am perhaps doing right in trying to explain
as clearly as possible not only what reasons we have
for believing in an external world, but also in what
sense I take them to be reasons.

I proceed, then with my explanation.   And there
is one thing, which, I think my illustration has
shown that I do *not* mean.   I have defined a reason
for a belief as a t ue proposition, which would not
be true unless the belief itself—what is believed—
were also true ; and I have used, as synonymous
with this form of words, the expressions :   A reason
for a belief is a true proposition from which the
truth of the belief *follows* from which it *could* be
validly inferred.   Now these expressions might
suggest the idea that I mean to restrict the word
" reason," to what, in the strictest sense, might be
called a *logical* reason—to propositions from which
the belief in question *follows*, according to the rules
of inference accepted by Formal Logic.   But I am
not using the words " follow," " validly inferred," in
this narrow sense ; I do *not* mean to restrict the
words " reason for a belief " to propositions from
which the laws of Formal Logic state that the
belief could be deduced.   The illustration which I
gave is inconsistent with this restricted meaning.
I said that the fact that a statement appeared in the
Times might be a good reason for believing that

that statement was true.   And I am using the word
" reason " in the wide and popular sense, in which
it really might be.   If, for instance, the *Times*
stated that the King was dead, we should think
that was a good reason for believing that the King
was dead ; we should think that the *Times* would
not have made such a statement as that unless the
King really were dead.   We should, indeed, not
think that the statement in the *Times* rendered it
absolutely *certain* that the King was dead.   But it
is extremely unlikely that the *Times* would make a
statement of this kind unless it were true ; and, in
that sense, the fact of the statement appearing in
the *Times* would render it *highly probable*--much
more likely than not—that the King was dead.
And I wish it to be understood that I am using the
words " reason for a belief " in this extremely wide
sense.   When I look for a good reason for our
belief in the existence of other people, I shall not
reject any proposition merely on the ground that it
only renders their existence probable—only shows
it to be more likely than not that they exist.
Provided that the proposition in question does
render it *positively probable* that they exist, then, if
it also conforms to the conditions which I am about
to mention, I shall call it a " good reason."

But it is not every proposition which renders it
probable that other people exist, which I shall
consider to be a good answer to my question.   I
have just explained that my meaning is wide in one
direction—in admitting *some* propositions which
render a belief merely probable ; but I have now to
explain that it is restricted in two other directions.
I do mean to exclude certain propositions which do
render that belief probable.   When I ask : What
reason have *we* for believing in the existence of
other people ? a certain ambiguity is introduced by
the use of the plural " we."   If each of several

different persons has a reason for believing that he himself exists, then it is not merely probable, but certain, according to the rules of Formal Logic, that, in a sense, *they* " have a reason for believing " that several people exist ; each has a reason for believing that he himself exists ; and, therefore, all of them, taken together, have reasons for supposing that several persons exist.   If, therefore, I were asking the question : What reason have *we* for believing in the existence of other persons ? in this sense, it would follow that if each of us has a reason for believing in his own existence, these reasons, taken together, would be a reason for believing in the existence of all of us.   But I am not asking the question in this sense : it is plain that this is not its natural sense.   What I do mean to ask is : Does *each single one* of us know any proposition, which is a reason for believing that *others* exist?   I am using " we," that is to say, in the sense of " each of us."   But again I do mean *each* of us : I am not merely asking whether some *one* man knows a proposition which is a reason for believing that other men exist.   It would be possible that some one man, or some few men, should know such a proposition, and yet the rest know no such proposition.   But I am not asking whether this is the case.   I am asking whether among propositions of the kind which (as we commonly suppose) all or almost all men know, there is any which is a reason for supposing that other men exist.   And in asking this question I am not begging the question by supposing that all men do exist.   My question might, I think, be put quite accurately as follows. There are certain kinds of belief which, as we commonly suppose, all or almost all men share.   I describe this kind of belief as " our " beliefs, simply as an easy way of pointing out which kind of belief I mean, but without assuming that all men do share them. And I then ask: Supposing a single man to have beliefs of this kind, which among them would be a good reason for supposing that other men existed having like beliefs?

This, then, is the first restriction which I put upon the meaning of my question. And it is, I think, a restriction which, in their natural meaning, the words suggest. When we ask: What reason have we for believing that other people exist? we naturally understand that question to be equivalent to: What reason has *each* of us for that belief? And this question again is naturally equivalent to the question: Which among the propositions that a single man believes, but which are of the kind which (rightly or wrongly) we assume all men to believe, are such that they would not be true unless some other person than that man existed? But there is another restriction which, I think, the words of my question also naturally suggest. If we were to ask anyone the question: How do you know that you did see that statement in the *Times*? and he were to answer "Because I did see it in the *Times* and in the *Standard* too," we should not think that he had given us a *reason* for the belief that he saw it in the *Times*. We should not think his answer a *reason*, because it asserts the very thing for which we require a reason. And similarly when I ask: How do we know that any thing or person exists, other than ourselves and what we directly perceive? What reason have we for believing this? I must naturally be understood to mean: What proposition, *other* than one which itself asserts or presupposes the existence of something beyond ourselves and our own perceptions, is a reason for supposing that such a thing exists? And this restriction obviously excludes an immense number of propositions of a kind which all of us do believe. We all of us believe an immense number of different propositions about the existence of things which we do not directly perceive, and many of these propositions are, in my sense, good reasons for believing in the existence of still other things. The belief in the existence of a statement in the *Times*, when we have not seen that statement, may, as I implied, be a good reason for believing that someone is dead. But no such proposition can be a good answer to my question, because it asserts the very kind of thing for which I require a reason : it asserts the existence of something other than myself and what I directly perceive. When I am asking : What reason have I for believing in the existence of anything but myself, my own perceptions, and what I do directly perceive? you would naturally understand me to mean : What reason, *other than* the existence of such a thing, have I for this belief?

Each of us, then, we commonly assume, believes some true propositions, which do not themselves assert the existence of anything other than himself, his own perceptions, or what he directly perceives. Each of us, for instance, believes that he himself has and has had certain particular perceptions : and these propositions are propositions of the kind I mean—propositions which do not themselves assert the existence of anything *other than* himself, his own perceptions, and what he directly perceives: they are, I think, by no means the only propositions of this kind, which most of us believe : but they *are* propositions of this kind. But, as I say, I am not assuming that each of us—each of several different people—does believe propositions of this kind. All that I assume is that at least one man does believe some such propositions. And then I ask : Which among those true propositions, which one man believes, are such that they would probably not be true, unless some other man existed and had certain particular perceptions? Which among them are such that it *follows* (in the wide sense, which I have explained) from their truth, that it is more likely than not that some other man has perceptions? This is the meaning of my question, so far as I have hitherto explained it : and I hope this meaning is quite clear. It is in this sense that I am asking : What reason have we for believing that other people exist? How do we know that they exist? This, indeed, is not *all* that I mean by that question: there is one other point—the most important one— which remains to be explained. But this is *part* of what I mean to ask ; and before I go on to explain what else I mean, I wish first to stop and enquire what is the answer to this part of my question. What is the answer to the question : Which among the true propositions, of a kind which (as we commonly assume) each of us believes, and which do not themselves assert the existence of anything other than that person himself, his own perceptions, or what he directly perceives, are such that they would probably not be true unless some other person existed, who had perceptions in some re- spects similar to his own?

Now to this question the answer is very obvious. It is very obvious that in this sense we have reasons for believing in the existence of other persons, and also what some of those reasons are. But I wish to make it quite plain that this is so : that in this sense one man *has* a reason for believing that another has certain perceptions. All that I am asking you to grant, is, you see, that some of you would not be having just those perceptions which you now have, unless I, as I read this paper, were perceiving more or less black marks on a more or less white ground ; or that I on the other hand, should not be having just those perceptions which I now have, unless some other persons than myself were hearing the sounds of my voice. And I am not asking you even to grant that this is certain—only that it is positively probable—more likely than not. Surely it is very obvious that this proposition is true. But I wish to make it quite clear what would be the consequences of denying that any such propositions are true—propositions which assert that the existence of certain perceptions in one man are a reason for believing in the existence of certain perceptions in another man—which assert that one man would probably not have had just those perceptions which he did have, unless some other man had had certain particular perceptions. It is plain, I think, that, unless some such propositions are true, we have no more reason for supposing that Alexander the Great ever saw an elephant, than for supposing that Sindbad the Sailor saw a Roc; we have no more reason for supposing that anybody saw Julius Cæsar murdered in the Senate House at Rome, than for supposing that somebody saw him carried up to Heaven in a fiery chariot. It is plain, I think, that if we have any reason at all for supposing that in all probability Alexander the Great did see an elephant, and that in all probability no such person as Sindbad the Sailor ever saw a Roc, part of that reason consists in the assumption that some other person would probably not have had just those perceptions which he did have, unless Alexander the Great had seen an elephant, and unless Sindbad the Sailor had not seen a Roc. And most philosophers, I think, are willing to admit that we have some reason, in some sense or other, for such propositions as these. They are willing to admit not only that some persons probably did see Julius Cæsar murdered in the Senate House; but also that some persons, other than those who saw it, had and have *some reason* for supposing that some one else probably saw it. Some sceptical philosophers might, indeed, deny both propositions; and to refute their views, I admit, other arguments are needed than any which I shall bring forward in this paper. But most philosophers will, I think, admit not only that facts, for which there is, as we say, good historical evidence, are probably true; but also that what we call good historical evidence really is in some sense a good reason for thinking them true. Accordingly I am going to assume that many propositions of the following kind are true. Propositions, namely, which assert that one man would probably not have certain perceptions which he does have, unless some other man had certain particular perceptions. That some of you, for instance, would probably not be having precisely the perceptions which you are having, unless I were having the perception of more or less black marks on a more or less white ground. And, in this sense, I say, we certainly have reasons for supposing that other people have perceptions similar, in some respects, to those which we sometimes have.

But when I said I was going to ask the question : What reason have we for supposing that other people exist? you will certainly not have thought that I merely meant to ask the question which I have just answered. My words will have suggested to you something much more important than merely this. When, for instance, I said that to the question " How do you know that?" the answer "I saw it in the *Times*" would be a satisfactory answer, you may have felt, as I felt, that it would not in all circumstances be regarded as such. The person who asked the question might, in some cases, fairly reply : " That is no answer : how do you know that, because you saw a thing in the *Times*, it is therefore true?" In other words he might ask for a *reason* for supposing that the occurrence of a particular statement in the *Times* was a reason for supposing that statement true. And this is a question to which we all believe that there may be an answer. We believe that, with some kinds of statements which the *Times* makes—some kinds of statements with regard to Fiscal Policy for example—the fact that the *Times* makes them is no reason for supposing them to be true : whereas with regard to other kinds of statements, which it makes, such a statement, for instance, as that the King was dead, the fact that it makes them *is* a reason for supposing them true. We believe that there are some kinds of statements, which it is very unlikely the *Times* would make, unless they were true ; and others which it is not at all unlikely that the *Times* might make, although they were not true. And we believe that a reason might be given for distinguishing, in this way, between the two different kinds of statement : for thinking that, in some cases (on points, for instance, which, as we should say, are not simple questions of fact) the *Times* is fallible, whereas in other cases, it is, though not absolutely infallible, very unlikely to state what is not true.

Now it is precisely in this further sense that I wish to consider : what reason have we for believing that certain particular things, other than ourselves, our own perceptions, and what we directly perceive, are real ? I have asserted that I do have certain perceptions, which it is very unlikely I should have, unless some other person had certain particular perceptions ; that, for instance, it is very unlikely I should be having precisely those perceptions which I am now having unless someone else were hearing the sound of my voice. And I now wish to ask : What reason have I for supposing that this is unlikely ? What reason has any of us for supposing that any such proposition is true? And I mean by "having a reason" precisely what I formerly meant. I mean : What other proposition do I know, which would not be true, unless my perception were connected with someone else's perception, in the manner in which I asserted them to be connected? Here again I am asking for *a good reason*; and am not asking a psychological question with regard to origin. Here again I am not asking for a reason, in the strict sense of Formal Logic; I am merely asking for a proposition which would probably not be true, unless what I asserted were true. Here again I am asking for some proposition of a kind which *each* of us believes; I am asking: What reason has *each* of us for believing that some of his perceptions are connected with particular perceptions of other people in the manner I asserted? —for believing that he would not have certain perceptions that he does have, unless some other person had certain particular perceptions? And here again I am asking for a *reason*—I am asking for some proposition *other* than one which itself asserts: When one man has a perception of such and such a particular kind, it *is* probable that another man has a perception or thought of this or that other kind.

But what kind of reason can be given for believing a proposition of this sort? For believing a proposition which asserts that, since one particular thing exists, it is probable that another particular thing also exists? One thing I think is plain, namely that we can have no good reason for believing such a proposition, unless we have good reason for believing some *generalisation*. It is commonly believed, for instance, that certain so-called flint arrow-heads, which have been discovered, were probably made by prehistoric men; and I think it is plain that we have no reason for believing this unless we have reason to suppose that objects which resemble these in certain particular respects are *generally* made by men—are *more often* made by men than by any other agency. Unless certain particular characteristics which those arrow-heads have were characteristics which belonged at least more frequently to articles of human manufacture than to any articles not made by men, it would surely be just as likely as not that these arrow-heads were *not* made by men—that they were, in fact not arrow-heads.   That is to say, unless we have reason to assert a *generalisation*—the generalisation that objects of a certain kind are *generally* made by men, we have no reason to suppose that these particular objects, which are of the kind in question, *were* made by men.   And the same, so far as I can see, is true universally.   If we ever have any reason for asserting that, since one particular thing exists, another probably exists or existed or will exist also part of our reason, at least, must consist in reasons for asserting some generalisation —for asserting that the existence of things of a particular kind is, more often than not, accompanied or preceded or followed by the existence of things of another particular kind.   It is, I think, sometimes assumed that an alternative to this theory may be found in the theory that the existence of one kind of thing "intrinsically points to," or is "intrinsically a sign or symbol of" the existence of another thing.   It is suggested that when a thing which thus points to the existence of another thing exists, then it is at least probable that the thing "pointed to" exists also.   But this theory, I think, offers no real alternative. For, in the first place, when we say that the existence of one thing A is a "sign of" or "points to" the existence of another thing B, we very commonly actually mean to say that when a thing like A exists, a thing like B *generally* exists too.   We may, no doubt, mean something else *too*; but this we do mean.   We say, for instance, that certain particular words, which we hear or read, are a "sign" that somebody has thought of the particular things which we call the meaning of those words. But we should certainly hesitate to admit that the hearing or reading of certain words could be called a "sign" of the existence of certain thoughts, unless it were true that when those words are heard or read, the thoughts in question *generally* have existed. If when those words were heard or read, the thoughts had generally *not* existed, we should say that, in one sense of the word at all events, the hearing of the words was *not* a sign of the existence of the thoughts. In this sense, therefore, to say that the existence of A "points to" or "is a sign of" the existence of B is actually to say that when A exists, B *generally* exists also. But, no doubt, the words "points to" "is a sign of" may be used in some other sense: they may, for instance, mean only that the existence of A *suggests* in some way the belief that B exists. And in such a case we certainly might know that the existence of A pointed to the existence of B, without knowing that when A existed B generally existed also. Let us suppose, then, that in some such sense A does "point to" the existence of B; can this fact give us a reason for supposing it even probable that B existed. Certainly it can, *provided* it is true that when A *does* point to the existence of B, B *generally* exists. But surely it can do so, only on this condition. If when A *points* to the existence of B, B, nevertheless, does *not* generally exist, then surely the fact that A points to the existence of B can constitute no probability that B does not exist: on the contrary it will then be probable that, even though A "points to" the existence of B, B does *not* exist. We have, in fact, only substituted the generalisation that A's *pointing to* B is generally accompanied by the existence of B, for the generalisation that A's *existence* is generally accompanied by the existence of B. If we are to have any reason for asserting that, when A *points to* or is a sign of the existence of B, B probably exists, we must still have a reason for some generalisation—for a generalisation which asserts that when one thing points to the existence of another, that other *generally* exists.

It is plain, then, I think, that if we are to find a reason for the assertion that some particular perception of mine would probably not exist, unless someone else were having or had had a perception of a kind which I can name, we must find a reason for *some* generalisation. And it is also plain, I think, that in many cases of this kind the generalisation must consist in an assertion that when one man has a certain kind of perception, some other man generally has had some other perception or belief. We assume, for instance, that when we hear or read certain words, somebody besides ourselves has thought the thoughts, which constitute the meaning of those words ; and it is plain, I think, that we have no reason for this assumption except one which is also a reason for the assumption that when certain words are heard or read, somebody generally has had certain thoughts. And my enquiry, therefore, at least includes the enquiry : What reasons have we for such generalisations as these ? for generalisations which assert a connection between the existence of a certain kind of perception in one man, and that of a certain kind of perception or belief in another man ?

And to this question, I think, but one answer can be given. If we have any reason for such generalisations at all, some reason must be given, in one way or another, by observation—by observation, understood in the wide sense in which it includes "experiment." No philosopher, I think, has ever failed to assume that observation does give a reason for *some* generalisations—for some propositions which assert that when one kind of thing exists, another generally exists or has existed in a certain relation to it. Even those who, like Hume, imply that observation cannot give a *reason* for anything, yet constantly appeal to observation in support of generalisations of their own. And even those who hold that observation can give no reason for any generalisation about the relation of one man's perceptions to another's, yet hold that it *can* give a reason for generalisations about the relation of some to others among a man's own perceptions. It is, indeed, by no means agreed *how* observation can give a reason for any generalisation. Nobody knows what reason we have, if we have any, for supposing that it can. But *that* it can, everyone, I think, assumes. I think, therefore, most philosophers will agree, that if we can find any reason at all for generalisations of the kind in which I am interested, a reason for *some* of them at all events must be found in observation. And what I propose to ask is : What reason can be found in observation for even a single proposition of the kind I have described? for a proposition which asserts that when one man has one kind of perception, another man generally has or has had another.

But, when it is said that observation gives us a reason for generalisations, two things may be meant neither of which I mean. In the first place, we popularly use " observation " in a sense in which we can be said to *observe* the perceptions, feelings and thoughts of other people : in which, therefore, we can be said to observe the very things with regard to which I am asking what reason we have for believing in their existence. But it is universally[1] agreed that there is a sense in which no man can observe the perceptions, feelings or thoughts of any other man. And it is to this strict sense that I

[1] Not now in 1921.

propose to confine the word. I shall use it in a
sense, in which we can certainly be said to observe
nothing but ourselves, our own perceptions, thoughts
and feelings, and what we directly perceive.   And
in the second place, it may be said that observations
made by another person may give *me* a reason for
believing some generalisation.   And it is certainly
the case that for many of the generalisations in
which we all believe, if we have a reason in observation at all, it is not in *our own* observation that we
have it : part of our reason, at all events, lies in
things which *other* people have observed but which
we ourselves have not observed.   But in asking
this particular question, I am not asking for reasons
of this sort.   The very question that I am asking
is :   What reason has any one of us for supposing
that any other person whatever has ever made any
observations ?   And just as, in the first meaning
which I gave to this question, it meant :   What
thing, that any single man observes is such that it
would probably not have existed, unless some other
man had made a particular observation?   So now
I am asking :   Which among the things, which *one
single man observes*, are such that they would
probably not have existed, unless it were true that
some of them generally stood in certain relations
to observations of some other person?   I am
asking :   Which among *my own* observations give
me a reason for supposing that some of them are
of a kind which are generally preceded or accompanied by observations of other people?   Which,
for instance, among my own observations give a
good reason for the generalisation that when I hear
certain words, somebody else has generally had
certain particular thoughts, or that whenever anyone
hears certain words, somebody else has generally
had the thoughts which constitute what we call the
meaning of those words?   I am asking :   Which

among the vast series of observations, which any one individual makes during his lifetime, give a good reason for any generalisation *whatever* of this kind—a generalisation which asserts that some of them are generally preceded by certain thoughts, perceptions or feelings in other persons? I quite admit that there are some generalisations of this kind for which the observations of *some* particular men will *not* give a reason. All that I ask is: Is there even *one* generalisation of this kind, for which the kind of observations, which (as we commonly assume) each man, or nearly every man does make, do give a reason? Among observations of the kind which (as we commonly assume) are common to you and to me, do yours, by themselves, give any reason for even *one* such generalisation? And do mine, by themselves, give any reason for even *one* such generalisation? And if they do, which, among these observations, is it which do so?

My question is, then: What reason do my own observations give me, for supposing that any perception whatever, which I have, would probably not occur, unless some other person had a certain kind of perception? What reason do my own observations give me for supposing, for instance, that I should not be perceiving what I do now perceive, unless someone were hearing the sound of my voice? What reason do your own observations give you for supposing that you would not be perceiving just what you are perceiving, unless I were perceiving more or less black marks on a more or less white ground? The question does, I think, appear to be a reasonable one; and most philosophers, I think, have assumed that there is an answer to it. Yet it may be said that there is no answer to it: that my own observations give me no reason whatever for any single proposition of this kind. There are certain philosophers (even apart from

thorough sceptics, with whom, as I have said, I am
not now arguing) who have denied that they do.
There are certain philosophers who hold that nothing
which any single one of us observes or can observe,
gives the slightest reason for supposing that any of
his own perceptions are generally connected with
certain perceptions in other people.   There are
philosophers who hold that the only generalisations
for which our own observations do give any warrant
are generalisations concerning the manner in which
our own perceptions, thoughts and feelings do and
probably will succeed one another ; and who conclude that, this being so, we have no reason whatever for believing in the existence of any other
people.   And these philosophers are, I think, right
in drawing this conclusion from this premiss.   It
does not, indeed, follow from their premiss that we
have not a reason in the sense which I first explained, and in which, I insisted, it must be admitted
that we have a reason.   It does not follow that
some of our perceptions *are* not such as would
probably not exist, unless some other person had
certain perceptions.   But, as I have urged, when
we say that we have a reason for asserting the
existence of something not perceived, we commonly
mean something more than this.   We mean not
only that, since what we perceive does exist, the
unperceived thing probably exists too ; we mean
also that we have some reason for asserting this
connection between the perceived and the unperceived.   And holding, as we do, that no reason can
be given for asserting such a connection, except
observation, we should say that, if observation gives
no reason for asserting it, we have *no* reason for
asserting it ; and having no reason for asserting this
conection between the perceived and the unperceived, we should say that we have none either for
asserting the even probable existence of the un-

perceived. This, I think, is what we commonly mean by saying that we have no reason to believe in the existence of a particular thing which we do not perceive. And hence, I think, those philosophers who hold that our own observations give us no reason whatever for any generalisation whatever concerning the connection of any of them with those of other people, are quite right in concluding that we have no reason to assert that any other person ever did have any particular thought or perception whatever. I think that the words of this conclusion, understood in their natural meaning, express precisely what the premiss asserts. We need not, indeed, conclude, as many of these philosophers are inclined to do, that, because we have no reason for believing in the existence of other people, it is therefore highly doubtful whether they do exist. The philosophers who advocate this opinion commonly refute themselves by assigning the existence of other people as part of their reason for believing that it is very doubtful whether any other people exist. That for which we have no reason may, nevertheless, be certainly true. And, indeed, one of the philosophers who hold most clearly and expressly that we do know not only the existence of other people but also that of material objects, is also one of those who deny most emphatically that our own observations can give any reason for believing either in the one or in the other. I refer to Thomas Reid. Reid, indeed, allows himself to use not only the word "observe," but even the word "perceive," in that wide sense in which it might be said that we observe or perceive the thoughts and feelings of others : and I think that the fact that he uses the words in this sense, has misled him into thinking that his view is more plausible and more in accordance with Common Sense than it really is : by using the words in this sense he is able to plead

that "observation" really does give a reason for
some of those generalisations, for which Common
Sense holds that "observation" (in a narrower
sense) does give a reason.   But with regard to what
we observe or perceive, in the strict sense to which
I am confining those words, he asserts quite explicitly that it gives us no reason either for believing
in the existence of material objects or for believing
in the existence of other minds.   Berkeley, he says,
has proved incontrovertibly that it gives us no
reason for the one, and Hume that it gives us no
reason for the other.

Now these philosophers may be right in holding
this.   It may, perhaps, be true that, in this sense,
my own observations give me no reason whatever
for believing that any other person ever has or will
perceive anything like or unlike what I perceive.
But I think it is desirable we should realise how
paradoxical are the consequences which must be
admitted, if this is true.   It must then be admitted
that the very large part of our knowledge, which we
suppose to have some basis in experience, is by no
means based upon experience, in the sense, and to
the extent, which we suppose.   We do for instance,
commonly suppose that there is some basis in
experience for the assertion that some people, whom
we call Germans, use one set of words to express
much the same meaning which we express by using
a different set of words.   But, if this view be
correct, we must admit that no person's experience
gives him any reason whatever for supposing that,
when he hears certain words, any one else has ever
heard or thought of the same words, or meant
anything by them.   The view admits, indeed, that
I do know that when I hear certain words,
somebody else has generally had thoughts more or
less similar to those which I suppose him to have
had : but it denies that my own observations could

ever give me the least reason for supposing that this is so. It admits that my own observations may give me reason for supposing that *if* anyone has ever had perceptions like mine in some respects, he will also have had other perceptions like others of mine : but it denies that they give me any reason for supposing that any one else has had a perception like one of mine. It admits that my own observations may give me reason for supposing that certain perceptions and thoughts in *one* person (*if* they exist) will be followed or preceded by certain other perceptions and thoughts in that person : but it denies that they give me any reason whatever for *any* similar generalisation concerning the connection of a certain kind of perception in one person with a certain kind of perception in another. It admits that I should not have certain perceptions, which I do have, unless someone else had had certain other perceptions ; but it denies that my own observations can give me any reason for saying so — for saying that I should not have had this perception, unless someone else had had that. No observations of mine, it holds, can ever render it probable that such a generalisation is true ; no observation of mine can ever confirm or verify such a generalisation. If we are to say that any such generalisation whatever is based upon observation, we can only mean, what Reid means, that it is based on a series of assumptions. When I observe this particular thing, I assume that *that* particular thing, which I do not observe, exists ; when I observe another particular thing, I again assume that a second particular thing, which I do not observe, exists ; when I observe a third particular thing, I again assume that a third particular thing, which I do not observe, exists. These assumed facts—the assumed fact that one observation of mine is accompanied by the existence of one particular kind of thing, and that another observation of mine is accompanied by the existence of a different particular kind of thing, will then give me a reason for different generalisations concerning the connection of different perceptions of mine with different external objects—objects which I do not perceive. But (it is maintained) nothing but a mass of such assumptions will give me a reason for any such generalisation.

Now I think it must be admitted that there is something paradoxical in such a view. I think it may be admitted that, in holding it, the philosopher of Common Sense departs from Common Sense at least as far in one direction as his opponents had done in another. But I think that there is some excuse for those who hold it : I think that, in one respect, they are more in the right than those who do not hold it—than those who hold that my own observations do give me a reason for believing in the existence of other people. For those who hold that my observations do give me a reason, have, I believe, universally supposed that the reason lies in a part of my observations, in which no such reason is to be found. This is why I have chosen to ask the question : *What* reason do my observations give me for believing that any other person has any particular perceptions or beliefs ? I wish to consider *which* among the things which I observe will give such a reason. For this is a question to which no answer, that I have ever seen, appears to me to be correct. Those who have asked it have, so far as I know, answered it *either* by denying that my observations give me any reason *or* by pointing to a part of my observations, which, as it seems to me, really do give none. Those who deny are, it seems to me, right in holding that the reason given by those who affirm is no reason. And their correct opinion on this point will, I think, partly serve to explain their denial. They have supposed that if our observations give us any reason at all for asserting the existence of other people, that reason must lie where it has been supposed to lie by those who hold that they do give a reason. And then, finding that this assigned reason is no reason, they have assumed that there is no other.

I am proposing then to ask : Which among the observations, which I make, and which (as we commonly suppose) are similar in kind to those which all or almost all men make, will give a reason for supposing that the existence of any of them is generally connected with the existence of certain kinds of perception or belief in other people ? And in order to answer this question, it is obvious we must first consider two others. We must consider, in the first place : Of what nature must observations be, if they are to give a reason for any generalisation asserting that the existence of one kind of thing is generally connected with that of another ? And we must consider in the second place : What kinds of things do we observe ?

Now to the first of these questions I am not going to attempt to give a complete answer. The question concerning the rules of Inductive Logic, which is the question at issue, is an immensely difficult and intricate question. And I am not going to attempt to say, what kind of observations are *sufficient* to justify a generalisation. But it is comparatively easy to point out that a certain kind of observations are *necessary* to justify a generalisation : and this is all that I propose to do. I wish to point out certain conditions which observations must satisfy, if they are to justify a generalisation ; without in any way implying that all observations which do satisfy these conditions, *will* justify a generalisation. The conditions, I shall mention, are ones which are certainly *not* sufficient to justify a generalisation ; but they are, I think, conditions, without which no generalisation can be justified.   If a particular kind of observations do *not* satisfy these conditions, we can say with certainty that those observations give us *no* reason for believing in the existence of other people ; though, with regard to observations which *do* satisfy them, we shall only be able to say that they *may* give a reason.

What conditions, then, must observations satisfy, if they are to justify a generalisation? Let us suppose that the generalisation to be justified is one which asserts that the existence of a kind of object, which we will call A, is generally preceded, accompanied, or followed by the existence of a kind of object, which we call B.   A, for instance, might be the hearing of a certain word by one person, and B the thought of that which we call the meaning of the word, in another person ; and the generalisation to be justified might be that when one person hears a word, not spoken by himself, someone else has generally thought of the meaning of that word. What must I have observed, if the generalisation that the existence of A is generally preceded by the existence of B, is to be justified by my observations? One first point, I think, is plain.   I must have observed both some object, which is in some respects like A, and which I will call a, and also some object in some respects like B which I will call β : I must have observed both a and β, and also I must have observed β preceding a. This, at least, I must have observed.   But I do not pretend to say *how* like a and β must be to A and B ; nor do I pretend to say how often I must have observed β preceding a, although it is generally held that I must have observed this more than once.   These are questions, which would have to be discussed if we were trying to discover what observations were *sufficient* to justify the generalisation that the existence of A is

generally preceded by that of B. But I am only
trying to lay down the minimum which is *necessary*
to justify this generalisation ; and therefore I am
content to say that we must have observed something more or less like B preceding something more
or less like A, at least once.

But there is yet another minimum condition. If
my observation of β preceding α is to justify the
generalisation that the *existence* of A is generally
preceded by the *existence* of B, it is plain, I think,
that both the β and the α, which I observed, must
have *existed* or been *real*; and that also the existence
of β must *really* have preceded that of α. It is
plain that if, when I observed α and β, α existed
but β did not, this observation could give me no
reason to suppose that on another occasion when A
existed, B *would* exist. Or again, if, when I
observed β preceding α, both β and α existed,
but the existence of β did not *really* precede that of
α, but, on the contrary, followed it, this observation
could certainly give me no reason to suppose that,
in general, the existence of A was *preceded* by the
existence of B. Indeed this condition that what is
observed must have been *real* might be said to be
included in the very meaning of the word "observation." We should, in this connection, say that we
had *not* observed β preceding α, unless β and α
were both real, and β had really preceded α. If I
say "I have *observed* that, on one occasion, my
hearing of the word 'moon' was followed by my
imagining a luminous silvery disc," I commonly
mean to include in my statement the assertion that
I did, on that occasion, really hear the word "moon,"
and really did have a visual image of a luminous
disc, and that my perception was really followed by
my imagination. If it were proved to me that this
had not really happened, I should admit that I had
not really observed it. But though this condition

that, if observation is to give reason for a generalisation, what is observed must be real, may thus be said to be implied in the very word "observation," it was necessary for me to mention the condition explicitly. It was necessary, because, as I shall presently show, we do and must also use the word "observation" in a sense in which the assertion "I observe A" by no means includes the assertion "A exists"—in a sense in which it *may* be true that though I did observe A, yet A did *not* exist.

But there is also, I think, a third necessary condition which is very apt to be overlooked. It may, perhaps, be allowed that observation gives some reason for the proposition that hens' eggs are generally laid by hens. I do not mean to say that any one man's observation can give a reason for this proposition : I do not assume either that it can or that it cannot. Nor do I mean to make any assumption as to what must be meant by the words "hens" and "eggs," if this proposition is to be true. I am quite willing to allow for the moment that if it is true at all, we must understand by "hens" and "eggs," objects very unlike that which we directly observe, when we see a hen in a yard, or an egg on the breakfast-table. I am willing to allow the possibility that, as some Idealists would say, the proposition "Hens lay eggs" is false, unless we mean by it : A certain kind of collection of spirits or monads sometimes has a certain intelligible relation to another kind of collection of spirits or monads. I am willing to allow the possibility that, as Reid and some scientists would say, the proposition "Hens lay eggs" is false, if we mean by it anything more than that : Certain configurations of invisible material particles sometimes have a certain spatio-temporal relation to another kind of configuration of invisible material particles. Or again I am willing to allow, with certain other philosophers, that we must, if it is to be true, interpret this proposition as meaning that certain kinds of sensations have to certain other kinds a relation which may be expressed by saying that the one kind of sensations "lay" the other kind. Or again, as other philosophers say, the proposition " Hens lay eggs " may possibly mean : Certain sensations of mine *would*, under certain conditions, have to certain other sensations of mine a relation which may be expressed by saying that the one set would "lay" the other set. But whatever the proposition "Hens' eggs are generally laid by hens" may *mean*, most philosophers would, I think, allow that, in some sense or other, this proposition was true. And they would also I think allow that we have *some* reason for it ; and that *part* of this reason at all events lies in observation : they would allow that we should have no reason for it unless certain things had been observed, which have been observed, Few, I think, would say that the existence of an egg "intrinsically points" to that of a hen, in such a sense that, even if we had had no experience of any kind concerning the manner in which objects like eggs are connected with animals like hens, the mere inspection of an egg would justify the assertion : A hen has probably existed.

I assume, then, that objects having all the characteristics which hens' eggs have (whatever these may be) are generally laid by hens (whatever hens may be) ; and I assume that, if we have any reason for this generalisation at all, observation gives us some reason for it. But now, let us suppose that the only observations we had made were those which we should commonly describe by saying that we had seen a hen laying an egg. I do not say that any number of such observations, by themselves, would be *sufficient* to justify our generalisation : I think it is plain that they would not. But let us suppose, for the moment, that we had observed nothing else which bore upon the connection between hens and eggs; and that, if therefore our generalisation was justified by any observations at all, it was justified by these. We are supposing, then, that the observations which we describe as "seeing hens lay eggs" give some reason for the generalisation that eggs of that kind are generally laid by hens. And if these observations give reason for this, obviously *in a sense* they give reason for the generalisation that the existence of such an egg is generally preceded by that of a hen; and hence also, they give us reason to suppose that if such an egg exists, a hen has probably existed also—that unless a hen had existed, the egg would not have existed. But the point to which I wish to call attention is that it is *only* in a limited sense that they do give reason for this. They only give us reason to suppose that, for each egg, there has existed a hen, which was at some time *near* the place where the egg in question then was, and which existed at a time *near* to that at which the egg began to exist. The only kind of hens, whose existence they do give us reason to suppose, are hens, of which each was at some time in spatial and temporal proximity (or, if Idealists prefer, in the relations which are the "intelligible counterparts" of these) to an egg. They give us no information at all about the existence of hens (if there are any) which never came within a thousand miles of an egg, or which were dead a thousand years before any egg existed. That is to say, they *do* give us reason to suppose that, if a particular egg exists, there has probably existed a hen which was at some time *near* that egg; but they give us no reason to suppose that, if a particular egg exists, there must have existed a hen which never came near that egg. They *do* give us reason to suppose that, for each egg, there has probably existed a hen which at some time stood to the egg in question in that relation which we have observed to hold between an egg and a hen, when we observed the hen laying an egg. But they give us no reason to infer from the existence of an egg any other kind of hen : any hen which *never* stood to the egg in the relation in which we have observed that some hens do stand to eggs.

What I wish to suggest is that this condition is a universal condition for sound inductions. If the observation of β preceding α can ever give us any reason at all for supposing that the existence of A is generally preceded by that of B, it can at most only give us reason to suppose that the existence of an A is generally preceded by that of a B *which stands to our A in the same relation in which β has been observed to stand to α*. It cannot give the least reason for supposing that the existence of an A must have been preceded by that of a B, which did *not* stand to A in the observed relation, but in some quite different one. If we are to have any reason to infer from the existence of an A the existence of such a B, the reason must lie in some different observations. That this is so, in the case of hens' eggs and hens, is, I think, obvious : and, if the rule is *not* universal, some reason should at least be given for supposing that it does apply in one case and not in another.

Having thus attempted to point out some conditions which seem to be necessary, though not *sufficient*, where observation is to give any reason for a generalisation, I may now proceed to my second preliminary question · What kinds of things do we observe ?

In order to illustrate how much and how little I mean by "observation" or "direct perception," I will take as an instance a very common visual perception. Most of us are familiar with the experience which we should describe by saying that we had seen a red book and a blue book side by side upon a shelf. What exactly can we be said to observe or directly perceive when we have such an experience? We certainly observe one colour, which we call blue, and a different colour, which we call red; each of these we observe as having a particular size and shape; and we observe also these two coloured patches as having to one another the spatial relation which we express by saying they are side by side. All this we certainly see or directly perceive *now*, whatever may have been the process by which we have come to perceive so much. But when we say, as in ordinary talk we should, that the objects we perceive are *books*, we certainly mean to ascribe to them properties, which, in a sense which we all understand, are not actually seen by us, at the moment when we are merely looking at two books on a shelf two yards off. And all such properties I mean to exclude as not being then *observed* or *directly perceived* by us. When I speak of what we *observe*, when we see two books on a shelf, I mean to limit the expression to that which is *actually seen*. And, thus understood, the expression does include colours, and the size and shape of colours, and spatial relations in three dimensions between these patches of colour, but it includes nothing else.

But I am also using observation in a sense in which we can be said actually to observe a movement. We commonly say that we can sometimes *see* a red billiard ball moving towards a white one on a green table. And, here again, I do not mean to include in what is directly perceived or observed, all that we mean by saying that the two objects perceived are billiard-balls. But I do mean to include what (we should say) we *actually see*. We actually see a more or less round red patch moving towards a more or less round white patch ; we *see* the stretch of green between them diminishing in size. And this perception is not merely the same as a series of perceptions—first a perception of a red patch with a green stretch of one size between it and the white ; then a perception of a red patch with a green stretch of a different size between it and the white ; and so on. In order to perceive a movement we must have a different perception from any one of these or from the sum of them. We must *actually see* the green stretch diminishing in size.

Now it is undoubtedly difficult, in some instances, to decide precisely what is perceived in this sense and what is not. But I hope I have said enough to show that I am using " perceive " and " observe " in a sense in which, on a given occasion, it is easy to decide that *some* things certainly are perceived, and other things, as certainly, are not perceived. I am using it in a sense in which we do perceive such a complex object as a white patch moving towards a red one on a green field ; but I am not using it in any sense in which we could be said to " perceive " or " observe " that what we saw moving was a billiard-ball. And in the same way I think we can distinguish roughly between what, on any given occasion, we perceive, as we say, " by any one of the other senses," and what we do not perceive by it. We can say with certainty that, on any given occasion, there are certain kinds of " content " which we are actually hearing, and others which we are *not* actually hearing ; though with regard to some again it is difficult to say whether we are actually hearing them or not. And similarly we can distinguish with certainty in some instances, between what we are on a given occasion, actually smelling or feeling, and what we are not actually smelling or feeling.

But now, besides these kinds of "things," "objects," or "contents," which we perceive, as we say, "by the senses," there is also another kind which we can be said to observe. Not only can I observe a red and blue book side by side ; I can also observe myself observing them. I can perceive a red patch moving towards a white, and I can also perceive my perception of this movement. And what I wish to make as plain as I can is that my perception of the movement of a coloured patch can at least be distinguished from that movement itself. I wish to make it plain that to observe a coloured patch moving is to observe one thing ; and to observe myself observing a coloured patch moving is another. When I observe my own perception of a movement, I observe something *more* than when I merely observe the movement, and something very different from the movement. I may perceive a red and a blue book side by side on a shelf ; and at another time I may perceive a red ball moving towards a white. The red and blue patch, of one shape, at rest side by side, are different from the red, of another shape, moving towards the white ; and yet, when I say that both are "perceived," I mean by "perceived" one and the same thing. And since, thus, two different things may both be perceived, there must also be some difference between each of them and what is meant by saying that it is perceived. Indeed, in precisely the same way in which I may observe a spatial relation between a red patch and a blue (when I observe them "side by side") I do, when I observe my own perception of them, observe a spatial relation between it and them. I observe a distance between my perception and the red and blue books which I perceive, comparable in magnitude with the breadth or height of the blue book, just as these are comparable in magnitude with one another. And

when I say I observe a distance between my
perception of a red book and that red book itself, I
do not mean that I observe a distance between my
eyes, or any other part of what I call my body, and
the red patch in question. I am talking not of my
eyes, but of my actual perception. I observe my
perception of a book to be near the book and
further from the table, in exactly the same sense in
which I observe the book to be near the shelf on
which it stands, and further from the table. And
just as, if the distance between a red patch and a
white is to be perceived, the red patch must be
different from the white, so, if I perceive a certain
distance between my perception and the red patch,
my perception must be different from the red patch
which I perceive.

I assume, then, that we observe, on the one hand,
coloured patches of certain shapes and sizes, and
their spatial relations to one another, together with
all the other kinds of "contents," which we should
usually be said to perceive "through the senses."
And, on the other hand, we also sometimes observe
our own perceptions of such "contents" and our
thoughts. And these two kinds of "content" are
different from one another : my perception of a red
patch with gold letters on it, is not itself a red patch
with gold letters on it ; and hence, when I observe
my perception of this patch, I observe something
different from that which I observe when I merely
perceive the patch. Either of these two kinds
of "content"—either colours, moving or at rest,
sounds, smells, and all the rest—or, on the other
hand, my perceptions of these—either of these
two kinds, or both, might conceivably, since both
are observed, give grounds for a generalisation
concerning what exists. But, as I have said, if
observations are to give any ground for such a
generalisation, it must be assumed that what is

observed *exists* or is *real*. And since, as I have
insisted, when I observe my *perception* of a red patch
with gold letters on it, I observe something different
from what I observed when I merely observed a red
patch with gold letters on it, it follows that to assume
the existence of my perception of this red and gold
is *not* the same thing as to assume the existence of
the red and gold itself.

But what, it may be asked, do I mean by this
property of "existence" or "reality," which may, it
would seem, belong to every content, which I
observe, or may again belong to none, or which
may belong to some and not to others? What is
this property which may belong to my perception of
a movement, and yet not belong to the movement
perceived, or which may again belong to the movement perceived and not to my perception of it, or
which may again belong to both or to neither?

It is necessary, I think, to ask this question at
this point, because there are some philosophers who
hold that, in the case of some kinds of "content,"
at all events, to say that they "exist" is to say that
they are "perceived." Some hold that to say "A
exists" is to say neither more nor less than "A is
perceived"—that the two expressions are perfect
synonyms; and others again would say that by "A
exists or is real" we may mean *more* than that "A
is perceived," but that we must at least mean this.
Now, I have hitherto used the word "existence"
pretty freely, and I think that, when I used it, I
used it in its ordinary sense. I think it will
generally have suggested to you precisely what I
meant to convey, and I think that, in some cases at
all events, it will not even have occurred to you to
doubt whether you did understand what I meant by
it. But, if these philosophers are right, then, if you
have understood what I meant by it, I have all along
been using it in a sense, which renders the end of

my last paragraph perfect nonsense. If these philosophers are right, then, when I assert that what *is* perceived may yet *not* exist, I am really asserting that what *is* perceived may yet *not* be perceived—I am contradicting myself. I am, of course, quite unaware that I am doing so. But these philosophers would say *either* you are contradicting yourself, *or* you are not using the word "exists" in its ordinary sense. And either of these alternatives would be fatal to my purpose. If I am not using the word in its ordinary sense, then I shall not be understood by anyone; and, if I am contradicting myself, then what I say will not be worth understanding.

Now, with one class of these philosophers—the class to which, I think, Berkeley belongs—I think I can put myself right comparatively easily. The philosophers I mean are those who say that it is only in the case of one particular class of "contents" (the kind of "content" which Berkeley calls "ideas") that to say "the 'content' A exists" is to say "A is perceived," and who admit that in the case of other contents—myself and my perceptions and thoughts, for example—to say that *these* exist or are real, is to say of them something different from this. These philosophers admit, that is to say, that the word "exists" has two different senses : and that in only one of these senses is it synonymous with the words "is perceived." When (they hold) I say of such a content as a red patch with gold letters on it that it "exists" I *do* mean that it is perceived; but when I say of my *perception* of such a patch that *it* exists, I do *not* mean that my perception is perceived but something different from this. Now, it would be nothing strange that one and the same word should be used in two different senses ; many words are used in many different senses. But it would, I think, be something very strange indeed, if in the case of

a word which we constantly apply to all sorts of
different objects, we should uniformly apply it to one
large class of object in the one sense and the one
sense only and the other large class in the other
sense and the other sense only. Usually, in the
case of such ambiguous words, it happens that,
in different contexts, we apply it to one and the
same object in *both* senses. We sometimes wish
to say of a given object that it has the one
property, and sometimes we wish to say of the
same object that it has the other property ; and
hence we apply the same word to the same object,
at one time in one sense, and at another in the other.
I think, therefore, that, even if there were these two
different senses of the word "existence," it would be
very unlikely that we should not commonly, in some
contexts, apply it in the sense, in which (as is
alleged) it does apply to perceptions, to "contents"
which are not perceptions. Indeed, I think, it is
quite plain that we constantly do ask, with regard
to what is not a perception, whether *it* exists, in
precisely the same sense, in which we ask, with
rega d to a perception, whether *it* exists. We ask
in precisely the same sense : Was the Roc a real
bird, or merely an imaginary one? and, did Sindbad's
perception of the Roc really exist, or is it a fiction
that he perceived a Roc? I think, therefore, that
the sense in which these philosophers admit that we
do apply the word "existence" to perceptions, is
one in which we also commonly apply it to "contents" other than perceptions. But, even if this is
not the case, I can set myself right with them by
a simple explanation. I need merely explain that
the sense in which I am proposing to enquire
whether a red patch exists, is precisely the sense in
which they admit that my perception of a red patch
does exist. And in this sense, it is plain that to
suppose that a thing may exist, which is not

perceived, or that it may *not* exist, although it is perceived, is at least not self-contradictory.

But there may be other philosophers who will say that, in the case of a perception also, to say that it exists or is real is to say that it is perceived—either that alone or something more as well. And to these philosophers I would first point out that they are admitting that the proposition "This perception is real" is significant. There is some sense or other in which we may say : "Alexander's perception of an elephant was real or did exist, but Sindbad's perception of a Roc was *not* real—never did exist" : the latter proposition is, in some sense or other, not self-contradictory. And then I would ask of them : When they say, that to call a perception "real" is to assert that it is perceived, do they mean by this that to call it real is to assert that it is *really* perceived, or not? If they say "No," then they are asserting that to call a perception "real" is merely to say that it was perceived in the sense in which Sindbad *did* perceive a Roc : they are asserting that to call it "real" is not to say, in any sense, that it was *really* perceived : they are asserting that to call a perception "real" is to say that it was perceived, in some sense quite other than that in which we ordinarily use the word : for we certainly commonly mean, when we say "A was perceived," that a perception of A was "real" : we should commonly say that Sindbad did *not* perceive a Roc—meaning that no such perception ever did exist. I do not think they do mean this ; and, in any case, if they do, I think it is plain that they are wrong. When we say that a perception is "real," we certainly do not mean merely that it is the object of another perception, which may itself be quite unreal—purely imaginary. I assume, therefore, that when they say : To call a perception "real" is to say that it is perceived ; they mean, what we should naturally understand, namely, that: To call it "real" is to say that it is *really* perceived—to say that it is the object of another perception, which is also *real* in the same sense. And, if they mean this, then what they say is certainly untrue. Their definition of reality is circular. It cannot be the case that the *only* sense in which a perception may be said to be real, is one in which to call it so is to assert that not it alone, but another perception is real also. It cannot be the case that the assertion "A is real" is *identical* with the assertion "A and B are both real," where A and B are different, and "real" is used in the same sense as applied to both. If it is to be true that the assertion "A is real" *ever*, in any sense, includes the assertion "A is *really* perceived," there must be another sense of the word "real," in which to assert "A is real" is to assert *less* than "A is *really* perceived"—the sense, namely, in which we here assert that the *perception* of A is real.

We find, therefore, that the other class of philosophers were at least right in this: they were right in allowing that the sense in which we commonly say that our perceptions exist is one in which "exist" does not include, even as a part of its meaning, "is perceived." We find that there is a common sense of the word "existence," in which to say "A exists" must mean *less* than "A is *really* perceived": since, otherwise, the only possible definition of the word "existence" would be a circular definition. And I may point out that two other definitions, which have been sometimes suggested by philosophers as giving what we commonly mean by "reality" or "existence" are vitiated by the same fault—they also are circular. Some philosophers have sometimes suggested that when we call a thing "real," we mean that it is "systematically connected" in some way with other things. But,

when we look into their meaning, we find that what
they mean is (what, indeed, is alone plausible)—
systematically connected with other *real* things.
And it may possibly be the case that we sometimes
use the word "real" in this sense : but, at least, it
must be certainly the case, that, if we do, we *also*
use it in another and simpler sense—the sense in
which it is employed in the proposed definition.
And other philosophers have suggested that what
we mean by "real" is—"connected in some way
with a purpose—helping or hindering, or the object
of a purpose." But if we look into their meaning,
we find they mean—connected with a *real* purpose.
And hence, even if we do sometimes mean by
"real," "connected with a *real* purpose," it is plain
we also sometimes mean by "real" something
simpler than this—that namely, which is meant by
"real" in the proposed definition.

It is certain, therefore, that we do commonly use
the word "existence" in a sense, in which to say
"A exists" is *not* to say "A is perceived," or "A is
systematically connected with other real things," or
"A is purposive." There is a simpler sense than
any of these—the sense in which we say that our
own perceptions do exist, and that Sindbad's perceptions did not exist. But when I say this, I am
by no means denying that what exists, in this
simple sense, may not always *also* exist in all the
others ; and that what exists in any of them may
not *also* always exist in this. It is quite possible
that what exists is always *also* perceived, and that
what is perceived always *also* exists. All that I am
saying is that, even if this is so, this proposition is
significant—is not merely a proposition about the
meaning of a word. It is not self-contradictory to
suppose that some things which exist are not perceived, and that some things which are perceived
do not exist.

But, it may be asked : What is this common simple sense of the word "exists"? For my own part, it seems to me to be so simple that it cannot be expressed in other words, except those which are recognised as its synonyms. I think we are all perfectly familiar with its meaning : it is the meaning which you understood me to have throughout this paper, until I began this discussion. I think we can perceive at once what is meant by asserting that my perception of black marks on a white ground is "real," and that no such perception as Sindbad's of a Roc was ever "real": we are perfectly familiar with the property which the one perception is affirmed to possess, aud the other to be without. And I think, as I have said, that this property is a simple one. But, whatever it is, this, which we ordinarily mean, is what I mean by "existence" or "reality." And this property, we have seen, is certainly neither identical with nor inclusive of that complex one which we mean by the words "is perceived."

I may now, then, at last approach the main question of my paper. Which among the "contents" which I observe will give me reason to suppose that my observation of some of them is generally preceded or accompanied or followed by the existence of certain particular perceptions, thoughts or feelings in another person? I have explained that the "contents" which I actually observe may be divided into two classes : on the one hand, those which, as we commonly say, we perceive "through the senses"; and, on the other hand, my perceptions of these last, my thoughts, and my feelings. I have explained that if any of these observed contents are to give reason for a generalisation about what exists, *they* must exist. And I have explained that with regard to both classes of "contents" I am using the word "exist" in precisely the same sense—a sense, in which it is certainly not self-contradictory to suppose that what *is* perceived, does not exist, and that what is *not* perceived, does exist ; and, in which, therefore, the assumption that a red patch with gold letters on it exists, is a *different* assumption from the assumption that my *perception* of a red patch with gold letters on it exists ; and the assumption that my *perception* of a red patch with gold letters on it exists, is a *different* assumption from the assumption that a red patch with gold letters on it exists.

What, then, that we observe, can give us any reason for believing that anyone else has certain particular perceptions, thoughts or feelings ? It has, I think, been very commonly assumed that the observation of my own perceptions, thoughts, and feelings, can, by itself, give me such a reason. And I propose, therefore, to examine this assumption. If, as I hope to show, it is false ; it will then follow, that if our own observation gives us any reason whatever, for believing in the existence of other persons, we must assume the existence, not only of our own perceptions, thoughts and feelings, but also of some, at least, among that other class of data, which I may now, for the sake of brevity, call "sense-contents" ; we must assume that some of them exist, in precisely the same sense in which we assume that our perceptions, thoughts, and feelings exist.

The theory which I propose to examine is, then, the following. My observation of my own thoughts, feelings, and perceptions may, it asserts, give me some reason to suppose that another person has thoughts, feelings, and perceptions similar to some of mine. Let us assume, accordingly, that my own thoughts, feelings, and perceptions do exist ; but that none of the "sense-contents," which I also observe, do so. Where among my perceptions am

I to look for any which might conceivably give me a reason for supposing the existence of other perceptions similar to my own? It is obvious where I must look. I have perceptions which I call perceptions of other people's bodies ; and these are certainly similar in many respects to other perceptions of my own body. But I also observe that certain kinds of perceptions of my own body are preceded by certain other perceptions, thoughts, or feelings of mine. I may, for instance, observe that when I perceive my hand suddenly catch hold of my foot in a particular way, this perception was preceded by a particular kind of feeling of pain. I may, perhaps, observe this often enough to justify the generalisation that the perception of that particular motion of my body is generally preceded by that particular feeling of pain. And in this way I may perhaps have reason for quite a number of generalisations which assert that particular kinds of perceptions of my own body are generally preceded by other particular kinds of perceptions, thoughts, or feelings of my own.

But I may also, no doubt, have the perception, which I call the perception of another person's hand catching hold of his foot, in a manner similar to that in which I have perceived my own hand catch hold of my own foot. And my perception of another person's hand catching hold of his foot may undoubtedly be similar in many respects to my perception of my own hand catching hold of my own foot. But I shall not observe the same kind of feeling of pain preceding my perception of *his* hand catching hold of his foot, which I have observed preceding my perception of *my* hand catching hold of my foot. Will my generalisation, then, give me any reason to suppose that nevertheless my perception of his hand catching hold of his foot *is* preceded by a similar feeling of pain, not in me but in him ? We undoubtedly do assume that when I perceive another person's body making movements similar to those which I have observed my own body making, this perception has generally been preceded by some feeling or perception of his similar to that which I have observed to precede my perception of similar movements in my own body. We do assume this ; and it is precisely the kind of generalisation, which, I have insisted, must be admitted to be true. But my present question is : Will such observations as I have described give any reason for thinking any such generalisation true ? I think it is plain that they will not give the slightest reason for thinking so. In the first place, all the perceptions which I call perceptions of another person's body differ very considerably from any of those which I call perceptions of my own. But I am willing to waive this objection. I am not offering any theory as to what degree of likeness is *sufficient* to justify a generalisation : and therefore I will allow that the degree of likeness *may* be sufficient. But there remains an objection which is, I think, quite fatal to the proposed inference. This objection is that the inference in question plainly does not satisfy the third condition which I suggested above as *necessary*, wherever any generalisation is to be justified by observation. I am willing to allow that my observations of the fact that my perception of a certain movement in my own body is preceded by a certain feeling of pain, *will* justify the generalisation that my perception of any such movement, whether in my own body *or* in that of another person, is generally preceded by a similar feeling of pain. And I allow, therefore, that when I perceive a certain movement in another's body, it *is* probable that the feeling of pain exists, though I do not perceive it. But, if it *is* probable that such a feeling of pain exists, such a feeling must stand *in the same relation* to my perception of the movement in another person's body, in which a similar feeling of pain has been observed by me to stand to my perception of such a movement in my own body. That is to say the only kind of feeling of pain, which my observations do justify me in inferring, if (as I admit they may) they justify me in inferring any at all, is a feeling of pain of *my own*. They cannot possibly justify the belief in the existence of any such feeling *except* one which stands to my perception in the same relation in which my feelings do stand to *my* perceptions—one, that is to say, which is my own. I have no more reason to believe that the feeling of pain which probably precedes my perception of a movement in another person's body can be the feeling *of another person*, than, in my former example, I had reason to suppose that the hen, whose existence probably preceded that of a given egg, could be a hen, which had never been near the egg in question. The two cases are exactly analogous. I observe a feeling of pain *of my own* preceding a perception *of my own*. I observe the two, that is to say, as standing to one another, in those relations (whatever they may be) in which any perception of mine stands to any other thought, perception or feeling of mine, and which are, at all events, different from any relation in which a perception or feeling of another person can stand to one of mine. I never perceive the feeling and the perception as standing in any other relation. In any case, therefore, where I do observe something like the perception, but do not observe the feeling, I can only be justified (*if* justified in inferring any feeling at all), in inferring an unperceived feeling *of my own*.

For this reason I think that no observations of my own perceptions, feelings or thoughts can give me the slightest reason for supposing a connection between any of them and any feeling, perception, or thought in another person. The argument is perfectly general, since *all* my perceptions, feelings and thoughts do have to one another those relations in virtue of which I call them mine ; and which, when I talk of a perception, feeling or thought as being *another person's*, I mean to say that it has *not* got to any of mine. I can, therefore, merely from observation of *this* class of data never obtain the slightest reason for belief in the existence of a feeling, perception, or thought which does *not* stand in these relations to one of mine—which *is*, that is to say, the feeling, perception or thought, of another person. But how different is the case, if we adopt the hypothesis, which I wish to recommend—if we assume the existence of that other class of data which I have called "sense-contents!" On this hypothesis, that which I perceive, when I perceive a movement of my own body, is *real*; that which I perceive when I perceive a movement of another's body is *real* also. I can now observe not merely the relation between my *perception* of a movement of my body and my own feelings, but also a relation between a *real* movement of my body and my own feelings. And there is no reason why I should not be justified in inferring that another person's feelings stand *in the same relation* to the real movements of his body, in which I observe my own feelings to stand to similar real movements of mine.

But there is another argument which may still be urged by those who hold that my own perceptions, thoughts, and feelings, by themselves, may be sufficient to justify a belief in the existence of other persons. It may be said : "Our observation of our own perceptions may be sufficient to *verify* or *confirm* the hypothesis that other persons exist. This hypothesis is one which "works." The assumption that other persons have particular thoughts, feelings and perceptions enables us to predict that they will have others and that our own perceptions will be modified accordingly : it enables us to predict future perceptions of our own ; and we find that these predictions are constantly verified. We observe that we do have the perceptions, which the hypothesis leads us to expect we should have. In short, our perceptions occur just as they would do, *if* the hypothesis were true ; our perceptions behave *as if* other persons had the perceptions, thoughts and feelings which we suppose them to have. Surely, then, they confirm the truth of the hypothesis—they give some reason to think it probably true ? "

All this, which I have supposed an opponent to urge, I admit to be true. I admit that the fact that an hypothesis works may give some reason to suppose it true. I admit that my perceptions occur just as they would do, if other people had the perceptions which I suppose them to have. I admit that that assumption enables me to make predictions as to future perceptions of my own, and that I observe these predictions to come true. I admit all this. But I admit it only in a sense in which it in no way conflicts with the position which I am maintaining. The words, which I have put into the mouth of a supposed opponent, may, in fact, mean three different things, which it is worth while to distinguish. In two of those meanings, which I shall admit to be true and which are what make them seem plausible, they do not deny what I assert. Only in the third sense are they an objection to my position : and in that sense they are false.

One of the meanings which I admit to be true is as follows :—I have not only admitted but insisted that some of my perceptions are just such as would occur if another person had certain particular feelings : I have insisted that I should not have just those perceptions which I do have, unless some other person had certain feelings and perceptions which I suppose him to have. And I admit further that the fact that I have one of the perceptions in question—for instance, that of another person's hand catching hold of his foot—this fact, *together with* the true assumption that I should not have this perception, unless some other person felt pain, will justify the assertion that another person has felt pain. In this sense, I admit, the fact that I perceive what I do perceive will give me reason to suppose that another person has felt pain. And, on the other hand, I also admit that the fact that I have this perception, *together with* the true assumption that when I have it another person has felt pain, may help to justify the assumption that the perception in question is one which I should not have had unless another person had felt pain—it helps to justify the generalisation that certain of my perceptions are just what would occur, *if* another person had felt pain. In general terms, that is to say, I admit that the occurrence of B, *together with* the assumption that B is just the sort of thing which would occur if A existed, will justify the assertion that A exists in that particular instance. And I also admit that the occurrence of B, *together with* the assumption that A exists in that particular instance, may help to justify the assumption that B is just the sort of thing which would exist, if A existed. In other words : When it is said that the observation of B's existence confirms or verifies the assumption that A exists, either of two things may be meant. It may be meant that, assuming B to be the sort of thing which would exist if A existed, the observation of B confirms the assumption that A exists *in this particular instance*. Or, on the other hand, it may be meant that, assuming

A to exist in this particular instance, the observation of B may confirm the generalisation, that B is just the sort of thing which would exist, if A existed. *Either* the one *or* the other of these two things is, I think, what is generally assumed, when it is assumed that what we do observe confirms or verifies the assumption that there exists some particular thing which we don't observe.   And I am admitting that both these assumptions are true.

But neither of them conflicts in any way with the position I am maintaining.   What I am maintaining is that no observation of my own perceptions, *by itself*, can confirm the generalisation that any one of them *is* just what would occur if another person had a particular feeling.   I admit this generalisation to be true ; and I admit that my observation of my own perceptions and feelings may give me *reason* to suppose that *if* another person has certain perceptions or feelings *he* will also have certain others. What I deny is that they give me the slightest reason to suppose that the existence of any such feeling or perception in another has any connection with the existence of any perception *of my own*— to suppose that any perception of my own is the sort of thing which would occur *if* another person had a particular feeling.   What therefore, my opponent must affirm is that the observation of a perception of my own *without* the assumption (which Reid makes) that in that particular instance any feeling or perception of another person, of any kind whatever, has preceded it, may give me reason to suppose that that perception of my own is of a kind which is generally preceded by a particular kind of feeling in another person.   And this, I think, is plainly false.

But there is yet a third thing which may be meant, and which I am willing to admit may be true.   It may be said : " I believe many generalisations of the following kind. I believe that when I have a perception A, some other person has generally had a feeling X ; I believe that the existence of the feeling X is generally followed, in the same person, by that of the feeling Y ; and I believe also that when another person has the feeling Y, I generally have the perception B. I believe all this." And it must, I think, be admitted that we do believe generalisations of this kind, and generalisations in which there are not merely two steps between A and B, but a great number of steps. "But then," it may be said, "my belief in this generalisation causes me, when I observe my perception A, to expect that I shall have the perception B ; and such expectations, I observe, are constantly realised." And this also, I think, must be admitted to be true. "But, finally," it may be said, " beliefs which produce expectations which are constantly realised are generally true. And hence the fact that these beliefs of mine about the connection of feelings in other persons with perceptions of my own do lead to expectations which are realised, gives me reason to suppose that these generalisations are true and hence that other persons do have particular kinds of feelings." And I am willing to admit that this also is true. I am willing to admit that true predictions can, as a rule, only be produced by true beliefs. The generalisation that this is so, is, indeed, one which can only be justified by the observations of beliefs, which are, in some way, independently proved to be true ; and hence, if it is to be justified, without assuming the existence of anything other than my own perceptions, thoughts, and feelings, it can only be justified by my observation that beliefs with regard to the manner in which *these* succeed one another generally lead to true predictions. Whether the observation of such beliefs *alone* could give sufficient reason for it, is, I think, doubtful ; but

I am willing to admit that it may be so. One thing, however, is, I think, quite plain : namely, that this generalisation "Beliefs which lead to true predictions are generally true" cannot be true, *unless* some other of the "contents" which I observe, beside my own perceptions, thoughts, and feelings, do exist. That is to say, in giving a reason for supposing the existence of other people, this generalisation also gives a reason for the very theory which I am advocating, namely, that some of those data which I have called "sense-contents" do exist. It does this, because it is quite certain that beliefs in generalisations about the existence of sense-contents *can* (and do) constantly lead to true predictions. The belief that when I have observed a fire of a certain size in my grate, something similar to what I have observed will continue to exist for a certain time, can, and constantly does, lead to the true prediction that, when I come back to my room in half an hour's time, I shall observe a fire of a certain size still burning. We make predictions on such grounds, I think, every day and all day long. And hence unless such beliefs as that what I observe when I see a fire burning *does* exist, *are* true, we certainly have no reason to suppose that beliefs which lead to true predictions are generally true. And hence on this hypothesis also it remains true : that, unless some of the contents which I observe *other* than my own perceptions, thoughts, and feelings, do exist, I cannot have the slightest reason for supposing that the existence of certain perceptions of my own is generally connected with that of certain perceptions, thoughts, or feelings in any other person.

I conclude therefore that, unless some of the observed data which·I have called sense-contents *do* exist, my own observations cannot give me the slightest reason for believing that anybody else has ever had any particular perception, thought, or feeling. And, having arrived so far towards an answer to my first question : How do we know that any other persons exist ?   I may now point out that precisely the same answer must be given to my second question: How do we know that *any* particular kind of thing exists, other than ourselves, our perceptions, thoughts, and feelings, and what we directly perceive ?   There is a view concerning what exists, which deserves, I think, much more respect than it generally receives from philosophers nowadays.   The view I mean is the view that material objects, such as they are conceived by physical science, do really exist.   It is held by some persons (and Reid is among them) that we *do* know of the existence, not only of other persons, but also of the movements of matter in space.   It is held that we do know, with considerable precision, what kinds of movements of matter generally precede my perception, when I have a particular perception.   It is held, for instance, that when I perceive a red and blue book side by side on a shelf, at a certain distance from me, there have existed, between two material objects, which may be called books, and another kind of material object, which may be called my eyes, certain wave-like motions of a material medium ; that there have existed two different sets of waves, of which the one is connected with my perception of red and the other with my perception of blue ; and that the relative heights and breadths of the two different sets of waves, and the relative velocity of their movements are very exactly known.   It is held that some men have a vast amount of very precise information about the existence of objects of this kind ; and I think the view that this is so deserves a great deal of respect. But what I wish now to point out is that no one's observation of his own perceptions, thoughts and feelings, can, by itself, give him the slightest reason for believing in the existence of any such material objects. All the arguments by which I have tried to show that this kind of observation alone can give me no reason to believe in the existence of any kind of perception or feeling in another person, apply, with at least equal force, to show that it can give me no reason to believe in the existence of any kind of material object. On the other hand, if we are to admit the principle that "Beliefs which lead to true predictions, are generally true," this principle will give us at least as much reason to believe in the existence of certain kinds of material objects as to believe in the existence of other persons ; since one of the most remarkable facts about beliefs in the existence of such objects is that they do so often lead to true predictions. But it must be remembered that we can have no reason for believing this principle itself, *unless* our own perceptions, thoughts and feelings are *not* the only kind of observed "content" which really does exist : we can have no reason for it, unless some such things as what I perceive, when I see a red and blue book side by side, do really exist.

It would seem, therefore, that if my own observations do give me any reason whatever for believing in the existence either of any perception in any other person or of any material object, it must be true that not only my own perceptions, thoughts and feelings, but also *some* of the other kinds of things which I directly perceive—colours, sounds, smells, etc.—do really exist : it must be true that some objects of this kind *exist* or are *real* in precisely the same simple sense in which my perceptions of them exist or are real. Is there then any reason to think that this is not true ? Is there any reason to think, for instance, that *none* of the colours which I perceive as occupying areas of certain shapes and sizes really

exist in the areas which they appear to occupy?
This is a question which I wished to discuss at
length, because I think that it is one in which there
are real difficulties. But I have given so much
space to other questions, that I can only deal with it
very briefly here.

Some philosophers are very fond of asserting that
a colour cannot exist except when it is perceived;
and it might possibly be thought that when I suggest
that colours do really exist, I am suggesting that
they do exist when they are not perceived. I wish,
therefore, briefly to point out that the question
whether anything does exist, when it is not perceived,
is one which I have not argued and shall not attempt
to argue in this paper. I have, indeed, tried to
show that since "exists" does not *mean* "is
perceived," it is, at least, conceivable that things
should exist, when they are not perceived. But I
have admitted that it is quite possible none *do* so:
it *may* be the case that whenever a thing exists, it is
also at the same time perceived, for anything that I
have said or shall say to the contrary. I think,
indeed, that, if such things as colours *do* exist, my
observation of their behaviour will justify me in
concluding that they also exist when I myself am,
at least, not aware of perceiving them: but since I
have not attempted to determine what kinds of
observation are sufficient to justify a generalisation,
I do not pretend to say whether this is so or not:
and still less do I pretend to say whether, *if* they
exist when *I* do not perceive them, we are justified
in supposing that someone else must be perceiving
them. The question whether anything exists, when
it is not perceived, and, if so, what things, seems to
me to be one which can only be settled by observation; and thus, I conceive, observation might
justify us in concluding that certain kinds of things—
pains, for example, do *not* exist, when they are not

perceived and that other kinds of things—colours, for example, *do* exist, when they are not perceived. The only way, in which, so far as I am aware, the theory I am advocating does conflict with ordinary Idealistic conclusions, is that it does suggest that things, which are *not* "spiritual," do *sometimes* exist, as really and as truly, as things which are.

The theory, therefore, that nothing exists, except when it is perceived, is no objection (even if it be true) to the supposition that colours do exist. What objections are there to this supposition? All serious objections to it are, I think, of one type. They all rest upon the assumption that, if a certain kind of thing exists at a certain time in a certain place, certain other kinds of things cannot exist at the same time in the same place. They are all, that is to say, of the same type as Berkeley's argument : that, though tbe same body of water may *appear* to be simultaneously both hot and cold (if one of the hands we plunge into it is warm and the other cold), yet the heat and the cold cannot both *really* be in the same body at the same time. And it is worth noticing that anyone who uses this argument must admit that he understands what is meant by " really existing in a given place," and that he means by it something *other* than " being perceived as in a given place." For the argument itself admits that *both* the heat *and* the cold *are* really *perceived* as being in the, same place, and that there is no difficulty in supposing that they are so ; whereas it urges that there *is* a difficulty in supposing that they both *really exist* in it.

Now there is one obvious defect in this type of argument, if designed to prove that *no* sensible quality exists at any place where it is perceived as being—a defect, which Berkeley himself admits in his " Principles," though he omits to notice it where he repeats the argument in his " Hylas." Even if we assume that the heat and the cold cannot *both* exist in the same place (and I admit that, in this case, the contrary assumption does seem repugnant to Common Sense), it does not follow that *neither* exists there.   That is to say this type of argument, even if we grant its initial assumption, will only entitle us to conclude that *some* sensible qualities which we perceive as being in a certain place at a certain time, do not exist in that place at that time. And this eonclusion, I am inclined to think, is true. In the case, for instance, of the so-called " images " which we perceive in a looking-glass, we may very readily admit that the colours and shapes which we perceive do *not* exist at the places where they appear to be—namely at various distances behind the glass. But yet, so far as I can see, we have no reason whatever for supposing that they do not, *except* the assumption that our observations give us reason to believe that *other* sensible qualities *do* exist in those positions behind the glass ; and the assumption that *where* these *other* sensible qualities do exist, those which we see in the glass do *not* exist.   I should, therefore, admit that *some* sensible qualities which we perceive as being in certain places, do *not* exist in those places, while still retaining my belief that others do.   And *perhaps* this explanation is the one which should also be adopted in the case of sensible qualities whieh appear to be at a great distance from us.   When, for instance, (as we say), " we see the moon," *what* we perceive (if the moon be full) is a round bright silver disc, of a small size, at a place very distant from us.   Does that silver disc exist at that place?   With what suppositions does the assumption that it *does* conflict?   Only, so far as I can see, with the supposition that the place in question is *really* occupied by a body such as science has taught us to suppose that the moon *really* is—a spherical body immensely larger than objects, in comparison with which the silver disc which we perceive is small ; *or else* with the supposition that the place in question is really occupied by some part of our atmosphere, or some part of the medium which science supposes to exist between our atmosphere and the moon ; *or else* with the supposition that the place in question is really occupied by what we might see, if the moon were nearer to us by many thousands of miles. Unless we suppose that some other object *is* in the place, in which the silver disc appears to be, and that this object is of a kind which cannot occupy the *same* place which is occupied by a silver disc, we have no reason to suppose that the silver disc does *not* really exist in the place where it appears to be. And, in this case, we *perhaps* have reason for both suppositions and should therefore conclude that the silver disc, which we perceive, does not exist in any real place.

Part, therefore, of these objections to our theory may, I think, be met by admitting that *some* of the sensible qualities which we perceive do not exist at the places where they appear to exist, though others do. But there is, I think, another class of cases, in which we may be justified in denying that two things which (it is asserted) cannot occupy the same space, really cannot. I will take an instance which is, I think, typical. When we look at a drop of blood with the naked eye, we perceive a small red spot, uniformly red all over. But when (as we say) we look at the *same* object under a microscope of a certain power, I am informed that we see a much larger spot, of similar shape, indeed, but *not* uniformly red—having, in fact, small red spots at different positions in a yellowish field. And if we were again to look at the *same* object through a microscope of much higher power still, we might perceive yet a third different arrangement of colours.   Is there any fatal objection to supposing that all *three* appearances—the uniform red spot, the yellowish field with reddish spots in it, and the third, whatever that may be—do all really occupy the same real spatial area?   I cannot see that there is. We are familiar with the idea that a given spatial area may contain parts which are invisible to us. And hence, I think it is quite conceivable that parts of a given area may be *really* occupied by one colour, while the whole is *really* occupied by another.   And this, I think, is what we actually *do* believe in many cases.   At all events, we certainly believe that the area which appears to be occupied by one colour really is *the same area* as that which appears to be occupied by another.   And, unless we assume that the area, in both cases, really is the same, we can certainly have no reason to deny that each colour does really occupy the area which it appears to occupy.

For these reasons I think that the difficulties in the way of supposing that *some* of the sensible qualities which we perceive as being in certain places, really exist in the places in which we perceive them to be, are not insuperable.   I have indeed not done justice to these difficulties ; but then, neither have I done justice to what is to be said on the other side.   At all events, I think it is plain that we have no reason to assert, in any case whatever, that a perceived colour does *not* really exist in the place where it is perceived as being, *unless* we assume that that very same place really is occupied by something else—*either* by some different sensible qualities *or* by material objects such as physical science supposes to exist.   But what reason can we give for such an assumption?   I have tried to show that our own observations can give us none, *unless* we assume that some of the sensible qualities, which we observe as occupying certain places, do really exist in those places. And, if this is so, then we must admit that neither he who believes (with Reid) in the existence of other minds and of matter also, nor he who believes in the existence of other minds and denies that of matter, can have, in his own observations, the slightest reason either for his assertion or for his denial : we must admit that he can have no reason for either assertion or denial, except one which consists in the assumption of the existence or non-existence of something which he does *not* observe—something, therefore, of the very same kind as that for which he gives it as a reason. I am very unwilling to suppose that this is the case : I am very unwilling to suppose that he who believes that Sindbad the Sailor really saw what the " Arabian Nights " represent him as seeing, has just as good reason (so far as his own observation goes) for believing this as he who denies it has for denying it. Still this may be the case. We *must*, perhaps, be content to assume as certain that for which our observation gives no reason : to assume such propositions as that Sindbad did *not* see a Roc, and that you *do* hear my voice. But if it is said that these things are certain ; then it also appears to me to be certain that the colours which I perceive do exist (*some* of them) where I perceive them. The more I look at objects round me, the more I am unable to resist the conviction that what I see does exist, as truly and as really, as my perception of it. The conviction is overwhelming.

This being, then, the state of the case, I think I may at least plead that we have grounds for suspense of judgment as to whether what I see does *not* really exist ; grounds, too, for renewed enquiry, more careful than such enquiry has sometimes been in the past.

WILLIAM JAMES' "PRAGMATISM"

My object in this paper is to discuss some of the things which Prof. William James says about truth in the recent book, to which he has given the above name.* In Lecture VI he professes to give an account of a theory, which he calls "the pragmatist theory of truth;" and he professes to give a briefer preliminary account of the same theory in Lecture II. Moreover, in Lecture VII, he goes on to make some further remarks about truth. In all these Lectures he seems to me to make statements to which there are very obvious objections; and my main object is to point out, as clearly and simply as I can, what seem to me to be the principal objections to some of these statements.

We may, I think, distinguish three different things which he seems particularly anxious to assert about truth.

(I) In the first place, he is plainly anxious to assert some connection between truth and "verification" or "utility." Our true ideas, he seems to say, are those that "work," in the sense that they are or can be "verified," or are "useful."

(II) In the second place, he seems to object to the view that truth is something "static" or "immutable." He is anxious to assert that truths are in some sense "mutable."

(III) In the third place, he asserts that "to an

* *Pragmatism: A New Name for some Old Ways of Thinking: Popular Lectures on Philosophy.* By William James. Longmans, Green, and Co., 1907.

unascertainable extent our truths are man-made products " (p. 242).

To what he asserts under each of these three heads there are, I think, serious objections; and I now propose to point out what seem to me to be the principal ones, under each head separately.

(I)

Professor James is plainly anxious to assert *some* connection between truth and "verification" or "utility." And that there is *some* connection between them everybody will admit. That *many* of our true ideas are verified; that *many* of them can be verified; and that *many* of them are useful, is, I take it, quite indisputable. But Professor James seems plainly to wish to assert something more than this. And one more thing which he wishes to assert is, I think, pretty plain. He suggests, at the beginning of Lecture VI, that he is going to tell us in what sense it is that our true ideas "agree with reality." Truth, he says, certainly *means* their agreement with reality; the only question is as to what we are to understand by the words "agreement" and "reality" in this proposition. And he first briefly considers the theory, that the sense in which our true ideas agree with reality, is that they "copy" some reality. And he affirms that some of our true ideas really do do this. But he rejects the theory, as a theory of what truth means, on the ground that they do not *all* do so. Plainly, therefore, he implies that no theory of what truth *means* will be correct, unless it tells us of some property which belongs to *all* our true ideas without exception. But his own theory is a theory of what truth means. Apparently, therefore, he wishes to assert that not only many but *all* our true ideas are or can be verified; that *all* of them are useful. And it is, I think, pretty plain that this is *one* of the things which he wishes to assert.

Apparently, therefore, Professor James wishes to assert that *all* our true ideas are or can be verified —that *all* are useful. And certainly this is not a truism like the proposition that *many* of them are so. Even if this were all that he meant, it would be worth discussing. But even this, I think, is not all. The very first proposition in which he expresses his theory is the following. "True ideas," he says (p. 201) "are those that we can assimilate, validate, corroborate and verify. False ideas are those that we cannot." And what does this mean? Let us, for brevity's sake, substitute the word "verify" alone for the four words which Professor James uses, as he himself subsequently seems to do. He asserts, then, that true ideas are *those which* we can verify. And plainly he does not mean by this merely that *some* of the ideas which we can verify are true, while plenty of others, which we can verify, are not true. The plain meaning of his words is that *all* the ideas which we can verify are true. No one would use them who did not mean this. Apparently, therefore, Professor James means to assert not merely that we can verify all our true ideas ; but also that all the ideas, which we can verify, are true. And so, too, with utility or usefulness. He seems to mean not merely that all our true ideas are useful ; but that all those which are useful are true. This would follow, for one thing, from the fact that he seems to use the words "verification" or "verifiability" and "usefulness" as if they came to the same thing. But, in this case too, he asserts it in words that have but one plain meaning. "The true" he says (p. 222) "is only the expedient in the way of our thinking." "The true" is *the* expedient : that is, *all* expedient thinking is true. Or again : "An idea is 'true' so long as to believe it is profitable to our lives" (p. 75). That is to say, *every* idea, which is profitable to our lives, is, while it is so, true. These words certainly have a plain enough meaning. Apparently, therefore, Professor James means to assert not merely that all true ideas are useful, but also that all useful ideas are true.

Professor James' words, then, do at least suggest that he wishes to assert all four of the following propositions. He wishes to assert, it would seem—

(1) That we can verify all those of our ideas, which are true.
(2) That all those among our ideas, which we can verify, are true.
(3) That all our true ideas are useful.
(4) That all those of our ideas, which are useful, are true.

These four propositions are what I propose first to consider. He does mean to assert them, at least. Very likely he wishes to assert something more even than these. He does, in fact, suggest that he means to assert, in addition, that these properties of "verifiability" and "utility" are the *only* properties (beside that of being properly *called* "true") which belong to all our true ideas and to none but true ideas. But this obviously cannot be true, unless all these four propositions are true. And therefore we may as well consider them first.

First, then, can we verify all our true ideas?

I wish only to point out the plainest and most obvious reasons why I think it is doubtful whether we can.

We are very often in doubt as to whether we did or did not do a certain thing in the past. We may have the idea that we did, and also the idea that we did not; and we may wish to find out which idea is the true one. Very often, indeed, I may believe very strongly, that I did do a certain thing; and somebody else, who has equally good reason to know, may believe equally strongly that I did not.

For instance, I may have written a letter, and may believe that I used certain words in it. But my correspondent may believe that I did not. Can we always verify either of these ideas? Certainly sometimes we can. The letter may be produced, and prove that I did use the words in question. And I shall then have verified my idea. Or it may prove that I did not use them. And then we shall have verified my correspondent's idea. But, suppose the letter has been destroyed; suppose there is no copy of it, nor any trustworthy record of what was said in it; suppose there is no other witness as to what I said in it, beside myself and my correspondent? Can we then always verify which of our ideas is the true one? I think it is very doubtful whether we can *nearly* always. Certainly we may often try to discover any possible means of verification, and be quite unable, for a time at least, to discover any. Such cases, in which we are unable, for a time at least, to verify either of two contradictory ideas, occur very commonly indeed. Let us take an even more trivial instance than the last. Bad whist-players often do not notice at all carefully which cards they have among the lower cards in a suit. At the end of a hand they cannot be certain whether they had or had not the seven of diamonds, or the five of spades. And, after the cards have been shuffled, a dispute will sometimes arise as to whether a particular player had the seven of diamonds or not. His partner may think that he had, and he himself may think that he had not. Both may be uncertain, and the memory of both, on such a point, may be well known to be untrustworthy. And, moreover, neither of the other players may be able to remember any better. Is it always possible to verify which of these ideas is the true one? Either the player did or did not have the seven of diamonds. This much is certain. One person thinks that he did, and another thinks he did not; and both, so soon as the question is raised, have before their minds both of these ideas—the idea that he did, and the idea that he did not. This also is certain. And it is certain that one or other of these two ideas is true. But can they always verify either of them? Sometimes, no doubt, they can, even after the cards have been shuffled. There may have been a fifth person present, overlooking the play, whose memory is perfectly trustworthy, and whose word may be taken as settling the point. Or the players may themselves be able, by recalling other incidents of play, to arrive at such a certainty as may be said to verify the one hypothesis or the other. But very often neither of these two things will occur. And, in such a case, is it always possible to verify the true idea? Perhaps, theoretically, it may be still possible. Theoretically, I suppose, the fact that one player, and not any of the other three, had the card in his hand, may have made some difference to the card, which *might* be discovered by some possible method of scientific investigation. Perhaps some such difference may remain even after the same card has been repeatedly used in many subsequent games. But suppose the same question arises again, a week after the original game was played. Did you, or did you not, last week have the seven of diamonds in that particular hand? The question has not been settled in the meantime; and now, perhaps, the original pack of cards has been destroyed. Is it still possible to verify either idea? Theoretically, I suppose, it may be still possible. But even this, I think, is very doubtful. And surely it is plain that, humanly and practically speaking, it will often have become quite impossible to verify either idea. In all probability it never will be possible for any man to verify whether I had the card or not on this particular occasion. No doubt we are here speaking of an idea, which some man *could have* verified at one time. But the hypothesis I am considering is the hypothesis that we never have a true idea, which we *can* not verify ; that is to say, which we cannot verify *after* the idea has occurred. And with regard to this hypothesis, it seems to me quite plain that *very often indeed* we have two ideas, one or other of which is certainly true ; and yet that, in all probability, it is no longer possible and never will be possible for any man to verify either.

It seems to me, then, that we very often have true ideas which we cannot verify ; true ideas, which, in all probability, no man ever will be able to verify. And, so far, I have given only comparatively trivial instances. But it is plain that, in the same sense, historians are very frequently occupied with true ideas, which it is doubtful whether they can verify. One historian thinks that a certain event took place, and another that it did not ; and both may admit that they cannot verify their idea. Subsequent historians may, no doubt, sometimes be able to verify one or the other. New evidence may be discovered or men may learn to make a better use of evidence already in existence. But is it certain that this will *always* happen ? Is it certain that *every* question, about which historians have doubted, will some day be able to be settled by verification of one or the other hypothesis ? Surely the probability is that in the case of an immense number of events, with regard to which we should like to know whether they happened or not, it never will be possible for any man to verify either the one hypothesis or the other. Yet it may be certain that either the events in question did happen or did not. Here, therefore, again, we have a large number of ideas—cases where many men doubt whether a thing did happen or did not, and have therefore the

idea both of its having happened and of its not
having happened—with regard to which it is certain
that half of them are true, but where it seems highly
doubtful whether any single one of them will ever
be able to be verified. No doubt it is just possible
that men will some day be able to verify every one
of them. But surely it is very doubtful whether
they will. And the theory against which I am
protesting is the positive assertion that we *can* verify
all our true ideas—that some one some day certainly
will be able to verify every one of them. This
theory, I urge, has all probability against it.

And so far I have been dealing only with ideas
with regard to what happened in the past. These
seem to me to be the cases which offer the most
numerous and most certain exceptions to the rule
that we can verify our true ideas. With regard to
particular past events, either in their own lives or in
those of other people, men very frequently have
ideas, which it seems highly improbable that any
man will ever be able to verify. And yet it is
certain that a great many of these ideas are true,
because in a great many cases we have both the
idea that the event did happen and also the idea
that it did not, when it is certain that one or other
of these ideas is true. And these ideas with regard
to past events would by themselves be sufficient for
my purpose. If, as seems certain, there are many
true ideas with regard to the past, which it is highly
improbable that anyone will ever be able to verify,
then, obviously, there is nothing in a true idea
which makes it certain that we can verify it. But
it is, I think, certainly not only in the case of ideas,
with regard to the past, that it is doubtful whether
we can verify all the true ideas we have. In the
case of many generalisations dealing not only with
the past but with the future, it is, I think, obviously
doubtful whether we shall ever be able to verify all

those which are true; although here, perhaps, in most cases, the probability that we shall not is not so great. But is it quite certain, that in all cases where scientific men have considered hypotheses, one or other of which must be true, either will ever be verified? It seems to be obviously doubtful. Take, for instance, the question whether our actual space is Euclidean or not. This is a case where the alternative has been considered; and where it is certain that, whatever be meant by "our actual space," it either is Euclidean or is not. It has been held, too, that the hypothesis that it is not Euclidean might, conceivably, be verified by observations. But it is doubtful whether it ever will be. And though it would be rash to say that no man ever will be able to verify either hypothesis; it is also rash to assert positively that we shall—that we certainly can verify the true hypotheses. There are, I believe, ever so many similar cases, where alternative hypotheses, one or other of which must be true, have occurred to men of science, and where yet it is very doubtful whether either ever will be verified. Or take, again, such ideas as the idea that there is a God, or the idea that we are immortal. Many men have had not only contradictory ideas, but contradictory beliefs, about these matters. And here we have cases where it is disputed whether these ideas have not actually been verified. But it seems to me doubtful whether they have been. And there is a view, which seems to me to deserve respect, that, in these matters, we never shall be able to verify the true hypothesis. Is it perfectly certain that this view is a false one? I do not say that it is true. I think it is quite possible that we shall some day be able to verify either the belief that we are immortal or the belief that we are not. But it seems to me doubtful whether we shall. And for this reason alone I should refuse to assent to the positive assertion that we certainly can verify all our true ideas.

When, therefore, Professor James tells us that "True ideas are those that we can assimilate, validate, corroborate and verify. False ideas are those that we cannot," there seems to be a serious objection to part of what these words imply. They imply that no idea of ours is true, unless we can verify it. They imply, therefore, that whenever a man wonders whether or not he had the seven of diamonds in the third hand at whist last night, neither of these ideas is true unless he can verify it. But it seems certain that in this, and an immense number of similar cases, one or other of the two ideas is true. Either, he did have the card in his hand or he did not. If anything is a fact, this is one. Either, therefore, Professor James' words imply the denial of this obvious fact, or else he implies that in *all* such cases we *can* verify one or other of the two ideas. But to this the objection is that, in any obvious sense of the words, it seems very doubtful whether we can. On the contrary it seems extremely probable that in a *very large* number of such cases no man ever will be able to verify either of the two ideas. There is, therefore, a serious objection to what Professor James' words imply. Whether he himself really means to assert these things which his words imply I do not know. Perhaps he would admit that, in this sense, we probably cannot verify nearly all our true ideas. All that I have wished to make plain is that there is, at least, an objection to what he says, whether to what he means or not. There is ample reason why we should refuse assent to the statement that none of our ideas are true, except those which we can verify.

But to another part of what he implies by the words quoted above, there is, I think, no serious objection. There is reason to object to the statement that we can verify all our true ideas; but to the statement that all ideas, which we can "assimilate, validate, corroborate and verify," are true, I see no serious objection. Here, I think, we might say simply that all ideas which we can verify are true. To this, which is the second of the four propositions, which I distinguished above (p. 35) as what Professor James seems to wish to assert, there is, I think, no serious objection, if we understand the word "verify" in its proper and natural sense. We may, no doubt, sometimes say that we have verified an idea or an hypothesis, when we have only obtained evidence which proves it to be probable, and does not prove it to be certain. And, if we use the word in this loose sense for incomplete verification, it is obviously the case that we may verify an idea which is not true. But it seems scarcely necessary to point this out. And where we really can *completely* verify an idea or an hypothesis, there, undoubtedly, the idea which we can verify is always true. The very meaning of the word "verify" is to find evidence which does really prove an idea to be true; and where an idea can be really proved to be true, it is of course, always true.

This is all I wish to say about Professor James' first two propositions, namely :—

(1) That no ideas of ours are true, except those which we can verify.
(2) That all those ideas, which we can verify, are true.

The first seems to me extremely doubtful—in fact, almost certainly untrue; the second on the other hand, certainly true, in its most obvious meaning. And I shall say no more about them. The fact is, I doubt whether either of them expresses anything which Professor James is really anxious to assert. I have mentioned them, only because his words do, in fact, imply them and because he gives those words a very prominent place. But I have already had occasion to notice that he seems to speak as if to say that we can verify an idea came to the same thing as saying it is useful to us. And it is the connection of truth with usefulness, not its connection with "verification," that he is, I think, really anxious to assert. He talks about "verification" only, I believe, because he thinks that what he says about it will support his main view that truth is what "works," is "useful," is "expedient," "pays." It is this main view we have now to consider. We have to consider the two propositions :—

(3) That all our true ideas are useful.
(4) That all ideas, which are useful, are true.

First, then : is it the case that all our true ideas are useful? Is it the case that none of our ideas are true, except those which are useful?

I wish to introduce my discussion of this question by quoting a passage in which Professor James seems to me to say something which is indisputably true. Towards the end of Lecture VI, he attacks the view that truths "have an unconditional claim to be recognised." And in the course of his attack the following passage occurs :—

"Must I," he says, "constantly be repeating the truth 'twice two are four' because of its eternal claim on recognition? or is it sometimes irrelevant? Must my thoughts dwell night and day on my personal sins and blemishes, because I truly have them ?—or may I sink and ignore them in order to be a decent social unit, and not a mass of morbid melancholy and apology ?"

"It is quite evident," he goes on, "that our obligation to acknowledge truth, so far from being unconditional, is tremendously conditional. Truth with a big T, and in the singular, claims abstractly to be recognised, of course ; but concrete truths in the plural need be recognised only when their recognition is expedient." (pp. 231-232).

What Professor James says in this passage seems to me so indisputably true as fully to justify the vigour of his language. It is as clear as anything can be that it would not be useful for any man's mind to be *always* occupied with the true idea that he had certain faults and blemishes ; or to be *always* occupied with the idea that twice two are four. It is clear, that is, that, if there are times at which a particular true idea is useful, there certainly are other times at which it would *not* be useful, but positively in the way. This is plainly true of nearly all, if not quite all, our true ideas. It is plainly true with regard to nearly all of them that, even if the occasions on which their occurrence is useful are many, the occasions on which their occurrence would *not* be useful are many more. With regard to most of them it is true that on most occasions they will, as Professor James says elsewhere, " be practically irrelevant, and had better remain latent."

It is, then, quite clear that almost any particular true idea *would* not be useful at all times and that the times at which it would *not* be useful, are many more than the times at which it would. And what we have to consider is whether, in just this sense in which it is so clear that most true ideas would *not* be useful at most times, it is nevertheless true that all our true ideas *are* useful. Is this so? Are all our true ideas useful?

Professor James, we see, has just told us that there are ever so many occasions upon which a particular true idea, such as that $2 + 2 = 4$, *would* not be useful—when, on the contrary, it would be positively in the way. And this seems to be indisputably clear. But is not something else almost equally clear? Is it not almost equally clear that cases, such as he says *would* not be useful, do sometimes actually happen? Is it not clear that we do actually sometimes have true ideas, at times when they are not useful, but are positively in the way? It seems to me to be perfectly clear that this does sometimes occur; and not sometimes only, but very commonly. The cases in which true ideas occur at times when they are useful, are, perhaps, far *more* numerous; but, if we look at men in general, the cases in which true ideas occur, at times when they are not useful, do surely make up positively a very large number. Is it not the case that men do sometimes dwell on their faults and blemishes, when it is *not* useful for them to do so? when they would much better be thinking of something else? Is it not the case that they are often unable to get their minds away from a true idea, when it is harmful for them to dwell on it? Still more commonly, does it not happen that they waste their time in acquiring pieces of inforation which are no use to them, though perhaps very useful to other people? All this seems to me to be undeniable—just as undeniable as what Professor James himself has said; and, if this is so, then, in one sense of the words, it is plainly not true that all, or nearly all, our true ideas are useful. *In one sense of the words.* For if I have the idea that $2+2=4$ on one day, and then have it again the next, I may certainly, in a sense, call the idea I have on one day *one* idea, and the idea I have on the next *another*. I have had two ideas that $2+2=4$, and not one only. Or if two different persons both think that I have faults, there have been two ideas of this truth and not one only. And in asking whether *all* our true ideas are useful, we might mean to ask whether *both* of these ideas were useful and not merely whether one of them was. In this sense, then, it is plainly not true that *all* our true ideas are useful. It is not true, that is, that every true idea is useful, *whenever it occurs.*

In one sense, then, it is plainly not true that all our true ideas are useful. But there still remains a perfectly legitimate sense in which it might be true. It might be meant, that is, not that every *occurrence* of a true idea is useful, but that every true idea is useful on at least one of the occasions when it occurs. But is this, in fact, the case? It seems to me almost as plain that it is not, as that the other was not. We have seen that true ideas are not by any means always useful on every occasion when they occur; though most that do occur many times over and to many different people are, no doubt, useful on some of these occasions. But there seems to be an immense number of true ideas, which occur but once and to one person, and never again either to him or to anyone else. I may, for instance, idly count the number of dots on the back of a card, and arrive at a true idea of their number; and yet, perhaps, I may never think of their number again, nor anybody else ever know it. We are all, it seems to me, constantly noticing trivial details, and getting true ideas about them, of which we never think again, and which nobody else ever gets. And is it quite certain that all these true ideas are useful? It seems to me perfectly clear, on the contrary, that many of them are not. Just as it is clear that many men sometimes waste their time in acquiring information which is useful to others but not to them, surely it is clear that they sometimes waste their time in acquiring information, which is useful to nobody at all, because nobody else ever acquires it. I do not say that it is never useful idly to count the number of dots on the back of a card. Plainly it is sometimes useful to be idle, and one idle employment may often be as good as another. But surely it is true that men *sometimes* do these things, when their time would have been better employed otherwise? Surely they sometimes get into the habit of attending to trivial truths, which it is as great a disadvantage that they should attend to as that they should constantly be thinking of their own thoughts and blemishes? I cannot see my way to deny that this is so; and therefore I cannot see my way to assert positively that all our true ideas are useful, even so much as on *one occasion*. It seems to me that there are many true ideas which occur but once, and which are not useful when they do occur. And if this be so, then it is plainly not true that *all* our true ideas are useful in any sense at all.

These seem to me to be the most obvious objections to the assertion that all our true ideas are useful. It is clear, we saw to begin with, that true ideas, which are sometimes useful, *would* not be useful at all times. And it seemed almost equally clear that they do sometimes occur at times when they are not useful. Our true ideas, therefore are not useful at every time when they actually occur. But in just this sense in which it is so clear that true ideas which are sometimes useful, nevertheless sometimes occur at times when they are not, it seems pretty plain that true ideas, which occur but once, are, some of them, not useful. If an idea, which is sometimes useful, does sometimes occur to a man at a time when it is irrelevant and in the way, why should not an idea, which occurs but once, occur at a time when it is irrelevant and in the way? It seems hardly possible to doubt that this does sometimes happen. But, if this be so, then it is not true that all our true ideas are useful, even so much as on one occasion. It is not true that none of our ideas are true, except those which are useful.

But now, what are we to say of the converse

proposition—the proposition that all those among our ideas, which are useful, are true? That we never have a useful idea, which is not true?

I confess the matter seems to me equally clear here. The assertion should mean that every idea, which is at any time useful, is true; that no idea, which is not true, is ever useful. And it seems hardly possible to doubt that this assertion is false. It is, in the first place, commonly held that it is sometimes right positively to deceive another person. In war, for instance it is held that one army is justified in trying to give the enemy a false idea as to where it will be at a given time. Such a false idea is sometimes given, and it seems to me quite clear that it is sometimes useful. In such a case, no doubt, it may be said that the false idea is useful to the party who have given it, but not useful to those who actually believe in it. And the question whether it is useful on the whole will depend upon the question which side it is desirable should win. But it seems to me unquestionable that the false idea is sometimes useful on the whole. Take, for instance, the case of a party of savages, who wish to make a night attack and massacre a party of Europeans but are deceived as to the position in which the Europeans are encamped. It is surely plain that such a false idea is sometimes useful on the whole. But quite apart from the question whether deception is ever justifiable, it is not very difficult to think of cases where a false idea, not produced by deception, is plainly useful— and useful, not merely on the whole, but to the person who has it as well. A man often thinks that his watch is right, when, in fact, it is slow, and his false idea may cause him to miss his train. And in such cases, no doubt, his false idea is *generally* disadvantageous. But, in a particular case, the train which he would have caught but for his false idea may be destroyed in a railway accident, or something may suddenly occur at home, which renders it much more useful that he should be there, than it would have been for him to catch his train. Do such cases never occur? And is not the false idea sometimes useful in some of them? It seems to me perfectly clear that it is *sometimes* useful for a man to think his watch is right when it is wrong. And such instances would be sufficient to show that it is not the case that every idea of ours, which is ever useful, is a true idea. But let us take cases, not, like these, of an idea, which occurs but a few times or to one man, but of ideas which have occurred to many men at many times. It seems to me very difficult to be sure that the belief in an eternal hell has not been often useful to many men, and yet it may be doubted whether this idea is true. And so, too, with the belief in a happy life after death, or the belief in the existence of a God; it is, I think, very difficult to be sure that these beliefs have not been, and are not still, often useful, and yet it may be doubted whether they are true. These beliefs, of course, are matters of controversy. Some men believe that they are both useful and true; and others, again, that they are neither. And I do not think we are justified in giving them as certain instances of beliefs, which are not true, but, nevertheless, have often been useful. But there is a view that these beliefs, though not true, have, nevertheless, been often useful; and this view seems to me to deserve respect, especially since, as we have seen, some beliefs, which are not true, certainly are sometimes useful. Are we justified in asserting positively that it is false? Is it perfectly certain that beliefs, which have often been useful to many men, may not, nevertheless, be untrue? Is it perfectly certain that beliefs, which are not true, have not often been useful to many men? The certainty may at least be doubted, and in any case it seems certain that some beliefs, which are not true, are, nevertheless, sometimes useful.

For these reasons, it seems to me almost certain that *both* the assertions which I have been considering are false. It is almost certainly false that all our true ideas are useful, and almost certainly false that all our useful ideas are true. But I have only urged what seem to me to be the most obvious objections to these two statements; I have not tried to sustain these objections by elaborate arguments, and I have omitted elaborate argument, partly because of a reason which I now wish to state. The fact is, I am not at all sure that Professor James would not himself admit that both these statements are false. I think it is quite possible he would admit that they are, and would say that he never meant either to assert or to imply the contrary. He complains that some of the critics of Pragmatism are unwilling to read any but the silliest of possible meanings into the statements of Pragmatism; and, perhaps, he would say that this is the case here. I certainly hope that he would. I certainly hope he would say that these statements, to which I have objected, are silly. For it does seem to me intensely silly to say that we can verify all our true ideas; intensely silly to say that every one of our true ideas is at some time useful; intensely silly to say that every idea which is ever useful is true. I hope Professor James would admit all these things to be silly, for if he and other Pragmatists would admit even as much as this, I think a good deal would be gained. But it by no means follows that because a philosopher would admit a view to be silly, when it is definitely put before him, he has not himself been constantly holding and implying that very view. He may quite sincerely protest that he never has either held or implied it, and yet he may all the time have been not only implying it but holding it—vaguely, perhaps, but really. A man may assure us, quite sincerely that he is not angry ; he may really think that he is not, and yet we may be able to judge quite certainly from what he says that he really is angry. He may assure us quite sincerely that he never meant anything to our discredit by what he said—that he was not thinking of anything in the least discreditable to us, and yet it may be plain from his words that he was actually condemning us very severely. And so with a philosopher. He may protest, quite angrily, when a view is put before him in other words than his own, that he never either meant or implied any such thing, and yet it may be possible to judge, from what he says, that this very view, wrapped up in other words, was not only held by him but was precisely what made his thoughts seem to him to be interesting and important. Certainly he may quite often imply a given thing which, at another time, he denies. Unless it were possible for a philosopher to do this, there would be very little inconsistency in philosophy, and surely everyone will admit that *other* philosophers are very often inconsistent. And so in this case, even if Professor James would say that he never meant to imply the things to which I have been objecting, yet in the case of two of these things, I cannot help thinking that he does actually imply them—nay more, that he is frequently actually vaguely thinking of them, and that his theory of truth owes its interest, in very great part, to the fact that he is implying them. In the case of the two views that all our true ideas are useful, and that all our useful ideas are true, I think this is so, and I do not mean merely that his *words* imply them. A man's *words* may often imply a thing, when he himself is in no way, however vaguely, thinking either of that thing or of anything which implies it ; he may simply have expressed himself unfortunately. But in the case of the two views that all our true ideas are useful, and all our useful ideas true, I do not think this is so with Professor James. I think that his thoughts seem interesting to him and others, largely because he is thinking, not merely of words, but of things which imply these two views, in the very form in which I have objected to them. And I wish now to give some reasons for thinking this.

Professor James certainly wishes to assert that there is *some* connection between truth and utility. And the connection which I have suggested that he has vaguely before his mind is this : that every true idea is, at some time or other, useful, and conversely that every idea, which is ever useful, is true. And I have urged that there are obvious objections to both these views. But now, supposing Professor James does not mean to assert either of these two things, what else can he mean to assert ? What else can he mean, that would account for the interest and importance he seems to attach to his assertion of connection between truth and utility ? Let us consider the alternatives.

And, first of all, he might mean that *most* of our true ideas are useful, and *most* of our useful ideas true. He might mean that most of our true ideas are useful at some time or other ; and even that most of them are useful, whenever they actually occur. And he might mean, moreover, that if we consider the whole range of ideas, which are useful to us, we shall find that by far the greater number of them are true ones ; that true ideas are far more often useful to us, than those which are not true. And all this, I think, may be readily admitted to be true. If this were all that he meant, I do not think that anyone would be very anxious to dispute it. But is it conceivable that this is *all* that he means ? Is it conceivable that he should have been so anxious to insist upon this admitted commonplace ? Is it conceivable that he should have been offering us this, and nothing more, as a theory of what truth means, and a theory worth making a fuss about, and being proud of ? It seems to me quite inconceivable that this should have been *all* that he meant. He must have had something more than this in his mind. But, if so, what more ?

In the passage which I quoted at the beginning, as showing that he does mean to assert that *all* useful ideas are true, he immediately goes on to assert a qualification, which must now be noticed. " The true," he says, " is only the expedient in the way of our thinking " (p. 222). But he immediately adds : " Expedient in the long run, and on the whole, of course ; for what meets expediently all the experience in sight won't necessarily meet all further experiences equally satisfactorily." Here, therefore, we have something else that he might mean. What is expedient *in the long run*, he means to say, is true. And what exactly does this mean ? It seems to mean that an idea, which is not true, may be expedient *for some time*. That is to say, it may occur *once*, and be expedient then ; and again, and be expedient then ; and so on, over a considerable period. But (Professor James seems to prophesy) if it is not true, there will come a time, when it will cease to be expedient. If it occurs again and again over a long *enough* period, there will at last, if it is not true, come a time when it will (for once at least) fail to be useful, and will (perhaps he means) *never* be useful again. This is, I think, what Professor James means in this passage. He means, I think, that though an idea, which is not true, may for some time be repeatedly expedient, there will at last come a time when its occurrence will, perhaps, *never* be expedient again, certainly will, for a time, not be *generally* expedient. And this a view which, it seems to me, may possibly be true. It is certainly possible that a time may come, in the far future, when ideas, which are not true, will hardly ever, if ever, be expedient. And this is all that Professor James seems here positively to mean. He seems to mean that, if you take time *enough*, false ideas will some day cease to be expedient. And it is very difficult to be sure that this is not true ; since it is very difficult to prophesy as to what may happen in the far future. I am sure I hope that this prophesy will come true. But in the meantime (Professor James seems to admit) ideas, which are not true, may, for an indefinitely long time, again and again be expedient. And is it conceivable that a theory, which admits this, is *all* that he has meant to assert ? Is it conceivable that what interests him, in his theory of truth, is merely the belief that, some day or other, false ideas will cease to be expedient? " In the long run, *of course*," he says, as if this were what he had meant all along. But I think it is quite plain that this is *not* all that he has meant. This may be one thing which he is anxious to assert, but it certainly does not explain the whole of his interest in his theory of truth.

And, in fact, there is quite a different theory which he seems plainly to have in his mind in other places. When Professor James says, " in the long run, *of course*," he implies that ideas which are expedient only for a *short* run, are very often not true. But in what he says elsewhere he asserts the very opposite of this. He says elsewhere that a belief is true " *so long as* to believe it is profitable to our lives " (p. 75). That is to say, a belief will be true, *so long as* it is useful, even if it is *not* useful in the long run! This is certainly quite a different theory; and, strictly speaking, it implies that an idea, which is useful even *on one occasion*, will be true. But perhaps this is only a verbal implication. I think very likely that here Professor James was only thinking of ideas, which can be said *to have a run*, though only a comparatively short one—of ideas, that is, which are expedient, not merely on one occasion, but *for some time*. That is to say, the theory which he now suggests, is that ideas, which occur again and again, perhaps to one man only, perhaps to several different people, over some space of time are, if they are expedient on most occasions within that space of time, true. This is a view which he is, I think, really anxious to assert; and if it were true, it would, I think, be important. And it is difficult to find instances which show, with certainty, that it is false. I believe that it is false; but it is difficult to prove it, because, in the case of some ideas it is so difficult to be certain that they ever were useful, and in the case of others so difficult to be certain that they are not true. A belief such as I spoke of before—the belief in eternal hell—is an instance. I think this belief has been, for a long time, useful, and that yet it is false. But it is, perhaps, arguable that it never has been useful; and many people on the other hand, would still assert that it is true. It cannot, therefore, perhaps, fairly be used as an instance of a belief, which is certainly not true, and yet has for some time been useful. But whether this view that all beliefs, which are expedient for some time, are true, be true or false; can it be all that Professor James means to assert? Can it constitute the whole of what interests him in his theory of truth?

I do not think it can. I think it is plain that he has in his mind something more than *any* of these alternatives, or than all of them taken together. And I think so partly for the following reason. He speaks from the outset as if he intended to tell us what *distinguishes* true ideas from those which are not true ; to tell us, that is to say, not merely of some property which belongs to all our true ideas ; nor yet merely of some property, which belongs to none but true ideas ; but of some property which satisfies *both* these requirements at once—which both belongs to all our true ideas, and *also* belongs to none but true ones. Truth, he says to begin with, means the agreement of our ideas with reality ; and he adds "as falsity their disagreement." And he explains that he is going to tell us what property it is that is meant by these words "agreement with reality." So again in the next passage which I quoted : " True ideas," he says "are those that we can assimilate, validate, corroborate and verify." But, he also adds, " False ideas are those that we cannot." And no one, I think, could possibly speak in this way, who had not in his head the intention of telling us what property it is which *distinguishes* true ideas from those which are not true, and which, therefore, not only belongs to all ideas which are true, but also to none that are not. And that he has this idea in his head and thinks that the property of being " useful " or "paying " is such a property, is again clearly shown by a later passage. " Our account of truth," he says (p. 218) " is an account of truths in the plural, of processes of leading, realised *in rebus*, and having only this quality in common, that they *pay*." *Only* this quality in common ! If this be so, the quality must obviously be one, which is *not* shared by any ideas which are *not* true ; for, if true ideas have any quality in common at all, they must have at least one such quality, which is *not* shared by those which are *not* true. Plainly, therefore, Professor James is intending to tell us of a property which belongs both to *all* true ideas and *only* to true ideas. And this property, he says, is that of "paying." But now let us suppose that he means by "paying," not "paying *once* at least," but, according to the alternative he suggests, "paying in the long run" or "paying for some time." Can he possibly have supposed that these were properties which belonged *both* to all true ideas *and also* to none but true ones? They may, perhaps, be properties which belong to *none but* true ones. I doubt, as I have said, whether the latter does; but still it is difficult to prove the opposite. But even if we granted that they belong to *none but* true ones, surely it is only too obvious that they do *not* fulfil the other requirement—that they do *not* belong to nearly all true ones. Can anyone suppose that *all* our true ideas pay "in the long run" or repeatedly for some time? Surely it is plain that an enormous number do not for the simple reason that an enormous number of them *have no run at all*, either long or short, but occur but once, and never recur. I believe truly that a certain book is on a particular shelf about 10.15 p.m. on December 21st, 1907; and this true belief serves me well and helps me to find it. But the belief that that book is there at that particular time occurs to no one else, and never again to me. Surely there are thousands of useful true beliefs which, like this, are useful but once, and never occur again; and it would, therefore, be preposterous to say that every true idea is useful "in the long run" or repeatedly for some time. If, therefore, we supposed Professor James to mean that "paying in the long run" or "paying repeatedly over a considerable period" were properties which belonged to all true ideas aud to none but true ones, we should be supposing him to mean something still more monstrous than if we suppose him to mean that "paying at least once" was such a property.

To sum up then :

I think there is no doubt that Professor James' interest in "the pragmatist theory of truth" is largely due to the fact that he thinks it tells us what distinguishes true ideas from those which are not true. And he thinks the distinction is that true ideas "pay," and false ones don't. The most natural interpretation of this view is : That every true idea pays at least once ; and that every idea, which pays at least once, is true. These were the propositions I considered first, and I gave reasons for thinking that *both* are false. But Professor James suggested elsewhere that what he means by "paying" is "paying in the long run." And here it seems possibly true that all ideas which "pay in the long run" are true ; but it is certainly false that all our true ideas "pay in the long run," if by this be meant anything more than "pay at least once." Again, he suggested that what he meant by paying was "paying for some time." And here, again, even if it is true (and it seems very doubtful) that all ideas which pay for some time are true, it is certainly false that all our true ideas pay for some time, if by this be meant anything more than that they pay "at least once."

This, I think, is the simplest and most obvious objection to Professor James' "instrumental" view of truth—the view that truth is what "works," "pays," is "useful." He seems certainly to have in his mind the idea that this theory tells us what distinguishes true ideas from false ones, and to be interested in it mainly for this reason. He has vaguely in his mind that he has told us of some property which belongs to all true ideas and to none but true ones ; and that this property is that of "paying." And the objection is, that, whatever we understand by "paying," whether "paying at least once," or "paying in the long run," or "paying for some time," it seems certain that none of these properties will satisfy *both* requirements. As regards the first, that of "paying at least once," it seems almost certain that it satisfies *neither:* it is neither true that all our true ideas "pay at least once," nor yet that every idea which pays at least once, is true. On the contrary, many true ideas never pay at all; and many ideas, which are not true, do pay on at least one occasion. And as regards the others, "paying in the long run" and "paying for some time," even if these do belong to none but true ideas (and even this seems very doubtful), they certainly neither of them satisfy the *other* requirement—neither of them belong to *all* our true ideas. For, in order that either of them may belong to an idea, that idea must pay at least once; and, as we have seen, many true ideas do not pay even once, and cannot, therefore, pay either in the long run or for some time. And, moreover, many true ideas, which do pay on one occasion, seem to pay on one occasion and one only.

And, if Professor James does not mean to assert any of these things, what is there left for him to mean? There is left in the first place, the theory that *most* of our true ideas do pay; and that *most* of the ideas which pay are true. This seems to me to be true, and, indeed, to be all that is certainly true in what he says. But is it conceivable that this is all he has meant? Obviously, these assertions tell us of no property at all which belongs to all true ideas, and to none but true ones; and, moreover, it seems impossible that he should have been so anxious to assert this generally admitted commonplace. What a very different complexion his whole discussion would have worn, had he merely asserted this—this quite clearly, and nothing but this, while admitting openly that many true ideas do not pay, and that many, which do pay, are not true!

And, besides this commonplace, there is only left for him to mean two one-sided and doubtful assertions to the effect that certain properties belong to none but true ideas. There is the assertion that all ideas which pay in the long run are true, and the assertion that all ideas which pay for some considerable time are true. And as to the first, it *may* be true; but it may also be doubted, and Professor James gives us no reason at all for thinking that it is true. Assuming that religious ideas have been useful in the past, is it quite certain that they may not permanently continue to be useful, even though they are false? That, in short, even though they are not true, they nevertheless will be useful, not only for a time, but in the long run? And as for the assertion that all ideas, which pay for a considerable time, are true, this is obviously more doubtful still. Whether certain religious ideas will or will not be useful in the long run, it seems difficult to doubt that many of them have been useful for a considerable time. And why should we be told dogmatically that all of these are true? This, it seems to me, is by far the most interesting assertion, which is left for Professor James to make, when we have rejected the theory that the property of being useful belongs to *all* true ideas, as well as to none but true ones. But he has given no reason for asserting it. He seems, in fact, to base it merely upon the general untenable theory, that utility belongs to *all* true ideas, and to none but true ones; that this is what truth means.

These, then, seem to me the plainest and most obvious objections to what Professor James says about the connection between truth and utility. And there are only two further points, in what he says under this head, that I wish to notice.

In the first place, we have hitherto been considering only whether it is true, as a matter of empirical fact, that all our true ideas are useful, and those which are not true, never. Professor James seems, at least, to mean that, *as a matter of fact*, this is so ; and I have only urged hitherto that *as a matter of fact*, it is not so. But as we have seen, he also asserts something more than this—he also asserts that this property of utility is the *only* one which belongs to all our true ideas. And this further assertion cannot possibly be true, if, as I have urged, there are many true ideas which do not possess this property ; or if, as I have urged, many ideas, which do possess it, are nevertheless not true. The objections already considered are, then, sufficient to overthrow this further assertion also. If there are any true ideas, which are not useful, or if any, which are useful, are not true, it cannot be the case that utility is the *only* property which true ideas have in common. There must be some property, other than utility, which is common to all true ideas ; and a correct theory as to what property it is that does belong to all true ideas, and to none but true ones, is still to seek. The empirical objections, hitherto given, are then sufficient objections to this further assertion also ; but they are not the only objections to it. There is another and still more serious objection to the assertion that utility is the *only* property which all true ideas have in common. For this assertion does not *merely* imply that, as a matter of fact, all our true ideas and none but true ideas are useful. It does, indeed, imply this ; and therefore the fact that these empirical assertions are not true is sufficient to refute it. But it also implies something more. If utility were the *only* property which all true ideas had in common, it would follow not merely that all true ideas are useful, but also that any idea, which was useful, *would* be true *no matter what other properties it might have or might fail to have.* There can, I think, be no doubt that Professor James does frequently speak as if this were the case ; and there is an independent and still more serious objection to this implication. Even if it were true (as it is not) that all our true ideas and none but true ideas are, as a matter of fact, useful, we should still have a strong reason to object to the statement that any idea, which was useful, *would* be true. For it implies that if such an idea as mine, that Professor James exists, and has certain thoughts, *were* useful, this idea would be true, *even if* no such person as Professor James ever did exist. It implies that, if the idea that I had the seven of diamonds in my hand at cards last night, *were* useful, this idea would be true, even if, in fact, I did not have that card in my hand. And we can, I think, see quite plainly that this is not the case. With regard to some kinds of ideas, at all events—ideas with regard to the existence of other people, or with regard to past experiences of our own—it seems quite plain that they would not be true, unless they "agreed with reality" in some other sense than that which Professor James declares to be the only one in which true ideas must agree with it. Even if my idea that Professor James exists were to "agree with reality," in the sense that, owing to it, I handled *other* realities better than I should have done without it, it would, I think, plainly not be true, unless Professor James really did exist—unless *he* were a reality. And this, I think, is one of the two most serious objections to what he seems to hold about the connection of truth with utility. He seems to hold that any idea, which was useful, *would* be true, *no matter what other properties it might fail to have.* And with regard to some ideas, at all events, it seems plain that they cannot be true, *unless* they have the property that what they believe to exist, really does or did exist. Beliefs in the existence of other people might be useful to me, even if I alone existed ; but, nevertheless, in such a case, they would not be true.

And there is only one other point, in what Professor James says in connection with the "instrumental" view of truth, upon which I wish to remark. We have seen that he seems sometimes to hold that beliefs are true, *so long as* they are "profitable to our lives." And this implies, as we have seen, the doubtful proposition than any belief which is useful for some length of time, is true. But this is not all that it implies. It also implies that beliefs are true *only* so long as they are profitable. Nor does Professor James appear to mean by this that they *occur*, only so long as they are profitable. He seems to hold, on the contrary, that beliefs, which are profitable for some time, do sometimes finally occur at a time when they are not profitable. He implies, therefore, that a belief, which occurs at several different times, may be true at some of the times at which it occurs, and yet untrue at others. I think there is no doubt that this view is what he is sometimes thinking of. And this, we see, constitutes a quite new view as to the connection between truth and utility—a view quite different from any that we have hitherto considered. This view asserts not that every true idea is useful at some time, or in the long run, or for a considerable period ; but that the truth of an idea may come and go, as its utility comes and goes. It admits that one and the same idea sometimes occurs at times when it is useful, and sometimes at times when it is not ; but it maintains that this same idea is true, at those times when it is useful, and not true, at those when it is not. And the fact that Professor James seems to suggest this view, constitutes, I think, a second most serious objection to what he says about the connection of truth and utility. It seems so obvious that utility is a property which comes and goes—which belongs to a given idea at one time, and does not belong to it at another, that anyone who says that the true is the useful naturally seems not to be overlooking this obvious fact, but to be suggesting that truth is a property which comes and goes in the same way. It is, in this way I think, that the "instrumental" view of truth is connected with the view that truth is "mutable." Professor James does, I think, imply that truth is mutable in just this sense—namely, that one and the same idea may be true at some of the times at which it occurs, and not true at others, and this is the view which I have next to consider.

(II)

Professor James seems to hold, generally, that "truth" is mutable. And by this he seems sometimes to mean that an idea which, when it occurs at one time, is true, *may*, when it occurs at another time, not be true. He seems to hold that one and the same idea *may* be true at one time and false at another. That it *may* be, for I do not suppose he means that all ideas do actually undergo this change from true to false. Many true ideas seem to occur but once, and, if so, they, at least, will not actually be true at one time and false at another, though, even with regard to these, perhaps Professor James means to maintain that they *might* be false at another time, if they were to occur at it. But I am not sure that he even means to maintain this with regard to *all* our true ideas. Perhaps he does not mean to say, with regard to *all* of them, even that they *can* change from true to false. He speaks, generally, indeed, as if truth were mutable ; but, in one passage, he seems to insist that there is a certain class of true ideas, none of which are mutable in this respect. "*Relations among purely mental ideas*," he says (p. 209), "form another sphere where true and false beliefs obtain, and here the beliefs are absolute or unconditional. When they are true they bear the name either of definitions or of principles. It is either a principle or a definition that 1 and 1 make 2, that 2 and 1 make 3, and so on; that white differs less from grey than it does from black; that when the cause begins to act the effect also commences. Such propositions hold of all possible 'ones,' of all conceivable 'whites,' 'greys,' and 'causes.' The objects here are mental objects. Their relations are perceptually obvious at a glance, and no sense-verification is necessary. Moreover, once true, always true, of those same mental objects. Truth here has an 'eternal' character. If you can find a concrete thing anywhere that is 'one' or 'white' or 'grey' or an 'effect,' then your principles will everlastingly apply to it." Professor James does seem here to hold that there are true ideas, which once true, are always true. Perhaps, then, he does not hold that *all* true ideas are mutable. Perhaps he does not even hold that all true ideas, *except* ideas of this kind, are so. But he does seem to hold at least that *many* of our true ideas are mutable. And even this proposition seems to me to be disputable. It seems to me that there is a sense in which it is the case with *every* true idea that, if once true, it is always true. That is to say, that every idea, which is true once, *would* be true at any other time at which it were to occur; and that every idea which does occur more than once, if true once, *is* true at every time at which it does occur. There seems to me, I say, to be *a sense* in which this is so. And this seems to me to be the sense in which it is most commonly and most naturally maintained that all truths are "immutable." Professor James seems to mean to deny it, even in this sense. He seems to me contsantly to speak as if there were *no* sense in which *all* truths are immutable. And I only wish to point out what seems to me to be the plainest and most obvious objection to such language.

And, first of all, there is one doctrine, which he seems to connect with this of his that "truths are mutable," with regard to which I fully agree with him. He seems very anxious to insist that reality is mutable : that it does change, and that it is not irrational to hope that in the future it will be different from and much better than it is now. And this seems to me to be quite undeniable. It seems to me quite certain that I do have ideas at one time which I did not have at another ; that change, therefore, doss really occur. It seems to me quite certain that in the future many things will be different from what they are now ; and I see no reason to think that they may not be much better. There is much misery in the world now ; and I think it is quite possible that some day there will really be much less. This view that *reality* is mutable, that *facts* do change, that some things have properties at one time which they do not have at other times, seems to me certainly true. And so far, therefore, as Professor James merely means to assert this obvious fact, I have no objection to his view. Some philosophers, I think, have really implied the denial of this fact. All those who deny the reality of time do seem to me to imply that nothing really changes or can change—that, in fact, reality is wholly immutable. And so far as Professor James is merely protesting against this view, I should, therefore, agree with him.

But I think it is quite plain that he does not mean *merely* this, when he says that truth is mutable. No one would choose this way of expressing himself if he merely meant to say that *some* things are mutable.   Truth, Professor James has told us, is a property of certain of our ideas.   And those of our ideas, which are true or false, are certainly only a part of the Universe.   Other things in the Universe might, therefore, change, even if our ideas never changed in respect of this property.   And our ideas themselves do undoubtedly change in some respects. A given idea exists in my mind at one moment and does not exist in it at another.   At one moment it is in my mind and not in somebody else's, and at another in somebody else's and not in mine.   I sometimes think of the truth that twice two are four when I am in one mood, and sometimes when I am in another.   I sometimes think of it in connection with one set of ideas and sometimes in connection with another set.   Ideas, then, are constantly changing in some respects.   They come and go ; and at one time they stand in a given relation to other things or ideas, to which at another time they do not stand in that relation.   In this sense, any given idea may certainly have a property at one time which it has not got at another time.   All this seems obvious ; and all this cannot be admitted, without admitting that reality is mutable—that *some* things change.   But obviously it does not seem to follow from this that there is *no* respect in which ideas are immutable.   It does not seem to follow that because ideas, and other things, change some of their properties, they necessarily change that one which we are considering—namely, "truth."   It does not follow that a given idea, which has the property of truth at one time, ever exists at any other time without having that property.   And yet that this *does* happen seems to be part of what is meant by saying that truth is mutable.   Plainly, therefore, to say this is to say something quite different from saying that *some* things are mutable. Even, therefore, if we admit that *some* things are mutable, it is still open to consider whether truth is so. And this is what I want now to consider. Is it the case that an idea which exists at one time, and is true then, ever exists at any other time, without being true? Is it the case that any idea ever changes from true to false? That it has the property of being true on one of the occasions when it exists, and that it has *not* this property, but that of being false instead, on some other occasion when it exists?

In order to answer this question clearly, it is, I think, necessary to make still another distinction. It does certainly seem to be true, *in a sense*, that a given idea may be true on one occasion and false on another. We constantly speak as if there were cases in which a given thing was true on one occasion and false on another; and I think it cannot be denied that, when we so speak, we are often expressing in a perfectly proper and legitimate manner something which is undeniably true. It is true now, I might say, that I am in this room; but to-morrow this will not be true. It is true now that men are often very miserable; but perhaps in some future state of society this will not be true. These are perfectly natural forms of expression, and what they express is something which certainly may be true. And yet what they do apparently assert is that something or other, which is true at one time, will not, or *perhaps* will not, be true at another. We constantly use such expressions, which imply that what is true at one time is not true at another; and it is certainly legitimate to use them. And hence, I think, we must admit that, *in a sense*, it is true that a thing may be true at one time which is not true at another; in that sense, namely, in which we use these expressions. And it is, I think, also plain that these things, which may be true at one time and false at another, may, *in a sense*, be ideas. We might even say : The idea that I am in this room, is true now ; but to-morrow it will not be true. We might say this without any strain on language. In any ordinary book—indeed, in any philosophical book, where the subject we are at present discussing was not being expressly discussed—such expressions do, I think, constantly occur. And we should pass them, without any objection. We should at once understand what they meant, and treat them as perfectly natural expressions of things undeniably true. We must, then, I think, admit that, *in a sense*, an idea may be true at one time, and false at another. The question is : In what sense? What is the truth for which these perfectly legitimate expressions stand?

It seems to me that in all these cases, so far as we are not merely talking of *facts*, but of true *ideas*, that the "idea" which we truly say to be true at one time and false at another, is merely the idea of a *sentence*— that is, of certain *words*. And we do undoubtedly call *words* "true." The words "I am at a meeting of the Aristotelian Society" are true, if I use them now ; but if I use the same words to-morrow, they would not be true. The words "George III is king of England" were true in 1800, but they are not true now. That is to say, a given set of words may undoubtedly be true at one time, and false at another ; and since we may have ideas of words as well as of other things, we may, in this sense, say the same of certain of our "ideas." We may say that some of our "ideas" (namely those of words) are true at one time and not true at another.

But is it conceivable that Professor James *merely* meant to assert that the same *words* are sometimes true at one time and false at another? Can this be *all* he means by saying that truth is mutable? I do not think it can possibly be so. No one, I think, in definitely discussing the mutability of truth, could say that true ideas were mutable, and yet mean (although he did not say so) that this proposition applied *solely* to ideas of words. Professor James must, I think, have been sometimes thinking that *other* ideas, and not merely ideas of words, do sometimes change from true to false. And this is the proposition which I am concerned to dispute. It seems to me that if we mean by an idea, not merely the idea of certain words, but the kind of idea which words express, it is very doubtful whether such an idea ever changes from true to false—whether any such idea is ever true at one time and false at another.

And plainly, in the first place, the mere fact that the same set of words, as in the instances I have given, really are true at one time and false at another, does not afford any presumption that anything which they stand for is true at one time and false at another. For the same words may obviously be used in different senses at different times; and hence though the same words, which formerly expressed a truth, may cease to express one, that may be because they now express a *different* idea, and not because the idea which they formerly expressed has ceased to be true. And that, in instances such as I have given, the words *do* change their meaning according to the time at which they are uttered or thought of, is I think, evident. If I use now the words "I am in this room," these words certainly express (among other things) the idea that my being in this room is contemporary with my present use of the words; and if I were to use the same words to-morrow, they would express the idea that my being in this room to-morrow, was contemporary with the use of them *then*. And since my use of them then would not be the same fact as my use of them now, they would certainly then express a different idea from that which they express now. And in general, whenever we use the present tense in its primary sense, it seems to me plain that we do mean something different by it each time we use it. We always mean (among other things) to express the idea that a given event is contemporary with our actual use of it ; and since our actual use of it on one occasion is always a different fact from our actual use of it on another, we express by it a different idea each time we use it. And similarly with the past and future tenses. If anybody had said in 1807 "Napoleon is dead," he would certainly have meant by these words something different from what I mean by them when I use them now. He would have meant that Napoleon's death occurred at a time previous to *his* use of those words ; and this would not have been true. But in this fact there is nothing to show that if he *had* meant by them what I mean now, his idea would not have been as true then as mine is now. And so, if I say "It will rain to-morrow," these words have a different meaning to-day from what they would have if I used them to-morrow. What we mean by "to-morrow" is obviously a different day, when we use the word on one day, from what we mean by it when we use it on another. But in this there is nothing to show that if the idea, which I *now* mean by "It will rain to-morrow," *were* to occur again to-morrow, it would not be true then, if it is true now. All this is surely very obvious. But, if we take account of it, and if we concentrate our attention not on the words but on what is meant by them, is it so certain that what we mean by them on any one occasion ever changes from true to false? If there were to occur to me to-morrow the very same idea which I now express by the words "I am in this room," is it certain that this idea would not be as true then as it is now? It is perhaps true that the *whole* of what I mean by such a phrase as this never does recur. But part of it does, and that a part which is true. Part of what I mean is certainly identical with part of what I should mean to-morrow by saying "I *was* in that room last night." And this part would be as true then, as it is now. And is there *any* part, which, if it were to recur at any time, would *not* then be true, though it is true now? In the case of all ideas or parts of ideas, which ever do actually recur, can we find a single instance of one, which is plainly true at one of the times when it occurs, and yet not true at another? I cannot think of any such instance. And on the other hand this very proposition that any idea (other than mere words) which is true once, would be true at any time, seems to me to be one of those truths of which Professor James has spoken as having an "eternal," "absolute," "unconditional" character—as being "perceptually obvious at a glance" and needing "no sense-verification." Just as we know that, if a particular colour differs more from black than from grey at one time, the same colour would differ more from black than from grey at any time, so, it seems to me, we can see that, if a particular idea is true at one time, the same idea would be true at any time.

It seems to me, then, that if we mean by an idea, not mere words, but the kind of idea which words express, any idea, which is true at one time when it occurs, *would* be true at any time when it were to occur; and that this is so, even though it is an idea, which refers to facts which are mutable. My being in this room is a fact which is now, but which certainly has not been at every time and will not be at every time. And the words "I *am* in this room," though they express a truth now, would not have expressed one if I had used them yesterday, and will not if I use them to-morrow. But if we consider the idea which these words *now* express—

namely, the idea of the connection of my being in this room with this particular time—it seems to me evident that anybody who had thought of that connection at any time in the past, would have been thinking truly, and that anybody who were to think of it at any time in the future would be thinking truly. This seems to me to be the sense in which truths are immutable—in which no idea can change from true to false. And I think Professor James means to deny of truths generally, if not of all truths, that they are immutable even in this sense. If he does not mean this there seems nothing left for him to mean, when he says that truths are mutable, except (1) that some *facts* are mutable, and (2) that the same *words* may be true at one time and false at another. And it seems to me impossible that he could speak as he does, if he meant *nothing more* than these two things. I believe, therefore, that he is really thinking that ideas which have been once true (*ideas*, and not merely words) do sometimes afterwards become false : that the very same idea is at one time true and at another false. But he certainly gives no instance which shows that this does ever occur. And how far does he mean his principle to carry him? Does he hold that this idea that Julius Cæsar was murdered in the Senate-House, though true now, may, at some future time cease to be true, if it should be more profitable to the lives of future generations to believe that he died in his bed? Things like this are what his words seem to imply ; and, even if he does hold that truths like this are *not* mutable, he never tries to tell us to what kinds of truths he would limit mutability, nor how they differ from such as this.

(III)

Finally, there remains the view that "to an unascertainable extent our truths are man-made products." And the only point I want to make about this view may be put very briefly.

It is noticeable that all the instances which Professor James gives of the ways in which, according to him, "our truths" are "made" are instances of ways in which our *beliefs* come into existence. In many of these ways, it would seem, false beliefs sometimes come into existence as well as true ones ; and I take it Professor James does not always wish to deny this. False beliefs, I think he would say, are just as much "man-made products" as true ones : it is sufficient for his purpose if true beliefs do come into existence in the ways he mentions. And the only point which seems to be illustrated by all these instances, is that in all of them the existence of a true belief does depend in some way or other upon the previous existence of something in some man's mind. They are all of them cases in which we may truly say : This man would not have had just that belief, had not some man previously had such and such experiences, or interests, or purposes. In some cases they are instances of ways in which the existence of a particular belief in a man depends upon *his own* previous experiences or interests or volitions. But this does not seem to be the case in all. Professor James seems also anxious to illustrate the point that one man's beliefs often depend upon the previous experiences or interests or volitions of *other* men. And, as I say, the only point which seems to be definitely illustrated in all cases is that the existence of a true belief does depend, *in some way or other*, upon something which has previously existed in some man's mind. Almost any kind of dependence, it would seem, is sufficient to illustrate Professor James' point.

And as regards this general thesis that almost all our beliefs, true as well as false, depend, in some way or other, upon what has previously been in some human mind, it will, I think, be readily admitted. It is a commonplace, which, so far as I know, hardly anyone would deny. If this is all that is to be meant by saying that our true beliefs are "man-made," it must, I think, be admitted that almost all, if not quite all, really are man-made. And this is all that Professor James' instances seem to me, in fact, to show.

But is this all that Professor James means, when he says that *our truths* are man-made? Is it conceivable that he only means to insist upon this undeniable, and generally admitted, commonplace? It seems to me quite plain that this is not all that he means. I think he certainly means to suggest that, from the fact that we "make" our true beliefs, something *else* follows. And I think it is not hard to see one thing more which he does mean. I think he certainly means to suggest that we not only make our true beliefs, but also that we *make them true*. At least as much as this is certainly naturally suggested by his words. No one would persistently say that we make *our truths*, unless he meant, at least, not merely that we make our true beliefs, but also that we make them true—unless he meant not merely that the existence of our true beliefs, but also that their *truth*, depended upon human conditions. This, it seems to me, is one consequence which Professor James means us to draw from the commonplace that the *existence* of our true beliefs depends upon human conditions. But does this consequence, in fact, follow from that commonplace? From the fact that we make our true beliefs, does it follow that we *make them true*?

In one sense, undoubtedly, even this does follow. If we say (as we may say) that no belief can be true, unless it exists, then it follows that, in a sense, the truth of a belief must always depend upon any conditions upon which its existence depends. If, therefore, the occurrence of a belief depends upon human conditions, so, too, must its truth. If the belief had never existed, it would never have been true; and therefore its truth must, in a sense, depend upon human conditions in exactly the same degree in which its existence depends upon them. This is obvious. But is this all that is meant? Is this all that would be suggested to us by telling us that we make our beliefs true?

It is easy to see that it is not. I may have the belief that it will rain to-morrow. And I may have "made" myself have this belief. It may be the case that I should not have had it, but for peculiarities in my past experiences, in my interests and my volitions. It may be the case that I should not have had it, but for a deliberate attempt to consider the question whether it will rain or not. This may easily happen. And certainly this particular belief of mine would not have been true, unless it existed. Its truth, therefore, depends, in a sense, upon any conditions upon which its existence depends. And this belief may be true. It will be true, if it does rain to-morrow. But, in spite of all these reasons, would anyone think of saying that, in case it is true, I had *made* it true ? Would anyone say that I had had any hand *at all* in making it true? Plainly no one would. We should say that I had a hand in making it true, if and only if I had a hand in *making the rain fall*. In every case in which we believe in the existence of anything, past or future, we should say that we had helped to make the belief true, if and only if we had helped to cause the existence of the fact which, in that belief, we believed did exist or would exist. Surely this is plain. I may believe that the sun will rise to-morrow. And I may have had a hand in "making" this belief; certainly it often depends for its existence upon what has been previously in my mind. And if the sun does rise, my belief will have been true. I have, therefore, had a hand in making a true belief. But would anyone say that, therefore, I had a hand in *making this belief true*? Certainly no one would. No one would say that anything had contributed to make this belief true, except those conditions (whatever they may be) which contributed to making the sun actually rise.

It is plain, then, that by "making a belief true," we mean something quite different from what Professor James means by "making" that belief. Conditions which have a hand in making a given true belief, may (it appears) have no hand at all in making it true ; and conditions which have a hand in making it true may have no hand at all in making *it*. Certainly this is how we use the words. We should never say that we had made a belief true, merely because we had made the belief. But now, which of these two things does Professor James mean ? Does he mean *merely* the accepted commonplace that we make our true beliefs, in the sense that almost all of them depend for their existence on what has been previously in some human mind ? Or does he mean also that we *make them true*—that their truth also depends on what has been previously in some human mind ?

I cannot help thinking that he has the latter, and not only the former in his mind. But, then, what does this involve ? If his instances of " truth-making " are to be anything to the purpose, it should mean that, whenever I have a hand in causing one of my own beliefs, I always have to that extent a hand in making it true. That, therefore, I have a hand in actually making the sun rise, the wind blow, and the rain fall, whenever I cause my beliefs in these things. Nay, more, it should mean that, whenever I " make " a true belief about the past, I must have had a hand in making this true. And if so, then certainly I must have had a hand in causing the French Revolution, in causing my father's birth, in making Professor James write this book. Certainly he implies that some man or other must have helped in causing almost every event, in which any man ever truly believed. That it was we who made the planets revolve round the sun, who made the Alps rise, and the floor of the Pacific sink—all these things, and others like them, seem to be involved. And it is these consequences which seem to me to justify a doubt whether, in fact "our truths are to an unascertainable extent man-made." That some of our truths are man-made—indeed, a great many— I fully admit. We certainly do make some of our beliefs true. The Secretary probably had a belief that I should write this paper, and I have made his belief true by writing it. Men certainly have the power to alter the world to a certain extent; and, so far as they do this, they certainly "make true" any beliefs, which are beliefs in the occurrence of these alterations. But I can see no reason for supposing that they "make true" *nearly* all those of their beliefs which are true. And certainly the only reason which Professor James seems to give for believing this—namely, that the *existence* of almost all their beliefs depends on them—seems to be no reason for it at all. For unquestionably a man does not "make true" nearly every belief whose *existence* depends on him; and if so, the question which of their beliefs and how many, men do "make true" must be settled by quite other considerations.

In conclusion, I wish to sum up what seems to me to be the most important points about this "pragmatist theory of truth," as Professor James represents it. It seems to me that, in what he says about it, he has in his mind some things which are true and others which are false; and I wish to tabulate separately the principal ones which I take to be true, and the principal ones which I take to be false. The true ones seem to me to be these :—

That *most* of our true beliefs are useful to us; and that *most* of the beliefs that are useful to us are true.

That the world really does change in some respects; that facts exist at one time, which didn't and won't exist at others; and that hence the world may be better at some future time than it is now or has been in the past.

That the very same words may be true at one time and false at another—that they may express a truth at one time and a falsehood at another.

That the existence of most, if not all, of our beliefs, true as well as false, does depend upon previous events in our mental history; that we should never have had the particular beliefs we do have, had not our previous mental history been such as it was.

That the truth, and not merely the existence, of *some* of our beliefs, does depend upon us. That we really do make some alterations in the world, and that hence we do help to "make true" all those of our beliefs which are beliefs in the existence of these alterations.

To all of these propositions I have no objection to offer. And they seem to me to be generally admitted common-places. A certain class of philosophers do, indeed, imply the denial of every one of them—namely, those philosophers who deny the reality of time. And I think that part of Professor James' object is to protest against the views of these philosophers. All of these propositions do constitute a protest against such views ; and so far they might be all that Professor James meant to assert. But I do not think that anyone, fairly reading through what he says, could get the impression that these things, and nothing more, were what he had in his mind. What gives colour and interest to what he says, seems to be obviously something quite different. And, if we try to find out what exactly the chief things are which give his discussion its colour and interest, it seems to me we may distinguish that what he has in his mind, wrapped up in more or less ambiguous language, are the following propositions, to all of which I have tried to urge what seem to me the most obvious objections :—

That utility is a property which distinguishes true beliefs from those which are not true ; that, therefore, *all* true beliefs are useful, and *all* beliefs, which are useful, are true—by "utility" being sometimes meant "utility on at least one occasion," sometimes "utility in the long run," sometimes "utility for some length of time."

That all beliefs which are useful for some length of time are true.

That utility is the *only* property which all true beliefs have in common : that, therefore, *if* it were useful to me to believe in Professor James' existence, this belief *would* be true, even if he didn't exist ; and that, *if* it were not useful to me to believe this, the belief *would* be false, even if he did.

That the beliefs, which we express by words, and not merely the words themselves, may be true at one time and *not* true at another ; and that this is a general rule, though perhaps there may be some exceptions.

That whenever the *existence* of a belief depends

to some extent on us, then also the *truth* of that belief depends to some extent on us ; in the sense in which this implies, that, when the existence of my belief that a shower will fall depends upon me, then, if this belief is true, I must have had a hand in making the shower fall : that, therefore, men must have had a hand in making to exist almost every fact which they ever believe to exist.

HUME'S PHILOSOPHY

In both of his two books on the Human Understanding, Hume had, I think, one main general object. He tells us that it was his object to discover "the extent and force of human understanding," to give us "an exact analysis of its powers and capacity." And we may, I think, express what he meant by this in the following way. He plainly held (as we all do) that some men sometimes entertain opinions which they cannot know to be true. And he wished to point out what characteristics are possessed by those of our opinions which we *can* know to be true, with a view of persuading us that any opinion which does *not* possess any of these characteristics is of a kind which we *cannot* know to be so. He thus tries to lay down certain rules to the effect that the *only* propositions which we can, any of us, know to be true are of certain definite kinds. It is in this sense, I think, that he tries to define the limits of human understanding.

With this object he, first of all, divides all the propositions, which we can even so much as conceive, into two classes. They are all, he says, either propositions about "relations of ideas" or else about "matters of fact." By propositions about "relations of ideas" he means such propositions as that twice two are four, or that black differs from white; and it is, I think, easy enough to see, though by no means easy to define, what kind of propositions it is that he means to include in this division. They are, he says, the only kind of propositions with regard to which we can have "intuitive" or "demonstrative" certainty. But the vast majority of the propositions in which we believe and which interest us most, belong to the other division : they are propositions about "matters of fact." And these again he divides into two classes. So far as his words go, this latter division is between "matters of fact, beyond the present testimony of our senses, or the records of our memory," on the one hand, and matters of fact for which we *have* the evidence of our memory or senses, on the other. But it is, I think, quite plain that these words do not represent quite accurately the division which he really means to make. He plainly intends to reckon along with facts for which we have the evidence of our *senses* all facts for which we have the evidence of *direct observation*—such facts, for instance, as those which I observe when I observe that I am angry or afraid, and which cannot be strictly said to be apprehended by my *senses*. The division, then, which he really intends to make is (to put it quite strictly) into the two classes—(1) propositions which assert some matter of fact which I am (in the strictest sense) *observing* at the moment, or which I have so observed in the past and now remember ; and (2) propositions which assert any matter of fact which I am not now observing and never have observed, or, if I have, have quite forgotten.

We have, then, the three classes—(1) propositions which assert "relations of ideas"; (2) propositions which assert "matters of fact" for which we have the evidence of direct observation or personal memory; (3) propositions which assert "matters of fact" for which we have *not* this evidence. And as regards propositions of the first two classes,

Hume does not seem to doubt our capacity for knowledge. He does not doubt that we can know *some* (though, of course, not *all*) propositions about "relations of ideas" to be true; he never doubts, for instance, that we can know that twice two are four. And he generally assumes also that each of us can know the truth of *all* propositions which merely assert some matter of fact which we ourselves are, in the strictest sense, directly observing, or which we have so observed and now remember. He does, indeed, in one place, suggest a doubt whether our memory is *ever* to be implicitly trusted, but he generally assumes that it *always* can. It is with regard to propositions of the third class that he is chiefly anxious to determine which of them (if any) we can know to be true and which not. In what cases can any man know any matter of fact which he himself has not directly observed? It is Hume's views on this question which form, I think, the main interest of his philosophy.

He proposes, first of all, by way of answer to it, a rule, which may, I think, be expressed as follows: No man, he says, can ever know any matter of fact, which he has not himself observed, unless he can know that it is connected by "the relation of cause and effect," with some fact which he *has* observed. And no man can ever know that any two facts are connected by this relation, except by the help of his own past *experience*. In other words, if I am to know any fact, A, which I have not myself observed, my past experience must give me some foundation for the belief that A is causally connected with some fact, B, which I have observed. And the only kind of past experience which can give me any foundation for such a belief is, Hume seems to say, as follows: I must, he says, have found *facts like* A "constantly conjoined" in the past with *facts like* B. This is what he *says*; but we must not, I think, press his words too strictly. I may, for instance, know that A is *probably* a fact, even where the conjunction of facts like it with facts like B has not been quite constant. Or instead of observing facts like A conjoined with facts like B, I may have observed a whole series of conjunctions—for instance, between A and C, C and D, D and E, and E and B ; and such a series, however long, will do quite as well to establish a causal connection between A and B, as if I had directly observed conjunctions between A and B themselves. Such modifications as this, Hume would, I think, certainly allow. But, allowing for them, his principle is, I think, quite clear. I can, he holds, never know any fact whatever, which I have not myself observed, unless I have observed similar facts in the past and have observed that they were "conjoined" (directly or indirectly) with facts similar to some fact which I do now observe or remember. In this sense, he holds, *all* our knowledge of facts, beyond the reach of our own observation, is founded on *experience*.

This is Hume's primary principle. But what consequences does he think will follow from it, as to the kind of facts, beyond our own observation, which we can know? We may, I think, distinguish three entirely different views as to its consequences, which he suggests in different parts of his work.

In the first place, where he is specially engaged in explaining this primary principle, he certainly seems to suppose that all propositions of the kind, which we assume most universally in everyday life, may be founded on experience in the sense required. He supposes that we have this foundation in experience for such beliefs as that "a stone will fall, or fire burn"; that Julius Cæsar was murdered ; that the sun will rise to-morrow ; that all men are mortal He speaks as if experience did not merely render such beliefs probable, but actually *proved* them to

be true.   The "arguments from experience" in
their favour are, he says, such as "leave no room
for doubt or opposition."   The only kinds of belief,
which he definitely mentions as *not* founded on
experience, are "popular superstitions" on the one
hand, and certain religious and philosophical beliefs,
on the other.   He seems to suppose that a few (a
very few) religious beliefs may, perhaps, be founded
on experience.   But as regards most of the specific
doctrines of Christianity, for example, he seems to
be clear that they are not so founded.   The belief
in miracles is not founded on experience ; nor is the
philosophical belief that every event is caused by
the direct volition of the Deity.   In short, it would
seem, that in this doctrine that our knowledge of
unobserved facts is confined to such as are "founded
on experience," he means to draw the line very
much where it is drawn by the familiar doctrine
which is called "Agnosticism."   We can know such
facts as are asserted in books on "history, ge-
ography or astronomy," or on "politics, physics and
chemistry," because such assertions may be "founded
on experience" ; but we cannot know the greater
part of the facts asserted in books "of divinity or
school metaphysics," because such assertions have
no foundation in experience.

This, I think, was clearly one of Hume's views.
He meant to fix the limits of our knowledge at a
point which would *exclude* most religious propositions
and a great many philosophical ones, as incapable of
being known ; but which would *include* all the other
kinds of propositions, which are most universally
accepted by common-sense, as capable of being
known.   And he thought that, so far as matters of
fact beyond the reach of our personal observation
are concerned, this point coincided with that at
which the possibility of "foundation on experience"
ceases.

But, if we turn to another part of his work, we find a very different view suggested. In a quite distinct section of both his books, he investigates the beliefs which we entertain concerning the existence of "external objects." And he distinguishes two different kinds of belief which may be held on this subject. "Almost all mankind, and philosophers themselves, for the greatest part of their lives," believe, he says, that "the very things they feel and see" *are* external objects, in the sense that they continue to exist, even when we cease to feel or see them. Philosophers, on the other hand, have been led to reject this opinion and to suppose (when they reflect) that what we actually perceive by the senses never exists except when we perceive it, but that there are other external objects, which do exist independently of us, and which *cause* us to perceive what we do perceive. Hume investigates both of these opinions, at great length in the *Treatise*, and much more briefly in the *Enquiry*, and comes to the conclusion, in both books, that neither of them can be "founded on experience," in the sense he has defined. As regards the first of them, the vulgar opinion, he does seem to admit in the *Treatise* that it is, in a sense, founded on experience ; but not, he insists, in the sense defined. And he seems also to think that, apart from this fact, there are conclusive reasons for holding that the opinion cannot be true. And as regards the philosophical opinion, he says that any belief in external objects, which we never perceive but which cause our perceptions, cannot possibly be founded on experience, for the simple reason that if it were, we should need to have directly observed some of these objects and their "conjunction" with what we do perceive, which *ex hypothesi*, we cannot have done, since we never do directly observe any external object.

Hume, therefore, concludes, in this part of his work, that we cannot know of the existence of any "external object" whatever. And though in all that he says upon this subject, he is plainly thinking only of *material* objects, the principles by which he tries to prove that we cannot know these must, I think, prove equally well that we cannot know any "external object" whatever—not even the existence of any other human mind. His argument is : We cannot directly observe any object whatever, except such as exist only when we observe them ; we cannot, therefore, observe any "constant conjunctions" except between objects of this kind : and hence we can have no foundation in experience for any proposition which asserts the existence of any other kind of object, and cannot, therefore, know any such proposition to be true. And this argument must plainly apply to all the feelings, thoughts and perceptions of other men just as much as to material objects. I can never know that any perception of mine, or anything which I do observe, must have been caused by any other man, because I can never directly observe a "constant conjunction" between any other man's thoughts or feelings or intentions and anything which I directly observe : I cannot, therefore, know that any other man ever had any thoughts or feelings—or, in short, that any man beside myself ever existed. The view, therefore, which Hume suggests in this part of his work, flatly contradicts the view which he at first seemed to hold. He now says we *cannot* know that a stone will fall, that fire will burn, or the sun will rise to-morrow. All that I can possibly know, according to his present principles, is that *I shall see* a stone fall, shall feel the fire burn, shall see the sun rise to-morrow. I cannot even know that any other men will see these things ; for I cannot know that any other men exist. For the same reason, I cannot know that Julius Cæsar was murdered, or that all men are mortal. For these are propositions asserting "external" facts—facts which don't exist only at the moment when I observe them; and, according to his present doctrine, I cannot possibly know any such proposition to be true. No man, in short, can know any proposition about "matters of fact" to be true, except such as merely assert something about *his own* states of mind, past, present or future—about these or about what *he himself* has directly observed, is observing, or will observe.

Here, therefore, we have a very different view suggested, as to the limits of human knowledge. And even this is not all. There is yet a third view, inconsistent with both of these, which Hume suggests in some parts of his work.

So far as we have yet seen, he has not in any way contradicted his original supposition that we can know *some* matters of fact, which we have never ourselves observed. In the second theory, which I have just stated, he does not call in question the view that I can know all such matters of fact as I know to be causally connected with facts which I have observed, nor the view that I can know some facts to be thus causally connected. All that he has done is to question whether I can know any *external* fact to be causally connected with anything which I observe; he would still allow that I may be able to know that future states of my own, or past states, which I have forgotten, are causally connected with those which I now observe or remember; and that I may know therefore, in some cases, what I shall experience in the future, or have experienced in the past but have now forgotten. But in some parts of his work he does seem to question whether any man can know even as much as this: he seems to question whether we can ever know any fact whatever to be causally connected with any other fact. For, after laying it down, as we saw above, that we cannot know any fact, A, to be causally connected with another, B, unless we have experienced in the past a constant conjunction between facts like A and facts like B, he goes on to ask what foundation we have for the conclusion that A and B *are* causally connected, even when we *have* in the past experienced a constant conjunction between them. He points out that from the fact that A has been constantly conjoined with B in the past, it does not follow that it ever will be so again. It does not follow, therefore, that the two really are causally connected in the sense that, when the one occurs, the other *always* will occur also. And he concludes, for this and other reasons, that *no argument* can assure us that, because they have been constantly conjoined in the past, therefore they really are causally connected. What, then, he asks, is the foundation for such an inference? *Custom*, he concludes, is the only foundation. It is nothing but custom which induces us to believe that, because two facts have been constantly conjoined on many occasions, therefore they will be so on *all* occasions. We have, therefore, no better foundation than custom for any conclusion whatever as to facts which we have not observed. And can we be said really to *know* any fact, for which we have no better foundation than this? Hume himself, it must be observed, never says that we can't. But he has been constantly interpreted as if the conclusion that we can't really know any one fact to be causally connected with any other, did follow from this doctrine of his. And there is, I think, certainly much excuse for this interpretation in the tone in which he speaks. He does seem to suggest that a belief which is *merely* founded on custom, can scarcely be one which we *know* to be true. And, indeed, he owns himself that, when he considers that this is our only foundation for any such belief, he is sometimes tempted to doubt whether we do know any fact whatever, except those which we directly observe. He does, therefore, at least suggest the view that every man's knowledge is entirely confined to those facts, which he is directly observing at the moment, or which he has observed in the past, and now remembers.

We see, then, that Hume suggests, at least, three entirely different views as to the consequences of his original doctrine. His original doctrine was that, as regards matters of fact beyond the| reach of our own actual observation, the knowledge of each of us is strictly limited to those for which we have a basis in our own experience. And his first view as to the consequences of this doctrine was that it does show us to be incapable of knowing a good many religious and philosophical propositions, which many men have claimed that they knew; but that it by no means denies our capacity of knowing the vast majority of facts beyond our own observation, which we all commonly suppose that we know. His second view, on the other hand, is that it cuts off at once all possibility of our knowing the vast majority of these facts; since he implies that we cannot have any basis in experience for asserting any *external* fact whatever—any fact, that is, except facts relating to our own actual past and future observations. And his third view is more sceptical still, since it suggests that we cannot really know any fact whatever, beyond the reach of our present observation or memory, even where we *have* a basis in experience for such a fact : it suggests that experience cannot ever let us *know* that any two things are causally connected, and therefore that it cannot give us *knowledge* of any fact based on this relation.

What are we to think of these three views, and

of the original doctrine from which Hume seems to infer them?

As regards the last two views, it may perhaps be thought that they are too absurd to deserve any serious consideration. It is, in fact, absurd to suggest that I do not know any external facts whatever; that I do not know, for instance, even that there are any men beside myself. And Hume himself, it might seem, does not seriously expect or wish us to accept these views. He points out, with regard to all such excessively sceptical opinions that we cannot continue to believe them for long together —that, at least, we cannot, for long together, avoid believing things flatly inconsistent with them. The philosopher may believe, when he is philosophising, that no man knows of the existence of any other man or of any material object; but at other times he will inevitably believe, as we all do, that he does know of the existence of this man and of that, and even of this and that material object. There can, therefore, be no question of making all our beliefs consistent with such views as this of never believing anything that is inconsistent with them. And it may, therefore, seem useless to discuss them. But in fact, it by no means follows that, because we are not able to adhere consistently to a given view, therefore that view is false; nor does it follow that we may not sincerely believe it, whenever we are philosophising, even though the moment we cease to philosophise, or even before, we may be forced to contradict it. And philosophers do, in fact, sincerely believe such things as this—things which flatly contradict the vast majority of the things which they believe at other times. Even Hume, I think, does sincerely wish to persuade us that we cannot know of the existence of external material objects—that this is a philosophic truth, which we ought, if we can, so long as we are philosophising, to believe. Many people, I think, are certainly tempted, in their philosophic moments, to believe such things; and, since this is so, it is, I think, worth while to consider seriously what arguments can be brought against such views. It is worth while to consider whether they are views which we ought to hold as philosophical opinions, even if it be quite certain that we shall never be able to make the views which we entertain at other times consistent with them. And it is the more worth while, because the question how we can prove or disprove such extreme views as these, has a bearing on the question how we can, in any case whatever, prove or disprove that we do really *know*, what we suppose ourselves to know.

What arguments, then, are there for or against the extreme view that no man can know any external fact whatever; and the still more extreme view that no man can know any matter of fact whatever, except those which he is directly observing at the moment, or has observed in the past and now remembers?

It may be pointed out, in the first place, that, if these views are true, then at least no man can possibly know them to be so. What these views assert is that I cannot know any external fact whatever. It follows, therefore, that I cannot know that there are any other men, beside myself, and that they are like me in this respect. Any philosopher who asserts positively that other men, equally with himself, are incapable of knowing any external facts, is, in that very assertion, contradicting himself, since he implies that he *does* know a great many facts about the knowledge of other men. No one, therefore, can be entitled to assert positively that human knowledge is limited in this way, since, in asserting it positively, he is implying that his own knowledge is not so limited. It cannot be proper, even in our philosophic moments, to take up such an attitude as this.

No one, therefore, can know positively that men in general, are incapable of knowing external facts. But still, although we cannot *know* it, it remains possible that the view should be a true one. Nay, more, it remains possible that a man should know that *he himself* is incapable of knowing any external facts, and that, *if* there are any other men whose faculties are only similar to his own, they also must be incapable of knowing any. The argument just used obviously does not apply against such a position as this. It only applies against the position that men in general positively are incapable of knowing external facts : it does not apply against the position that the philosopher himself is incapable of knowing any, or against the position that there are *possibly* other men in the same case, and that, if their faculties are similar to the philosopher's, they certainly would be in it. I do not contradict myself by maintaining positively that *I* know no external facts, though I do contradict myself if I maintain that I am only one among other men, and that no man knows any external facts. So far, then, as Hume merely maintains that *he* is incapable of knowing any external facts, and that there *may* be other men like him in this respect, the argument just used is not valid against his position. Can any conclusive arguments be found against it ?

It seems to me that such a position must, in a certain sense, be quite incapable of disproof. So much must be granted to any sceptic who feels inclined to hold it. Any valid argument which can be brought against it must be of the nature of a *petitio principii* : it must beg the question at issue. How is the sceptic to prove to himself that he does know any external facts ? He can only do it by bringing forward some instance of an external fact,

which he does know ; and, in assuming that he does
know this one, he is, of course, begging the question.
It is therefore quite impossible for any one to *prove*,
in one strict sense of the term, that he does know
any external facts.   I can only prove that I do, by
assuming that in some particular instance, I actually
do know one.   That is to say, the so-called proof
must assume the very thing which it pretends to
prove.   The only proof that we do know external
facts lies in the simple fact that we do know them.
And the sceptic can, with perfect internal consistency, deny that he does know any.   But it can,
I think, be shown that he has no reason for denying
it.   And in particular it may, I think, be easily seen
that the arguments which Hume uses in favour of
this position have no conclusive force.

    To begin with, his arguments, in both cases,
depend upon the two original assumptions, (1) that
we cannot know any fact, which we have not observed, unless we know it to be causally connected
with some fact which we have observed, and (2)
that we have no reason for assuming any causal
connection, except where we have experienced some
instances of conjunction between the two facts
connected.   And both of these assumptions may, of
course, be denied.   It is just as easy to deny them,
as to deny that I do know any external facts.   And,
if these two assumptions did really lead to the
conclusion that I cannot know any, it would, I
think, be proper to deny them : we might fairly
regard the fact that they led to this absurd conclusion as disproving them.   But, in fact, I think it
may be easily seen that they do not lead to it.

    Let us consider, first of all, Hume's most sceptical
argument (the argument which he merely suggests).
This argument suggests that, since our only reason
for supposing two facts to be causally connected is
that we have found them constantly conjoined in

the past, and since it does not follow from the fact
that they have been conjoined ever so many times,
that they *always* will be so, therefore we cannot
know that they always will be so, and hence cannot
know that they are causally connected. But obviously the conclusion does not follow. We must,
I think, grant the premiss that, from the fact that
two things have been conjoined, no matter how
often, it does not strictly *follow* that they *always* are
conjoined. But it by no means follows from this
that we may not *know* that, as a matter of fact,
when two things are conjoined sufficiently often,
they are also *always* conjoined. We may quite
well *know* many things which do not logically follow
from anything else which we know. And so, in
this case, we may *know* that two things are causally
connected, although this does not logically follow
from our past experience, nor yet from anything
else that we know. And, as for the contention that
our belief in causal connections is merely based on
.*custom*, we may, indeed, admit that custom would
not be a, sufficient *reason* for concluding the belief
to be true. But the mere fact (if it be a fact) that
the belief is only caused by custom, is also no
sufficient reason for concluding that we can *not*
know it to be true. Custom *may* produce beliefs,
which we do know to be true, even though it be
admitted that it does not *necessarily* produce them.

And as for Hume's argument to prove that we
can never know any *external* object to be causally
connected with anything which we actually observe,
it is, I think, obviously fallacious. In order to
prove this, he has, as he recognises, to disprove
both of two theories. He has, first of all, to
disprove what he calls the vulgar theory—the
theory that we can know the very things which we
see or feel to be external objects ; that is to say,
can know that these very things exist at times when

we do not observe them. And even here, I think, his arguments are obviously inconclusive. But we need not stay to consider them, because, in order to prove that we cannot know any external objects, he has also to disprove what he calls the philosophic theory—the theory that we can know things which we do observe, to be caused by external objects which we never observe. If, therefore, his attempt to disprove this theory fails, his proof that we cannot know any external objects also fails ; and I think it is easy to see that his disproof does fail. It amounts merely to this : That we cannot, *ex hypothesi*, ever observe these supposed external objects, and therefore cannot observe them to be constantly conjoined with any objects which we do observe. But what follows from this ? His own theory about the knowledge of causal connection is not that in order to know A to be the cause of B, we must have observed A *itself* to be conjoined with B ; but only that we must have observed objects *like* A to be constantly conjoined with objects *like* B. And what is to prevent an external object from being *like* some object which we have formerly observed ? Suppose I have frequently observed a fact *like* A to be conjoined with a fact *like* B : and suppose I now observe B, on an occasion when I do not observe anything like A. There is no reason, on Hume's principles, why I should not conclude that A does exist on this occasion, even though I do not observe it ; and that it is, therefore, an external object. It will, of course, differ from any object which I have ever observed, in respect of the simple fact that it is *not* observed by me, whereas they were. There is, therefore, this one respect in which it must be *unlike* anything which I have ever observed. But Hume has never said anything to show that unlikeness in this single respect is sufficient to invalidate the

inference. It may quite well be like objects which
I have observed in all other respects ; and this
degree of likeness may, according to his principles,
be quite sufficient to justify us in concluding its
existence. In short, when Hume argues that we
cannot possibly learn by experience of the existence
of any external objects, he is, I think, plainly
committing the fallacy of supposing that, because
we cannot, *ex hypothesi*, have ever observed any
object which actually is "external," therefore we
can never have observed any object *like* an external
one. But plainly we may have observed objects
like them in all respects except the single one that
these have been observed whereas the others have
not. And even a less degree of likeness than this
would, according to his principles, be quite sufficient
to justify an inference of causal connection.

Hume does not, therefore, bring forward any
arguments at all sufficient to prove either that he
cannot know any one object to be causally connected
with any other or that he cannot know any external
fact. And, indeed, I think it is plain that no conclusive argument could possibly be advanced in
favour of these positions. It would always be at
least as easy to deny the argument as to deny that
we do know external facts. We may, therefore,
each one of us, safely conclude that we do know
external facts ; and, if we do, then there is no reason
why we should not also know that other men do
the same. There is no reason why we should not,
in this respect, make our philosophical opinions
agree with what we necessarily believe at other
times. There is no reason why I should not con-
fidently assert that I do really *know* some external
facts, although I cannot prove the assertion except
by simply assuming that I do. I am, in fact, as
certain of this as of anything ; and as reasonably
certain of it. But just as I am certain that I do

know *some* external facts, so I am also certain that there are others which I do not know. And the question remains : Does the line between the two fall, where Hume says it falls ? Is it true that the only external facts I know are facts for which I have a basis in my own experience ? And that I cannot know any facts whatever, beyond the reach of my own observation and memory, except those for which I have such a basis ?

This, it seems to me, is the most serious question which Hume raises. And it should be observed that his own attitude towards it is very different from his attitude towards the sceptical views which we have just been considering. These sceptical views he did not expect or wish us to accept, except in philosophic moments. He declares that we cannot, in ordinary life, avoid believing things which are inconsistent with them ; and, in so declaring, he, of course, implies incidentally that they are false : since he implies that he himself has a great deal of knowledge as to what we can and cannot believe in ordinary life. But, as regards the view that our knowledge of matters of fact beyond our own observation is entirely confined to such as are founded on experience, he never suggests that it is impossible that all our beliefs should be consistent with this view, and he does seem to think it eminently desirable that they should be. He declares that any assertion with regard to such matters, which is not founded on experience, can be nothing but "sophistry and illusion" ; and that all books which are composed of such assertions should be "committed to the flames." He seems, therefore, to think that here we really have a test by which we may determine what we should or should not believe, on all occasions : any view on such matters, for which we have no foundation in experience, is a view which we cannot know to be

even probably true, and which we should *never*
accept, if we can help it.   Is there any justification
for this strong view ?

It is, of course, abstractly possible that we do
really know, *without* the help of experience, some
matters of fact, which we never have observed.
Just as we know matters of fact, which we *have*
observed, without the need of any further evidence,
and just as we know, for instance, that $2 + 2 = 4$,
without the need of any proof, it is possible that we
may know, directly and immediately, without the
need of any basis in experience, some facts which
we never have observed.   This is certainly possible,
in the same sense in which it is possible that I do not
really know any external facts : no conclusive disproof
can be brought against either position.   We must
make assumptions as to what facts we do know and
do not know, before we can proceed to discuss
whether or not all of the former are based on
experience ; and none of these assumptions can, in
the last resort, be conclusively proved.   We may
offer one of them in proof of another ; but it will
always be possible to dispute the one which we offer
in proof.   But there are, in fact, certain kinds of
things which we universally assume that we do know
or do not know, just as we assume that we do know
some external facts ; and if among all the things
which we know as certainly as this, there should
turn out to be none for which we have no basis in
experience, Hume's view would I think, be as fully
proved as it is capable of being.   The question is :
Can it be proved in this sense ?   Among all the
facts beyond our own observation, which we know
most certainly, are there any which are certainly not
based upon experience ?   For my part, I confess,
I cannot feel certain what is the right answer to this
question : I cannot tell whether Hume was right or
wrong.   But if he was wrong—if there are any

matters of fact, beyond our own observation, which we know for certain, and which yet we know directly and immediately, without any basis in experience, we are, I think, faced with an eminently interesting problem.   For it is, I think, as certain as anything can be that there are *some* kinds of facts with regard to which Hume was right—that there are *some* kinds of facts which we cannot know without the evidence of experience.   I could not know, for instance, without some such evidence, such a fact as that Julius Cæsar was murdered.   For such a fact I must, in the first instance, have the evidence of other persons ; and if I am to know that their evidence is trustworthy, I must have some ground in experience for supposing it to be so.   There are, therefore, some kinds of facts which we cannot know without the evidence of experience and observation.   And if it is to be maintained that there are others, which we can know without any such evidence, it ought to be pointed out exactly what kind of facts these are, and in what respects they differ from those which we cannot know without the help of experience.   Hume gives us a very clear division of the kinds of propositions which we can know to be true.   There are, first of all, some propositions which assert "relations of ideas " ; there are, secondly, propositions which assert "matters of fact" which we ourselves are actually observing, or have observed and now remember ; and there are, thirdly, propositions which assert "matters of fact" which we have never actually observed, but for believing in which we have some foundation in our past observations. And it is, I think, certain that some propositions, which we know as certainly as we know anything, do belong to each of these three classes.   I know, for instance, that twice two are four ; I know by direct observation that I am now seeing these words,

that I am writing, and by memory that this after-
noon I saw St. Paul's ; and I know also that Julius
Cæsar was murdered, and I have some foundation
in experience for this belief, though I did not myself
witness the murder.   Do any of those propositions,
which we know as certainly as we know these and
their like, *not* belong to either of these three classes ?
Must we add a fourth class consisting of propositions
which resemble the two last, in respect of the fact
that they do assert " matters of fact," but which
differ from them, in that we know them neither by
direct observation nor by memory, nor yet as a
result of previous observations ?   There may,
perhaps, be such a fourth class ; but, if there is, it
is, I think, eminently desirable that it should be
pointed out exactly what propositions they are which
we do know in this way ; and this, so far as I know,
has never yet been done, at all clearly, by any
philosopher.

THE STATUS OF SENSE-DATA

THE term "sense-data" is ambiguous ; and there-fore I think I had better begin by trying to explain what the class of entities is whose status I propose to discuss.

There are several different classes of mental events, all of which, owing to their intrinsic resemblance to one another in certain respects, may, in a wide sense, be called "sensory experiences," although only some among them would usually be called "sensations." There are (1) those events, happening in our minds while we are awake, which consist in the experiencing of one of those entities, which are usually called "images," in the narrowest sense of the term. Everybody distinguishes these events from sensations proper ; and yet everybody admits that "images" intrinsically resemble the entities which are experienced in sensations proper in some very important respect. There are (2) the sensory experiences we have in dreams, some of which would certainly be said to be experiences of images, while others might be said to be sensations. There are (3) hallucinations, and certain classes of illusory sensory experiences. There are (4) those experiences, which used to be called the having of "after-images," but which psychologists now say ought rather to be called "after-sensations." And there are, finally, (5) that class of sensory experiences, which are immensely commoner than any of the above, and which may be called *sensations proper*, if we agree to use this term in such a way as to exclude experiences of my first four sorts.

Every event, of any one of these five classes, consists in the fact that an entity, of some kind or other, *is experienced*. The entity which is experienced may be of many different kinds ; it may, for instance, be a patch of colour, or a sound, or a smell, or a taste, etc ; or it may be an image of a patch of colour, an image of a sound, an image of a smell, an image of a taste, etc. But, whatever be its nature, the entity which *is* experienced must in all cases be distinguished from the fact or event which consists in its being experienced ; since by saying that it is experienced we mean that it has a relation of a certain kind to something else. We can, therefore, speak not only of *experiences* of these five kinds, but also of the entities which *are experienced in* experiences of these kinds ; and the entity which is experienced *in* such an experience is never identical with the experience which consists in its being experienced. But we can speak not only of the entities which *are* experienced in experiences of this kind, but also of *the sort* of entities which are experienced in experiences of this kind ; and these two classes may again be different. For a patch of colour, even if it were not actually experienced, would be an entity *of the same sort* as some which are experienced in experiences of this kind : and there is no contradiction in supposing that there are patches of colour, which yet are not experienced ; since by calling a thing a patch of colour we merely make a statement about its intrinsic quality, and in no way assert that it has to anything else any of the relations which may be meant by saying that it is experienced. In speaking, therefore, of *the sort of* entities which are experienced in experiences of the five kinds I have mentioned, we do not necessarily confine ourselves to those which actually *are* experienced in some such experience : we leave it an open question whether the two classes are identical or not.   And the class of entities, whose status I wish to discuss, consists precisely of all those, whether experienced or not, which are *of the same sort* as those which are experienced in experiences of these five kinds.

I intend to call this class of entities the class of *sensibles*; so that the question I am to discuss can be expressed in the form : What is the status of sensibles? And it must be remembered that images and after-images are just as much " sensibles," in my sense of the term, as the entities which are experienced in sensations proper ; and so, too, are any patches of colour, or sounds, or smells, etc, (if such there be), which are not experienced at all.

In speaking of sensibles as *the sort of* entities which are experienced in sensory experiences I seem to imply that all the entities which are experienced in sensory experiences have some common characteristic other than that which consists in their being so experienced.   And I cannot help thinking that this is the case, in spite of the fact that it is difficult to see what intrinsic character can be shared in common by entities so different from one another as are patches of colour, sounds, smells, tastes, etc.   For, so far as I can see, some non-sensory experiences may be exactly similar to sensory ones in all intrinsic respects, except that what is experienced in them is different in kind from what is experienced in any sensory experience : the relation meant by saying that in them something *is experienced* may be exactly the same in kind, and so may the experient.   And, if this be so, it seems to compel us to admit that the distinction between sensory and non-sensory experiences is derived from that between sensibles, and non-sensibles and not *vice versâ*.   I am inclined, therefore, to think that all sensibles, in spite of the great differences between them, have some common intrinsic property, which we recognise, but which is unanalysable ; and that, when we call an experience sensory, what we mean is not only that in it something is experienced in a particular way, but also that this something has this unanalysable property. If this be so, the ultimate definition of "sensibles" would be merely all entities which have this unanalysable property.

It seems to me that the term "sense-data" is often used, and may be correctly used, simply as a synonym for "sensibles"; and everybody, I think, would expect me, in discussing the status of sense-data, to discuss, among other things, the question whether there are any sensibles which are not "given." It is true that the etymology of the term "sense-data" suggests that nothing should be called a sense-datum, but what *is* given ; so that to talk of a non-given sense-datum would be a contradiction in terms. But, of course, etymology is no safe guide either as to the actual or the correct use of terms ; and it seems to me that the term "sense-data" is often, and quite properly, used merely for *the sort of* entities that are given in sense, and not in any way limited to those which are actually given. But though I think I might thus have used "sense-data" quite correctly instead of "sensibles," I think the latter term is perhaps more convenient ; because though nobody ought to be misled by etymologies, so many people in fact are so. Moreover the term "sense-data" is sometimes limited in yet another way, viz, to the sort of sensibles which are experienced in *sensations proper* ; so that in this sense "images" would not be "sense-data." For both these reasons, I think it is perhaps better to drop the term "sense-data" altogether, and to speak only of "sensibles."

My discussion of the status of sensibles will be divided into two parts. I shall first consider how, in certain respects, they are related to our minds ; and then I shall consider how, in certain respects, they are related to physical objects.

(I)

(1) We can, I think, distinguish pretty clearly at least one kind of relation which sensibles, of all the kinds I have mentioned, do undoubtedly sometimes have to our minds.

I do now see certain blackish marks on a whitish ground, and I hear certain sounds which I attribute to the ticking of my clock. In both cases I have to certain sensibles—certain blackish marks, in the one case, and certain sounds, in the other—a kind of relation with which we are all perfectly familiar, and which may be expressed, in the one case, by saying that I actually *see* the marks, and in the other, by saying that I actually *hear* the sounds. It seems to me quite evident that the relation to the marks which I express by saying that I *see* them, is not different in kind from the relation to the sounds which I express by saying that I *hear* them. "Seeing" and "hearing," when thus used as names for a relation which we may have to sensibles, are not names for different relations, but merely express the fact that, in the one case, the kind of sensible to which I have a certain kind of relation is a patch of colour, while, in the other case, the kind of sensible to which I have the same kind of relation is a sound. And similarly when I say that I feel warm or smell a smell these different verbs do not express the fact that I have a different kind of relation to the sensibles concerned, but only that I have the *same* kind of relation to a different kind of sensible. Even when I call up a visual image of a sensible I saw yesterday, or an auditory image of a sound I heard yesterday, I have to those images exactly the same kind of relation which I have to the patches of colour I now see and which I had yesterday to those I saw then.

But this kind of relation, which I sometimes have to sensibles of all sorts of different kinds, images as well as others, is evidently quite different in kind from another relation which I may also have to sensibles. After looking at this black mark, I may turn away my head or close my eyes, and then I no longer *actually* see the mark I saw just now. I may, indeed, have (I myself actually do have at this moment) a visual *image* of the mark before my mind; and to this image I do now have exactly the same kind of relation which I had just now to the mark itself. But the image is not identical with the mark of which it is an image; and to the mark itself it is quite certain that I have *not* now got the same kind of relation as I had just now, when I was actually seeing it. And yet I certainly may *now* have to that mark itself a kind of relation, which may be expressed by saying that I am *thinking of* it or remembering it. I can *now* make judgments about *it itself*—the very sensible which I did see just now and am no longer seeing : as, for instance, that I did then see it and that it was different from the image of it which I am now seeing. It is, therefore, quite certain that there is a most important difference between the relation I have to a sensible when I am actually seeing or hearing it, and any relation (for there may be several) which I may have to the same sensible when I am only thinking of or remembering it. And I want to express this difference by using a particular term for the former relation. I shall express this relation, which I certainly do have to a sensible when I actually see or hear it, and most certainly do not have to it, when I only think of or remember it, by saying that there is in my mind a *direct apprehension* of it. I have expressly chosen this term because, so far as I know, it has not been used hitherto as a technical term ; whereas all the terms which have been so used, such as "presented," "given," "perceived," seem to me to have been spoilt by ambiguity. People sometimes, no doubt, use these terms as names for the kind of relation I am concerned with. But you can never be sure, when an entity is said to be "given" or "presented" or "perceived," that what is meant is simply and solely that it has to someone that relation which sensibles do undoubtedly have to me when I actually see or hear them, and which they do *not* have to me when I only think of or remember them.

I have used the rather awkward expression "There is in my mind a direct apprehension of this black mark," because I want to insist that though, when I see the mark, the mark certainly has to *something* the fundamental relation which I wish to express by saying that it is directly apprehended, and though the event which consists in its being directly apprehended by that something is certainly a mental act of *mine* or which occurs in my mind, yet the something which directly apprehends it may quite possibly not be anything which deserves to be called "I" or "me." It is quite possible, I think, that there is *no* entity whatever which deserves to be called "I" or "me" or "my mind"; and hence that nothing whatever is ever directly apprehended by *me*. Whether this is so or not, depends on the nature of that relation which certainly does hold between all those mental acts which are *mine*, and does not hold between any of mine and any of yours; and which holds again between all those mental acts which are yours, but does not hold between any of yours and any of mine. And I do not feel at all sure what the correct analysis of this relation is. It may be the case that the

relation which unites all those acts of direct apprehension which are mine, and which is what we
mean to say that they have to one another when
we say they are all mine, really does consist in
the fact that one and the same entity is *what*
directly apprehends in each of them : in which case
this entity could properly be called "me," and it
would be true to say that, when I see this black
mark, *I* directly apprehend it. But it is also quite
possible (and this seems to me to be the view which
is commonest amongst psychologists) that the entity
which directly apprehends, in those acts of direct
apprehension which are mine, is numerically
different in every different act ; and that what I
mean by calling all these different acts *mine* is
either merely that they have some kind of relation
to *one another* or that they all have a common
relation to some other entity, external to them,
which may or may not be something which
deserves to be called "me." On any such view,
what I assert to be true of this black mark, when I
say that it is seen by me, would not be simply that
it is directly apprehended by me, but something
more complex in which, besides direct apprehension,
some other quite different relation was also involved.
I should be asserting *both* (1) that the black mark
is being directly apprehended by *something*, *and* (2)
that this act of direct apprehension has to something
else, external to it, a quite different relation, which
is what makes it an act of *mine*.   I do not know
how to decide between these views, and that is why
I wished to explain that the fundamental relation
which I wish to call direct apprehension, is one
which quite possibly never holds between *me* and
any sensible. But, once this has been explained, I
think no harm can result from using the expression
"I directly apprehend A" as a synonym for "A
direct apprehension of A occurs in my mind."   And

in future I shall so speak, because it is much more convenient.

The only other point, which seems to me to need explanation, in order to make it quite clear what the relation I call "direct apprehension" is, concerns its relation to *attention* ; and as to this I must confess I don't feel clear.   In every case where it is quite clear to me that I am directly apprehending a given entity, it seems also clear to me that I am, more or less, attending to it ; and it seems to me possible that what I mean by "direct apprehension" may be simply identical with what is meant by "attention," in *one* of the senses in which that word can be used.   That it can, at most, only be identical with *one* of the relations meant by attention seems to me clear, because I certainly can be said to attend, in some sense or other, to entities, which I am not directly apprehending : I may, for instance, think, with attention, of a sensible, which I saw yesterday, and am certainly not seeing now.   It is, therefore, clear that to say I am attending to a thing and yet am *not* directly apprehending it, is not a contradiction in terms : and this fact alone is sufficient to justify the use of the special term "direct apprehension."   But whether to say that I am directly apprehending a given thing and yet am *not* attending to it, in any degree at all, is or is not a contradiction in terms, I admit I don't feel clear.

However that may be, one relation, in which sensibles of all sorts do sometimes stand to our minds, is the relation constituted by the fact that we directly apprehend them : or, to speak more accurately, by the fact that events which consist in their being directly apprehended are *in* our minds, in the sense in which to say that an event is *in* our minds means merely that it is a mental act of *ours*—that it has to our other mental acts that relation (whatever it may be) which we mean by saying that they are all mental acts *of the same individual.* And it is clear that to say of a sensible that it is directly apprehended by me, is to say of it something quite different from what I say of a mental act of mine, when I say that this *mental act is in my mind*: for nothing is more certain than that an act of direct apprehension or belief may be in my mind, without being itself directly apprehended by me. If, therefore, by saying that a sensible is *in our minds* or is *ours*, we mean merely that it is directly apprehended by us, we must recognise that we are here using the phrases "in our minds" or "ours" in quite a different sense from that in which we use them when we talk of our mental acts being "in our minds" or "ours." And why I say this is because I think that these two relations are very apt to be confused. When, for instance, we say of a given entity that it is "experienced," or when the Germans say that it is "erlebt," it is sometimes meant, I think, merely that it is directly apprehended, but sometimes that it is in my mind, in the sense in which, when I entertain a belief, this act of belief is in my mind.

But (2) it seems to me to be commonly held that sensibles are often in our minds in some sense quite other than that of being directly apprehended by us or that of being thought of by us. This seems to me to be often what is meant when people say that they are "immediately experienced" or are "subjective modifications"; though, of course, both expressions are so ambiguous, that when people say that a given entity is immediately experienced or is a subjective modification, they *may* mean merely that it is directly apprehended. And since I think this view is held, I want to explain that I see no reason whatever for thinking that sensibles ever are experienced by us in any other sense than that of being directly apprehended by us.

Two kinds of argument, I think, are sometimes used to show that they are.

(*a*) It is a familiar fact that, when, for instance, we are in a room with a ticking clock, we may seem suddenly to become aware of the ticks, whereas, so far as we can tell, we had previously not heard them at all. And it may be urged that in these cases, since the same kind of·stimulus was acting on our ears all the time, we must have *experienced* the same kind of sensible sounds, although we did not directly apprehend them.

But I think most psychologists are now agreed that this argument is quite worthless. There seem to me to be two possible alternatives to the conclusion drawn. It may, I think, possibly be the case that we did directly apprehend the ticks all the time, but that we cannot afterwards remember that we did, because the degree of attention (if any) with which we heard them was so small, that in ordinary life we should say that we did not attend to them at all. But, what, I think, is much more likely is that, though the same stimulus was acting on our ears, it failed to produce any mental effect whatever, because our attention was otherwise engaged.

(*b*) It is said that sometimes when we suddenly become aware, say, of the eighth stroke of a striking clock, we can *remember* earlier strokes, although we seem to ourselves *not* to have directly apprehended them. I cannot say that I have ever noticed this experience in myself, but I have no doubt that it is possible. And people seem inclined to argue that, since we can remember the earlier strokes, we must have experienced them, though we did not directly apprehend them.

But here again, the argument does not seem to me at all conclusive. I should say, again, that it is possible that we did directly apprehend them, but

only with a very slight degree of attention (if any).
And, as an alternative, I should urge that there is
no reason why we should not be able to remember
a thing, which we never experienced at all.

I do not know what other arguments can be
used to show that we sometimes *experience* sensibles
in a sense quite other than that of directly apprehending them.   But I do not know how to show
that we do not; and since people whose judgment
I respect, seem to hold that we do, I think it is
worth while to say something as to what this sense
of " experience " can be, in case it does occur.

I have said that sometimes when people say that
a given entity is " experienced " they seem to mean
that it belongs to some individual, in the sense in
which my acts of belief belong to me. To say that
sensibles were experienced by me in this sense
would, therefore, be to say that they sometimes
have to my acts of belief and acts of direct apprehension the same relation which these have to one
another—the relation which constitutes them *mine*.
But that sensibles ever have this kind of relation
to my mental acts, is a thing which I cannot believe.
Those who hold that they are ever experienced at
all, in some sense other than that of being directly
apprehended, always hold, I think, that, whenever
they are directly apprehended by us, they also, at
the same time, have to us this other relation as well.
And it seems to me pretty clear that when I do
directly apprehend a sensible, it does *not* have to
me the same relation which my direct apprehension
of it has.

If, therefore, sensibles are ever experienced by us
at all, in any sense other than that of being directly
apprehended by us, we must, I think, hold that they
are so in an entirely new sense, quite different both
from that in which to be experienced means to be
directly apprehended, and from that in which to be

experienced means to occur in some individual's mind. And I can only say that I see no reason to think that they ever are experienced in any such sense. If they are, the fact that they are so is presumably open to the inspection of us all ; but I cannot distinguish any such fact as occurring in myself, as I can distinguish the fact that they are directly apprehended. On the other hand, I see no way of showing that they are *not* experienced in some such sense ; and perhaps somebody will be able to point it out to me. I do not wish to assume, therefore, that there *is* no such sense ; and hence, though I am inclined to think that the *only* sense in which they are experienced is that of being directly apprehended, I shall, in what follows, use the phrase " experienced " to mean *either* directly apprehended *or* having to something this supposed different relation, if such a relation there be.

(3) We may now, therefore, raise the question : Do sensibles ever exist at times when they are not being experienced at all ?

To this question it is usual to give a negative answer, and two different *a priori* reasons may be urged in favour of that answer.

The first is what should be meant by Berkeley's dictum that the *esse* of sensibles is *percipi.* This should mean, whatever else it may mean, at least this : that to suppose a sensible to exist and yet *not* to be experienced in self-contradictory. And this at least seems to me to be clearly false. Anything which was a patch of colour would be a sensible ; and to suppose that there are patches of colour which are not being experienced is clearly not self-contradictory, however false it may be.

It may, however, be urged (and this is the second argument) that, though to suppose a thing to be a sensible and *yet* not experienced is not self-contradictory, yet we can clearly see that nothing can have the one property without having the other. And I do not see my way to deny that we may be able to know, *a priori* that such a connection holds between two such properties. In the present case, however, I cannot see that it does hold, and therefore, so far as *a priori* reasons go, I conclude that there is no reason why sensibles should not exist at times when they are not experienced.

It may, however, be asked : Is there any reason to suppose that they ever do? And the reason, which weighs with me most, is one which applies, I think, to a certain class of sensibles *only ;* a class which I will try to define by saying that it consists of those which *would* (under certain conditions which actually exist) be experienced in a *sensation proper, if only* a living body, having a certain constitution, existed under those conditions in a position in which no such body does actually exist. I think it is very probable that this definition does not define at all accurately the kind of sensibles I mean ; but I think that what the definition aims at will become clearer when I proceed to give my reasons for supposing that sensibles, of a kind to be defined in *some* such way, do exist unexperienced. The reason is simply that, in Hume's phrase, I have " a strong propensity to believe " that, *e.g.*, the visual sensibles which I directly apprehend in looking at this paper, still exist unchanged when I merely alter the position of my body by turning away my head or closing my eyes, *provided* that the physical conditions outside my body remain unchanged. In such a case it is certainly true in some sense that I *should* see sensibles like what I saw the moment before, *if only* my head were still in the position it was at that moment or my eyes unclosed. But if, in such a case, there is reason to think that sensibles which I should see, if the position of my body were altered, exist in spite of the fact that I do not experience them, there is, I think, an equal reason to suppose it in other cases. We must, for instance, suppose that the sensibles which I should see now, if I were at the other end of the room, or if I were looking under the table, exist at this moment, though they are not being experienced. And similarly we must suppose that the sensibles which *you* would see, if you were in the position in which I am now, exist at this moment, in spite of the fact that they may be more or less different from those which I see, owing to the different constitution of our bodies. All this implies of course, that a vast number of sensibles exist at any moment, which are not being experienced at all. But still it implies this only with regard to sensibles of a strictly limited class, namely sensibles which would be experienced *in a sensation proper*, if a body, having a certain constitution, were in a position in which it is not, under the given physical conditions. It does not, for instance, imply that any *images*, of which it may be true that I *should* have them, under present physical conditions, if the position of my body were altered, exist now ; nor does it imply that sensibles which *would* be experienced by me now in a sensation proper, if the physical conditions external to my body were different from what they are, exist now.

I feel, of course, that I have only succeeded in defining miserably vaguely the kind of sensibles I mean ; and I do not know whether the fact that I have a strong propensity to believe that sensibles of a kind to be defined in some such way, do exist unexperienced, is any good reason for supposing that they actually do. The belief may, of course, be a mere prejudice. But I do not know of any certain test by which prejudices can be distinguished from reasonable beliefs. And I cannot help thinking that there may be a class of sensibles, capable of

definition in *some* such way, which there really is
reason to think exist unexperienced.

But, if I am not mistaken, there is an empirical
argument which, though, even if it were sound, it
would have no tendency whatever to show that *no*
sensibles exist unexperienced, would, if it were
sound, show that this very class of sensibles, to
which alone my argument for unexperienced
existence applies, certainly do not so exist.   This,
it seems to me, is the most weighty argument which
can be used upon the subject ; and I want, therefore,
to give my reasons for thinking that it is fallacious.

The argument is one which asserts that there is
abundant empirical evidence in favour of the view
that the existence of the sensibles which we experience at any time, always depends upon the
condition of our nervous system : so that, even where
it also depends upon external physical conditions,
we can safely say that sensibles, which we should
have experienced, if only our nervous system had
been in a different condition, certainly do not exist,
when it is not in that condition.   And the fallacy of
this argument seems to me to lie in the fact that it
does not distinguish between the existence of the
sensibles *which* we experience and *the fact that we
experience them.*   What there *is* evidence for is that
our experience of sensibles always depends upon the
condition of our nervous system ; that, according as
the condition of the nervous system changes,
different sensibles are *experienced,* even where other
conditions are the same.   But obviously the fact that
our experience of a given sensible depends upon the
condition of our nervous system does not directly
show that the existence of *the sensible experienced*
always also so depends.   The fact that I am now
experiencing this black mark is certainly a different
fact from the fact that this black mark now exists.   And
hence the evidence which does tend to show that

the former fact would not have existed if my nervous system had been in a different condition, has no tendency to show that the latter would not have done so either. I am sure that this distinction ought to be made ; and hence, though I think there may be other reasons for thinking that the very existence of the sensibles, which we experience, and not merely the fact that we experience them *does* always depend upon the condition of our nervous systems, it seems to me certain that this particular argument constitutes no such reason.

And I think that those who suppose that it does are apt to be influenced by an assumption, for which also, so far as I can see, there is no reason. I have admitted that the only reason I can see for supposing that sensibles which we experience ever exist unexperienced, seems to lead to the conclusion that the sensibles which would be seen by a colour-blind man, if he occupied exactly the position which I, who am not colour-blind, now occupy, exist now, just as much as those which I now see. And it may be thought that this implies that the sensibles, which he would see, and which would certainly be very different from those which I see, are nevertheless at this moment in exactly the same place as those which I see. Now, for my part, I am not prepared to admit that it is impossible they should be in the same place. But the assumption against which I wish to protest, is the assumption that, if they exist at all, they *must* be in the same place. I can see no reason whatever for this assumption. And hence any difficulties there may be in the way of supposing that they could be in the same place at the same time as the sensibles which I see, do not at all apply to my hypothesis, which is only that they exist *now*, *not* that they exist *in the same place* in which mine do.

On this question, therefore, as to whether sensibles ever exist at times when they are not experienced, I have only to say (1) that I think there is certainly no good reason whatever for asserting that *no* sensibles do; and (2) that I think perhaps a certain amount of weight ought to be attached to our instinctive belief that certain kinds of sensibles do; and that here again any special arguments which may be brought forward to show that, whether some sensibles exist unexperienced or not, *this* kind certainly do not, are, so far as I can see, wholly inconclusive.

(II)

I now pass to the question how sensibles are related to physical objects. And here I want to say, to begin with, that I feel extremely puzzled about the whole subject. I find it extremely difficult to distinguish clearly from one another the different considerations which ought to be distinguished; and all I can do is to raise, more or less vaguely, certain questions as to how certain *particular* sensibles are related to certain *particular* physical objects, and to give the reasons which seem to me to have most weight for answering these questions in one way rather than another. I feel that all that I can say is very tentative.

To begin with, I do not know how "physical object" is to be defined, and I shall not try to define it. I shall, instead, consider certain propositions, which everybody will admit to be propositions *about* physical objects, and which I shall assume that I know to be true. And the question I shall raise is as to how these propositions are to be interpreted—*in what sense* they are true; in considering which, we shall at the same time consider how they are related to certain sensibles.

I am looking at two coins, one of which is a half-crown, the other a florin. Both are lying on the ground; and they are situated obliquely to

G

my line of sight, so that the visual sensibles which I directly apprehend in looking at them are visibly elliptical, and not even approximately circular. Moreover, the half-crown is so much farther from me than the florin that *its* visual sensible is visibly smaller than that of the florin.

In these circumstances I am going to assume that I know the following propositions to be true ; and no one, I think, will deny that we can know such propositions to be true, though, as we shall see, extremely different views may be taken as to what they mean.   I know (*a*) that, in the ordinary sense of the word "see" I am *really seeing two coins ;* an assertion which includes, if it is not identical with, the assertion that the visual experiences, which consist in my direct apprehension of those two elliptical patches of colour, *are* sensations proper, and are not either hallucinations nor mere experiences of "images" ; (*b*) that the upper sides of the coins are *really* approximately circular, and not merely elliptical like the visual sensibles ; (*c*) that the coins *have* another side, and an inside, though I don't see it ; (*d*) that the upper side of the half-crown is really *larger* than that of the florin, though its visual sensible is *smaller* than the visual sensible of the upper side of the florin : (*e*) that both coins continue to exist, even when I turn away my head or shut my eyes ; but in saying this, I do not, of course, mean to say that there is absolutely *no* change in them ; I daresay there must be *some* change, and I do not know how to define exactly what I do mean.   But we can, I think, say at least this : viz., that propositions (*b*), (*c*), and (*d*) will still be true, although proposition (*a*) has ceased to be true.

Now all these propositions are, I think, typical propositions of the sort which we call propositions about physical objects; and the two coins themselves *are* physical objects, if anything is.   My question is : *In what sense* are these propositions true?

And in considering this question, there are, I think, two principles which we can lay down as certain to begin with ; though they do not carry us very far.

The one is (*a*) that the upper side of the coin, which I am said to *see*, is not simply identical with the visual sensible which I *directly apprehend* in seeing it.   That this is so might be thought to follow absolutely from each of the two facts which I have called (*b*) and (*d*) ; but I am not quite sure that it does follow from either of these or from both together : for it seems to me just possible that the two sensibles in question, though *not* circular *in my private space*, may yet be circular in *physical* space ; and similarly that though the sensible of the half-crown is smaller than that of the florin *in my private space*, it may be larger *in physical space*.   But what I think it does follow from is the fact that another person may be seeing the upper side of the coin in exactly the same sense in which I am seeing it, and yet his sensible be certainly different from mine. From this it follows absolutely that the upper side of the coin cannot be identical with *both* sensibles, since they are *not* identical with one another.   And though it does not follow absolutely that it may not be identical with *one* of the two, yet it does follow that we *can* get a case in which it is not identical with *mine* and I need only assume that the case I am taking is such a case.

From this it follows that we must distinguish that sense of the word " see " in which we can be said to " see " a physical object, from that sense of the word in which " see " means merely to directly apprehend a visual sensible.   In a proposition of the form " I see A," where A is a name or description of some physical object, though, if this proposition is to be true, there must be some visual sensible, B, which I am directly apprehending, yet the proposition " I see A " is certainly not always, and probably never, identical in meaning with the proposition " I directly apprehend B." In asserting " I see A " we are asserting not only that we directly apprehend some sensible but also something else about this sensible—it may be only some proposition of the form, " and this sensible has certain other properties," or it may be some proposition of the form " and *I know* this sensible to have certain other properties." Indeed we have not only to distinguish that sense of the word " perceive " in which it is equivalent to " directly apprehend," from *one* sense in which we can be said to perceive a physical object ; we have also to distinguish at least two different senses in which we can be said to perceive physical objects, different both from one another and from " directly apprehend." For it is obvious that though I should be said to be now seeing *the half-crown*, there is a narrower, and more proper, sense, in which I can only be said to *see* one side of it—*not* its lower side or its inside, and not therefore the whole half-crown.

The other principle, which we can lay down to start with is (β) that my knowledge of all the five propositions (*a*) to (*e*), is based, in the last resort, on experiences of mine consisting in the direct apprehension of sensibles and in the perception of relations between directly apprehended sensibles. It is *based* on these, in at least this sense, that I should never have known any of these propositions if I had never directly apprehended any sensibles nor perceived any relations between them.

What, in view of these two principles, can be the sense in which my five propositions are true ?

(1) It seems to me possible that the only *true*

interpretation which can be given to any of them is an interpretation of a kind which I can only indicate rather vaguely as follows : Namely, that all of them express only a kind of fact which we should naturally express by saying that, *if* certain conditions were fulfilled, I or some other person, *should* directly apprehend certain other sensibles. For instance the only *true* thing that can be meant by saying that I really see *coins* may be some such thing as that, *if* I were to move my body in certain ways, I should directly apprehend *other* sensibles, *e.g.* tactual ones, which I should not directly apprehend as a consequence of these movements, if these present visual experiences of mine were mere hallucinations or experiences of "images." Again, the only true thing that can be meant by saying that the upper sides of the coins are *really* approximately circular may be some such thing as that, *if* I were looking straight at them, I should directly apprehend circular sensibles. And similarly, the only true interpretation of (*c*) may be some such fact as that, *if* I were to turn the coins over, or break them up, I *should* have certain sensations, of a sort I can imagine very well ; of (*d*) that *if* I were at an equal distance from the half-crown and the florin, the sensible, I should then see corresponding to the half-crown would be bigger than that corresponding to the florin, whereas it is now smaller ; of (*e*) that, *if*, when my eyes were closed, they had been open instead, I should have seen certain sensibles.

It is obvious, indeed, that if any interpretation on these lines *is* the only true interpretation of our five propositions, none of those which I have vaguely suggested comes anywhere near to expressing it in its ultimate form. They cannot do so for the simple reason that, in them, the conditions under which I *should* experience certain other sensibles are themselves expressed in terms of *physical objects*, and not

in terms of sensibles and our experience of them.
The conditions are expressed in such terms as "if I
were to move my body," "if I were to look straight
at the coins," "if I were to turn the coins over,"
etc. ; and all these are obviously propositions, which
must themselves again be interpreted in terms of
sensibles, if our original five propositions need to be
so. It is obvious, therefore, that any *ultimate*
interpretation of our five propositions, on these
lines, would be immensely complicated ; and I
cannot come anywhere near to stating exactly what it
would be. But it seems to me possible that *some*
such interpretation could be found, and that it is the
only true one.

The great recommendation of this view seems
to me to be that it enables us to see, more clearly
than any other view can, how our knowledge of
physical propositions can be based on our experien e
of sensibles, in the way in which principle (β)
asserts it to be. If, when I know that the coins
are round, all that I know is some such thing as
that if, after experiencing the sensibles I do now
experience, I were to experience still others, I
should finally experience a third set, we can
understand, as clearly as we can understand how
any knowledge can be obtained by induction at all,
how such a knowledge could be based on our
previous experience of sensibles, and how it could
be verified by our subsequent experience.

On the other hand, apart from the difficulty of
actually giving any interpretation on these lines,
which will meet the requirements, the great objection to it seems to me to be this. It is obvious
that, on this view, though we shall still be allowed
to say that the coins *existed* before I saw them, are
circular etc., all these expressions, if they are to be
true, will have to be understood in a Pickwickian
sense. When I know that the coins existed before

I saw them, what I know will not be that anything
whatever existed at that time, in the sense in which
those elliptical patches of colour exist now. *All* that
I know will be simply that, since the elliptical patches
exist now, it is true, that, *if* certain unrealised conditions had been realised, I should have had certain
sensations that I have not had ; or, *if* certain conditions, which may or may not be realised in the future,
were to be so, I *should* have certain experiences.
Something like this will actually be the *only true* thing
that can be meant by saying that the coins existed
before I saw them.   In other words, to say of a
physical object that it *existed* at a given time will
always consist merely in saying of some sensible,
not that *it* existed at the time in question, but something quite different and immensely complicated.
And thus, though, when I know that the coins
exist, what I know will be merely some proposition
about these sensibles which I am directly apprehending, yet this view will not contradict principle
(*a*) by *identifying* the coins with the sensibles.   For
it will say that to assert a given thing of the *coins* is
not equivalent to asserting the *same thing* of the
sensibles, but only to asserting of them something
quite different.

   The fact that these assertions that the coins exist,
are round, etc., will, on this view, only be true in
this outrageously Pickwickian sense, seems to me to
constitute the great objection to it.   But it seems
to me to be an objection only, so far as I can
see, because I have a " strong propensity to believe "
that, when I know that the coins existed before I
saw them, *what* I know is that something existed at
that time, in the very same sense in which those
elliptical patches now exist.   And, of course, this
belief *may* be a mere prejudice.   It *may* be that
when I believe that I *now* have, in my body, blood
and nerves and brain, *what* I believe is only true, if

it does *not* assert, in the proper sense of the word "existence," the *present* existence of anything whatever, other than sensibles which I directly apprehend, but only makes assertions as to the kind of experiences a doctor *would* have, if he dissected me. But I cannot feel at all sure that my belief, that, when I know of the present existence of these things (as I think I do), I am knowing of the present existence (in the proper sense) of things other than any sensibles which I or any one else am now directly apprehending, is a mere prejudice. And therefore I think it is worth while to consider what, if it is not, these things, of whose existence I know, can be.

(2) It is certain that if, when I know that that half-crown existed before I saw it, I am knowing that something existed at that time in other than a Pickwickian sense, I only know this something *by description*; and it seems pretty clear that the description by which I know it is as *the* thing which has a certain connection with this sensible which I am now directly apprehending. But *what* connection? We cannot simply say, as many people have said, that by "that half-crown" I mean *the* thing which *caused* my experience of this sensible; because events which happen between the half-crown and my eyes, and events in my eyes, and optic nerves, and brains are just as much *causes* of my experiences as the half-crown itself. But it may perhaps be the case that the half-crown has some particular *kind* of causal relation to my experience, which these other events have not got—a kind which may be expressed, perhaps, by saying that it is its "source." And hence, when I know that that half-crown is circular, I may perhaps be knowing that the *source* of this experience is circular.

But what sort of a thing can this "source" be?

One kind of view, which I think is very commonly held, is that it is something "spiritual" in its nature, or something whose nature is utterly unknown to us. And those who hold this view are apt to add, that it is not really "circular," in any sense at all; nor is the "source" of my half-crown experience, in any sense at all, "bigger" than that of my florin experience. But if this addition were seriously meant, it would, of course, amount to saying that propositions (*b*) and (*d*) are not true, in any sense at all; and I do not think that those who make it, really mean to say this. I think that what they mean is only that the only sense in which those "sources" are circular, and one bigger than the other, is one in which to say this merely amounts to saying that the sensibles, which they *would* cause us to experience, under certain conditions, *would* be circular, and one bigger than the other. In other words, in order to give a true interpretation to the propositions that the coins are circular and one bigger than the other, they say that we must interpret them in the same kind of way in which view (1) interpreted them; and the only difference between their view and view (1), is that, whereas *that* said that you must give a Pickwickian interpretation *both* to the assertion that the coins *exist*, *and* to the assertion that they are *circular*, they say that you must *not* give it to the former assertion, and must to the latter.

To this view my objection is only that any reason there may be for saying that the "sources" exist in other than a Pickwickian sense, seems to me to be also a reason for saying that they are "circular" in a sense that is not Pickwickian. I have just as strong a propensity to believe that they are really circular, in a simple and natural sense, as that they exist in such a sense: and I know of no better reason for believing either.

G *

(3) It may be suggested, next, that these "sources," instead of being something spiritual in their nature or something of a nature utterly unknown, consist simply of sensibles, of a kind which I have previously tried to define; namely of all those sensibles, which anybody *would*, under the actual physical conditions, experience in *sensations proper* of which the half-crown and the florin were the source, *if* their bodies were in any of the positions relatively to those coins, in which they would get sensations from them at all. We saw before that it seems *possible* that all these sensibles do really exist at times when they are not experienced, and that some people, at all events, seem to have a strong propensity to believe that they do. And in favour of the view that some such huge collection of sensibles *is* the upper side of the half-crown, is the fact that we do seem to have a strong propensity to believe that any particular sensible, which we directly apprehend in looking at the upper side of the half-crown, and of our direct apprehension of which the upper side is the source, is *in the place* in which the upper side is. And that *some* sense might be given to the expression "in the same place as," in which it could be true that sensibles of all sorts of different shapes and sizes, and of all sorts of different colours, were in the same place at the same time, seems to me to be possible. But the objection to this view seems to me to be the same as to the last; namely that if the upper side of the half-crown were identical with such a collection of sensibles, then the only sense in which it could be said to be "circular," or bigger than that of the florin, would certainly be very Pickwickian, though not the same as on that view.

(4) If, for the reasons given, we reject both (1), (2), and (3) as interpretations of our five pro-

positions, the only alternative I can think of that remains, is one which is roughly identical, so far as I can see, with Locke's view.   It is a view which asserts that the half-crown and the florin really did exist (in the natural sense) before I saw them ; that they really are approximately circular (again in the natural sense) ; that, therefore, they are not composed of sensibles which I or others should directly apprehend under other conditions ; and that therefore also neither these sensibles (even if such do now exist) nor those which I am now directly apprehending are in the place in which the coins are.   It holds, therefore, that the coins do really *resemble* some sensibles, in respect of the "primary" qualities which these have ; that they really are round, and one larger than the other, in much the same sense in which some sensibles are round and some larger than others.   But it holds also that no sensibles which we ever do directly apprehend, or should directly apprehend, if at a given time we were in other positions, are *parts* of those coins ; and that, therefore, there is no reason to suppose that any parts of the coins have any of the "secondary qualities"—colour, etc.—which any of these sensibles have.

On this view, it is plain, there is nothing to prevent us from holding that, as suggested in I (3), all sorts of unexperienced sensibles do exist.   We are only prevented from holding that, if they do, those which have the same source all exist in the *same place* as their source.   And the natural view to take as to the status of sensibles generally, relatively to physical objects, would be that none of them, whether experienced or not, were ever in the same place as any physical object.   That none, therefore, exist "anywhere" in physical space ; while, at the same time, we can also say, as argued in I (2), that none exist "in the mind," except in the sense that some are directly apprehended by some minds. And the only thing that would need to be added, is that some, and some only, *resemble* the physical objects which are their source, in respect of their shape.

To this view I can see no objection except the serious one that it is difficult to answer the questions : How can I ever come to know that these sensibles have a " source " at all ? And how do I know that these " sources " are circular ? It would seem that, if I do know these things at all, I must know *immediately*, in the case of *some* sensibles, both that they have a source and what the shape of this source is. And to this it may be objected that this is a kind of thing which I certainly cannot know immediately. The argument in favour of an interpretation of type (1) seems to me to rest wholly on the assumption that there are only certain kinds of facts which I can know immediately ; and hence that if I believe I know a fact, which is not of this kind, and which also I cannot have learnt immediately, my belief must be a mere prejudice. But I do not know how it can be shown that an assertion of the form : Facts of certain kinds are the only ones you can know immediately ; is itself not a prejudice. I do not think, therefore, that the fact that, if this last view were true, we should have to admit that we know immediately facts of a kind which many people think we cannot know immediately, is a conclusive objection to it.

THE CONCEPTION OF REALITY

THE fourth chapter of Mr. Bradley's *Appearance and Reality* is a chapter headed "Space and Time," and he begins the chapter as follows :—

"The object of this chapter is far from being an attempt to discuss fully the nature of space or of time. It will content itself with stating our main justification for regarding them as appearances. It will explain why we deny that, *in the character which they exhibit*, they either *have* or *belong* to reality."*

Here, it will be seen, Mr. Bradley states that, in his opinion, Time, *in a certain character*, neither has nor belongs to reality ; this is the conclusion he wishes to maintain. And to say that Time *has not* reality would seem to be plainly equivalent to saying that Time *is not* real. However, if anybody should doubt whether the two phrases are meant to be equivalent, the doubt may be easily set at rest by a reference to the concluding words of the same chapter, where Mr. Bradley uses the following very emphatic expression : "Time," he says, "like space, has most evidently proved *not to be real*, but to be a contradictory appearance" (p. 43). Mr. Bradley does, then, say here, in so many words, that Time *is not* real. But there is one other difference between this statement at the end of the chapter, and the statement at the beginning of it,

---

* *Appearance and Reality* (2nd edn.), p. 35. The Italics are mine.

which we must not forget to notice. In the statement at the beginning he carefully qualifies the assertion " Time neither has nor belongs to reality " by saying " Time, *in the character which it exhibits*, neither has nor belongs to reality," whereas in the final statement this qualification is not inserted ; here he says simply " Time is not real." This qualification, which is inserted in the one place and omitted in the other, might, of course. be meant to imply that, in some *other* character—some character which it does *not* exhibit—Time *has* reality and does belong to it. And I shall presently have something to say about this distinction between Time in one character and Time in another, because it might be thought that this distinction is the explanation of the difficulty as to Mr. Bradley's meaning, which I am going to point out.

However, so far it is clear that Mr. Bradley holds that *in some sense*, at all events, the whole proposition " Time is not real " can be truly asserted. And, now, I want to quote a passage in which he says things which, at first sight, seem difficult to reconcile with this view. This new passage is a passage in which he is not talking of Time in particular, but of "appearances" in general. But, as we have seen, he does regard Time as one among appearances, and I think there is no doubt that what he here declares to be true of all appearances is meant to be true of Time, among the rest. This new passage is as follows :—

" For the present," he says,* " we may keep a fast hold upon this, that appearances *exist*. That is absolutely certain, and to deny it is nonsense. And whatever exists must *belong to reality*. This is also quite certain, and its denial once more is self-contradictory. Our appearances, no doubt, may be a beggarly show, and their nature to an unknown

* *Op. cit.* pp. 131-2

extent may be something which, *as it is*, is *not* true
of reality.   That is one thing, and it is quite another thing to speak as if these facts had no actual
existence, or as if there could be anything but
reality to which they might belong.   And I must
venture to repeat that such an idea would be sheer
nonsense.   What appears, for that sole reason, most
indubitably *is;* and there is no possibility of con-
juring its being away from it."

That is the passage which seems to me to raise a
difficulty as to his meaning when contrasted with
the former passage.   And the reason why it seems
to me to raise one is this.   In the former passage
Mr. Bradley declared most emphatically that Time
is not real; he said: "Time has *most evidently*
proved not to be real."   Whereas in this one he
seems to declare equally emphatically that Time
does exist, and *is*.   And his language here again is
as strong as possible.   He says it is sheer nonsense
to suppose that Time does *not* exist, is *not* a fact,
does *not* belong to reality.   It looks, therefore, as if
he meant to make a distinction between "being
real" on the one hand, and "existing," "being a
fact," and "being" on the other hand—as if he
meant to say that a thing may exist, and be, and be
a fact, and yet *not* be real..   And I think there is,
at all events, some superficial difficulty in understanding this distinction.   We might naturally think
that to say "Time exists, is a fact, and is," is
equivalent to saying that it is real.   What more, we
might ask, can a man who says that Time *is* real
mean to maintain about it than that it exists, is a
fact, and is?   All that most people would mean by
saying that time is real could, it would seem, be
expressed by saying "There is such a thing as
Time."   And it might, therefore, appear from this
new passage as if Mr. Bradley fully agreed with the
view that most people would express by saying

" Time is real "—as if he did not at all mean to contradict anything that most people believe about Time.   But, if so, then what are we to make of his former assertion that, nevertheless, Time is *not* real ? He evidently thinks that, in asserting this, he is asserting something which is *not* mere nonsense ; and he certainly would not have chosen this way of expressing what he means, unless he had supposed that what he is here asserting about Time is incompatible with what people *often* mean when they say " Time is real."   Yet, we have seen that he thinks that what he is asserting is *not* incompatible with the assertions that Time is, and is a fact, and exists.   He must, therefore, think that when people say " Time is real " they often, at least, mean something *more* than merely that there *is* such a thing as Time, something therefore, which may be denied, without denying this.   All the same, there is, I think, a real difficulty in seeing that they ever *do* mean anything more, and, *if* they do, what more it is that they can mean.

The two expressions " There *is* such a thing as so and so " and " So and so is real " are certainly sometimes and quite naturally used as equivalents, even if they are not always so used.   And Mr. Bradley's own language implies that this is so. For, as we have seen, in the first passage, he seems to identify belonging to reality with being real. The conclusion which he expresses in one place by saying that Time does not belong to reality he expresses in another by saying that it is not real ; whereas in the second passage he seems to identify the meaning of the same phrase " belonging to reality " with *existing ;* he says that whatever exists must belong to reality, and that it is self-contradictory to deny this.   But if both being real and existing are identical with belonging to reality, it would seem they must be identical with one another.

And, indeed, in another passage in the Appendix to the 2nd Edition (p. 555) we find Mr. Bradley actually using the following words : " Anything," he says, " that in any sense *is*, qualifies the absolute reality and so is real." Moreover, as we have seen, he declares it to be nonsense to deny that Time *is* ; he must, therefore, allow that, *in a sense*, at all events, it is nonsense to deny that Time is real. And yet this denial is the very one he has made. Mr. Bradley, therefore, does seem himself to allow that the word " real " may, *sometimes* at all events, be properly used as equivalent to the words " exists," " is a fact," " is." And yet his two assertions cannot both be true, unless there is *some* sense in which the whole proposition " Tine is real " is *not* equivalent to and cannot be inferred from " Time is," or " Time exists," or " Time is a fact."

It seems, then, pretty clear that Mr. Bradley must be holding that the statement " Time is real " is in *one* sense, *not* equivalent to " Time exists " ; though he admits that, in *another* sense, it is. And I will only quote one other passage which seems to make this plain.

" If," he says later on (p. 206) " Time is not unreal, I admit that our Absolute is a delusion ; but, on the other side, it will be urged that time cannot be mere appearance. The change in the finite subject, we are told, is a matter of direct experience ; it is a fact, and hence it cannot be explained away. And so much of course is indubitable. Change is a fact and, further, *this fact, as such*, is *not* reconcilable with the Absolute. And, if we could not in any way perceive how *the fact* can be *unreal*, we should be placed, I admit, in a hopeless dilemma . . . But our real position is very different from this. For time has been shown to contradict itself, and so to be appearance. With this, its discord, we see at once, may pass as an element into a wider harmony.   And with this, the *appeal to fact* at once becomes worthless."

"It is mere superstition to suppose that an appeal to experience can prove *reality*.   That I find something in existence in the world or in my self, shows that this something *exists*, and it cannot show *more*. Any deliverance of consciousness—whether original or acquired—is but a ' 'liverance of consciousness. It is in no case an oracle and a revelation which we have to accep   ᴄ is a fact, like other facts, to be dealt with ; and ᴄhere is no presumption anywhere that any *fact* is better than appearance."

Here Mr. Bradley seems plainly to imply that to be "real" is something *more* and other than to be a fact or to exist.   This is the distinction which I think he means to make, and which, I think, is the real explanation of his puzzling language, and this is the distinction which I am going presently to discuss.   But I want first to say something as to that other distinction, which I said might be supposed to be the explanation of the whole difficulty— the distinction implied by the qualification "Time, *in the character which it exhibits*" ; the suggestion that, when we talk of "Time," we may sometimes mean Time in one character, sometimes in another, and that what is true of it in the one character may not be true of it in the other.   It might, I think, be suggested that this is the explanation of the whole difficulty.   And I want briefly to point out why I think it cannot be the only explanation.

Stated very badly and crudely, the difficulty which requires explanation is this : Mr. Bradley says, "It is sheer nonsense to say Time is not real."   But this thing which he says it is sheer nonsense to say is the very thing which he himself had formerly said.   He had said, "Time has most evidently proved not to be real."   Now, Mr. Bradley certainly does not mean to say that this proposition of his own is sheer nonsense; and yet he says, in words, that it *is* sheer nonsense. This is the difficulty. What is the explanation? Quite obviously, the explanation can only take one possible form. **Mr.** Bradley must be holding that the words " Time is real" may have two different *senses*. In one sense, the denial of them is sheer nonsense; in the other sense, so far from being sheer nonsense, denial of them is, according to him, evidently true. Now, what are these two different senses, between which the difference is so enormous? It is here that the two different explanations come in.

The first and, as I think, the wrong explanation (though I think Mr. Bradley's words do give some colour to it) is this. It might be said : " The whole business is perfectly easy to explain. When Mr. Bradley says that Time is *not* real, what he means is that Time, *in the character which it exhibits*, is not real. Whereas, when he says, Time does exist, is a fact, and is, and that it is nonsense to deny this, what he means is that Time does exist, *in some other character*—some character *other* than that which it exhibits. He does *not* mean to make any distinction, such as you suppose, between two meanings of the word 'real'—the one of them merely equivalent to 'exists,' 'is,' 'is a fact,' and the other meaning something very different from this. The only distinction he means to make is a distinction between *two* meanings of 'Time' or of the whole sentence 'Time is real.' He distinguishes between the meaning of this sentence, when it means, 'Time in the character which it exhibits, is real,' which meaning, he says, is evidently false; and its meaning when it means, 'Time in *some other* character, is real,' and this meaning, he says, is evidently true. This is the complete explanation of your supposed puzzle, which is, in fact, therefore, very easy to solve."

This, I think, might be offered as an explanation of Mr. Bradley's meaning. And it must be admitted that it *would* furnish a complete explanation of the particular puzzle I have just stated, it would completely absolve Mr. Bradley from the charge of inconsistency ; and would show that where he appears to contradict himself about the reality of Time, the contradiction is verbal only and not real. We might, indeed, object to this distinction between Time in one character and Time in another ; on the ground that anything which has not got the character which Time exhibits, but only some *other* character, ought not to be called Time at all. We are, indeed, perfectly familiar with the conception that one and the same thing may *at one time* possess a character which it does *not* possess at another, so that what is true of it at one time may not be true of it at another. We are, that is, familiar with the idea of a thing *changing* its character. But Time itself as a whole obviously cannot change its character in this sense. Mr. Bradley cannot mean to say that it possesses the character " which it exhibits " and in which it is unreal *at one time*, and possesses some other character, in which it is real, at *some other time*. And hence we might say it is certainly wrong to speak as if Time itself could have two incompatible characters ; since nothing can have two incompatible characters, unless it has them *at different times*. And this is an objection which does seem to apply to Mr. Bradley's doctrine in any case, since he does in any case seem to imply this distinction between Time in one character and Time in another, whether this distinction is the complete explanation of our particular puzzle or not. Yet this objection would not necessarily be more than an objection to Mr. Bradley's words ; it would not necessarily be an objection to his meaning. Where he seems to imply that Time, in some character other than that which it exhibits, may be fully real, he may only mean that something completely different from Time, but which does in some sense correspond to it, is fully real; and if he does mean this, our objection would only amount to an objection to his giving the name of "Time" to this supposed counterpart of Time; we might say, and I think justly, that it is misleading to speak of this counterpart of Time as if it were Time itself in some other character; but this would go no way at all to show that there may not really be such a counterpart of Time, which *is* real, while Time itself is unreal. We might ask, too, what this supposed counterpart of Time is like, or (to put it in Mr. Bradley's way) what the precise character is, in which Time *is* real? And I think Mr. Bradley would admit that he cannot tell us. But this, you see, would also be no objection to his actual doctrine. He might quite well know, and be right in saying, that there is and must be a real *counterpart* of Time, completely different in character from Time, as we know it, even though he has not the least idea what this counterpart is like.

We must, therefore, admit that this proposed explanation of our puzzle would be a complete explanation of it. It would completely vindicate Mr. Bradley from the charge of inconsistency, and would give us, as his doctrine, a doctrine to which we have hitherto found no objection except verbal ones.

But, nevertheless, I think it is a wrong explanation, and I want to explain why. If we were to suppose that this distinction between Time in one character and Time in another were the only one on which Mr. Bradley meant to rely, we should have as his doctrine this : We should have to suppose him to affirm most emphatically that Time, in the character which it exhibits, neither is real, *nor* exists, *nor* is a fact, *nor* is.   We should have to suppose him to be using all these four expressions always as strict equivalents, and to mean that it is *only* in its other character that Time either exists, or is a fact, or is.   And if he did mean this, there would, of course, be no doubt whatever that he does mean to contradict the common view with regard to Time; since, of course, what most people mean by "Time" is what he chooses to call "Time in the character which it exhibits."   Yet, his language, even in the passages that I quoted, seems to me to indicate that he does not mean this.   I think, on the contrary, he means to affirm emphatically that Time *even* in the character which it exhibits, does exist, *is* a fact, and indubitably *is*, though it is *not* real in that character.   In the second passage, for instance, where he insists so emphatically that appearances do exist, are facts, and indubitably *are*, he is, I think, plainly talking of appearances, in the character which they exhibit—or, as he there puts it, their nature, *as it is*—he does, I think, mean that appearances, even in this character, are facts, exist, and are, though, in this character, they are not "true of reality."   And, so again in the third passage, where he says, Change *is* a fact, and this fact, *as such*, is not reconcilable with the Absolute; this language is surely quite inexcusable, unless he means that Change, as such—change, in the *character which it exhibits*—change, *as it is*, *is* a fact: though, of course, he holds that *in* this character it certainly is not real.   I think, therefore, we have to assume that Mr. Bradley means to make a distinction not merely between Time, in one character, and Time in another, but also between "real," in one sense, and "real" in another.   His meaning is not so simple as it would be, if he were merely making a distinction between Time in one character and Time in another, and it is not, after all, at all plain whether he means to contradict what ordinary people hold about Time or not.   He does not mean to assert that Time, *as such*, *neither* is real, *nor* exists, *nor* is a fact, *nor* is ; but, on the contrary, that Time, even *as such*, does exist, *is* a fact, and *is* ; *but*, nevertheless, is not real.   This, at least, is what I am going to assume him to mean.   And on this assumption, we are brought face to face with the question as to the meaning of the word "real," and also as to the meaning of these other words "exists," "is a fact," and "is."   Mr. Bradley seems to admit, we have seen, that "real" may *sometimes* be properly used as *merely* equivalent to these other phrases.   We are, however, now supposing that he also holds that in another sense they are not equivalent, but that "real" means something more than the others, so that it is quite consistent to maintain that Time is *not* "real," and yet *does* exist, is a fact, and is.   In holding this I think he is mistaken ; and what I want to do is to explain, as clearly as I can, what sort of a mistake I take him to be making, and what seems to me to be the source of this mistake.   I may, perhaps, be quite wrong in thinking that Mr Bradley has made this mistake, and that it is in any degree the source of the distinction he seems to draw between "reality" and "existence." To maintain that it is so is no part of my main object.   My main object is simply to make clear the nature of this particular mistake, whether committted by Mr. Bradley or not, and that it is a mistake ; because it seems to me that it is a mistake which it is very easy to make, and very important to avoid.   I am, of course, not concerned at all to discuss the question whether Time *is* real or not, but only to discuss the question what sort of things would have to be true, if it were unreal, and whether

if those things were true it could still be true that
Time either exists, or is, or is a fact.

Now, to begin with, I think I know pretty well,
in part at least, what Mr. Bradley means when he
says that it is unreal.   I think that part at least of
what he means is just what he *ought* to mean—just
what anyone else would mean if he said that Time
was unreal, and what any ordinary person would
understand to be meant, if he heard those words.
But I can conceive that, when I have explained as
well as I can what this is that he *ought* to mean,
some people may be inclined to dispute whether he
means any such thing at all.   They may say that
he is using the word "real" exclusively in some
highly unusual and special sense, so that in asserting
that "Time is unreal" he is by no means denying
any part of what ordinary people would mean by
saying that "Time is real."   And that some special
sense may *come in* to his meaning I am prepared to
admit.   I do think it is possible that *part* of what
Mr. Bradley is asserting may be something which
no unsophisticated person would think of expressing
in the same way, and I will admit, therefore, that he
does not, very likely, mean by "Time is unreal"
merely what other people would mean by this
phrase, but something else *as well*.   What, however, I cannot help thinking is that, even if he
means something more, he *does* mean what ordinary
people would mean *as well*: that what they would
mean is at least a *part* of his meaning.   And if even
this is disputed, if it is maintained that he is using
the words *exclusively* in some special sense, I own I
do not know how to argue the question.   If anybody really does take the view that, when he says
"Time is unreal," absolutely all that he means is
something which is in no way incompatible with
what most people would mean by saying "Time is
real," I do not know how to show that this view is

wrong. I can only say that if this *had* been all
that he meant, I cannot believe that he would have
expressed his view in the form "Time is unreal."
The only further argument I shall bring in favour
of my view that he does mean what he ought to
mean will take the form of an answer to one possible
argument which might be brought against it.   When
I have explained what he *ought* to mean by saying
that "Time is unreal," it will be quite clear that this
is something which is in fact incompatible with the
truth of the propositions that Time *is*, or *exists*, or
is a fact.   And it might be urged that the fact that
it is thus incompatible is a strong argument against
the view that Mr. Bradley does mean what he
ought to mean, since, if he had meant it, he could
hardly have failed to perceive that what he meant
was inconsistent with these propositions, whereas,
as we have seen, he certainly does not perceive this.
I have an answer to that argument, which consists
in giving an explanation, which I think a plausible
one, as to how he could come to think that the
propositions are *not* inconsistent, when in fact they
are.

What, then, *ought* Mr. Bradley to mean by
"Time is unreal"?   What would most people mean
by this proposition?   I do not think there is much
difficulty in discovering what sort of thing they
would mean by it.   Of course, Time, with a big T,
seems to be a highly abstract kind of entity, and to
define *exactly* what can be meant by saying of an
entity of that sort that it is unreal does seem to
offer difficulties.   But if you try to translate the
proposition into the concrete, and to ask what it
implies, there is, I think, very little doubt as to the
sort of thing it implies.   The moment you try to do
this, and think what it really comes to, you at once
begin thinking of a number of different *kinds* of
propositions, all of which plainly must be untrue, if

Time is unreal. If Time is unreal, then plainly
nothing ever happens before or after anything else ;
nothing is ever simultaneous with anything else ; it
is never true that anything is past ; never true that
anything will happen in the future ; never true that
anything is happening now ; and so on. You can
at once think of a considerable number of kinds of
propositions (and you could easily add to the list),
the falsehood of all of which is plainly implied by
saying that Time is unreal. And it is clear, also,
that to say that the falsehood of all propositions of
these kinds is implied is equivalent to saying that
there are no facts of certain corresponding kinds—
no facts which consist in one event happening before
another ; none which consist in an event being past
or future, and so on. That is to say, what "Time
is unreal" implies is that, in the case of a large
number of different *properties* which are such that,
if they *did* belong to anything, what they belonged
to would be facts having some common characteristic, which we might express by calling them
"temporal facts," the properties in question do, in
fact, belong to nothing. It implies that the property
of being a fact which consists in one event following
another belongs to nothing ; that that of being a
past event belongs to nothing, and so on. And
why it implies that all those different special properties belong to nothing is, I think we may say,
because what it *means* is that the general property
which I have called that of being a "temporal fact"
belongs to nothing. To say that the property of
being a temporal fact belongs to nothing *does imply*
that such special properties as that of being a fact
which consists in one event following another, or
that of being a fact which consists in something
being past, also belong to nothing ; in exactly the
same way as to say that the property of being
"coloured" belongs to nothing *implies* with regard

to the special properties "being red," "being blue," etc., that they also belong to nothing. We may, then, I think, say that what "Time is unreal" *means* is simply "The property of being a temporal fact belongs to nothing," or, to express this in the way in which it would be expressed in ordinary life, "There *are* no temporal facts." And this being so, we have explained the usage of "unreal," where it is predicated of Time with a capital T, by reference to a much more common and perfectly familiar usage of the term. The use of "is unreal" in the phrase "Time is unreal" has been defined by reference to its use in the phrase "Temporal facts are unreal." And its use in this phrase is, so far as I can see, exactly the same as in hosts of phrases with which we are perfectly familiar ; it is, I think, *the* commonest and by far the most important use of the term "unreal." The use is that in which we use it when we say, "Unicorns are unreal," "Griffins are unreal," "Chimæras are unreal," and so on. It is the usage in which unreal is equivalent to "imaginary" ; and in which to say "Unicorns are unreal" means the same as "There are no unicorns" or "Unicorns do not exist." In just the same way the proposition "Temporal facts are unreal," into which we have translated "Time is unreal," means the same as "There are no temporal facts," or "Temporal facts do not exist," or "Temporal facts are imaginary."

I think, then, that what Mr. Bradley *ought* to mean by "Time is unreal" can be defined by reference to one particular usage of the word "real" —or, if you like to put it that way, to one particular one among the conceptions for which the term "reality" may stand. And this particular conception seems to me to be by far the commonest and most important of those for which the term does stand. I want, therefore, before going on, to dwell a little upon its nature; although I daresay that all that I have to say is perfectly familiar and perfectly well understood by every one here. Of course, it has often been said before, but I think it is still very far from being generally understood.

I think, perhaps, the point I want to insist on can be brought out in this way. I have just said that we have pointed out one particular one, and that the most important, among the conceptions for which the term "reality" may stand; and that is an excusable way of saying what we have done. But it would, I think, be more correct to say that we have pointed out one particular, and that the most important, usage of the terms "real" and "unreal," and that one of the peculiarities of this usage is that it is such that the terms "real" and "unreal" cannot, when used in this way, be properly said to stand for any conception whatever. I will try to explain what I mean. We have said that what "Lions are real" *means* is that some particular property or other—I will say, for the sake of brevity, *the* property of being a lion, though that is not strictly accurate, does in fact *belong to* something—that there are things which have it, or, to put it in another way, that the conception of being a lion is a conception which does apply to some things—that there are things which *fall under* it. And similarly what "Unicorns are *unreal*" means is that the property of being a unicorn belongs to *nothing*. Now, if this is so, then it seems to me, in a very important sense, "real" and "unreal" do *not* in this usage stand for any conceptions at all. The only *conceptions* which occur in the proposition "Lions are real" are, on this interpretation, plainly, (1) the conception of being a lion, and (2) the conception of belonging to something, and perfectly obviously "real" does not stand for either of these. In the case of the first that is obvious; but it is worth while pointing out that it is also true of the second.

For if "is real" did stand for "belongs to something," then the proposition "Lions are real" would stand, not for the assertion that the property of "being a lion" belongs to something, but for the assertion that lions themselves *are properties which belong to something*; and it is quite obvious that what we mean to assert is not any such nonsense as this. "Real," therefore, does not, in this proposition, stand for the conception of "belonging to something;" nor yet, quite plainly, does it stand for the conception of "being a lion." And hence, since these are the only two conceptions which do occur in the proposition, we may, I think, say that "real," in this usage, does not stand for any conception at all. To say that it did would be to imply that it stood for some property of which we are asserting that everything which has the property of "being a lion" *also* has this other property. But we are not, in fact, asserting any such thing. We are not asserting of any property called "reality" that it belongs to lions, as in the proposition "Lions are mammalian" we *are* asserting of the property of "being a mammal" that *it* belongs to lions. The two propositions "Lions are real" and "Lions are mammalian," though grammatically similar, are in reality of wholly different forms; and one difference between them may be expressed by saying that whereas "mammalian" does stand for a property or conception, the very point of this usage of "real" is that it does not.

To return to Mr. Bradley. "Time is unreal" *ought* to mean, according to me, "Temporal facts are unreal," in the sense I have tried to explain. And I cannot help thinking that this which he *ought* to mean is, in part at least, what Mr. Bradley *does* mean when he says "Time is unreal," though

possibly he also means something else as well.
But if so, it is quite clear, I think, that what he
means is inconsistent with its being true that Time
exists or that there is such a thing as Time.   To
say that Time exists or that there is such a thing, is
to assert at least, that there are some temporal
facts : it may assert more than this, but it does
assert this, at least.   And this, we have seen, is
exactly what is denied when it is said that Time is
unreal.   " Time is unreal " just means " Temporal
facts are unreal," *or* " there are no temporal facts," *or*
" Temporal facts do not exist."   And just this is
also what is meant by " Time does not exist " or
" There is no such thing as Time."   There is, in
fact, nothing. else for these expressions to mean.
What, therefore, Mr. Bradley *ought* to mean and
(according to me) does mean by " Time is unreal "
is, in fact, inconsistent with what he ought to mean
by " Time exists " or by " Time is."   And yet
plainly he does not think that it is so.   Is it possible
to explain why he should have failed to perceive the
inconsistency ?

I think his failure can be explained as follows.
It may have been noticed that, in the passages I
quoted from him, he insists in one place, that to
deny that appearances exist is not merely false but
self-contradictory, and in another appeals to the
principle that " any deliverance of consciousness is
but a deliverance of consciousness " in support of
his contention that what *is* a fact need, nevertheless,
not be real.   And the fact that he does these two
things does, I think, give colour to the suggestion
that the reason why he thinks that what is unreal
may yet exist, and be a fact, and be, is the following.
It is undoubtedly the case that, even if temporal
facts are unreal, *i.e.*, there *are* no such things, we
can and do *think of them*, just as it is undoubtedly
the case that, though unicorns are unreal, we can

and do imagine them. In other words, "temporal facts" and "unicorns" are both quite certainly "deliverances of consciousness," at least in the sense that they are "objects of thought"; being "objects of thought" they are, in a wide sense, "appearances" also, and I cannot help thinking that Mr. Bradley supposes that, merely because they are so, they *must* at least BE. "How" (I imagine he would ask) "can a thing 'appear' or even 'be thought of' unless it is there to appear and to be thought of? To say that it appears or is thought of, and that yet there is no such thing, is plainly self-contradictory. A thing cannot have a property, unless it is there to have it, and, since unicorns and temporal facts *do* have the property of being thought of, there certainly must be such things. When I think of a unicorn, what I am thinking of is certainly not nothing; if it were nothing, then, when I think of a griffin, I should also be thinking of nothing, and there would be no difference between thinking of a griffin and thinking of a unicorn. But there certainly is a difference; and what can the difference be except that in the one case what I am thinking of is a unicorn, and in the other a griffin? And if the unicorn is what I am thinking of, then there certainly must *be* a unicorn, in spite of the fact that unicorns are unreal. In other words, though in one sense of the words there certainly *are* no unicorns—that sense, namely, in which to assert that there are would be equivalent to asserting that unicorns are real—yet there *must* be *some* other sense in which there *are* such things; since, *if* there were not, we could not think of them."

Perhaps, it may be thought that the fallacy involved in this argument is too gross for it to be possible that Mr. Bradley should have been guilty of it. But there are other passages in *Appearance*

and Reality—particularly what he says about Error
—which look to me as if he certainly was guilty of
it.   I suppose it will be quite obvious to everyone
here that it is a fallacy; that the fact that we can
think of unicorns is not sufficient to prove that, in
any sense at all, there *are* any unicorns.   Yet, I am
not sure that I know myself what is *the* mistake
involved in thinking that it *is* sufficient, and I am
going, therefore, to try to put as clearly as I can,
what I think it is, in the hope that somebody may
be able, if I am wrong, to correct me.

The main mistake, I suppose, is the mistake of
thinking that the proposition " Unicorns are thought
of " is a proposition of the same form as " Lions are
hunted "; or the proposition " I am thinking of a
unicorn " of the same form as " I am hunting a
lion "; or the proposition " Unicorns are objects of
thought " of the same form as " Lions are objects
of the chase."   Of the second proposition in each of
these three pairs, it is in fact the case that it could
not be true unless there were lions—at least one.
Each of them does, in fact, assert both with regard
to a certain property—which we will call that of
" being a lion "—that there *are* things which possess
it, and also with regard to another—that of being
hunted—that some of the things which possess the
former possess this property too.   But it is obvious
enough to common sense that the same is by no
means true of the *first* proposition in each pair, in
spite of the fact that their grammatical expression
shows no trace of the difference.   It is perfectly
obvious that if I say " I am thinking of a unicorn,"
I am not saying both that there is a unicorn and
that I am thinking of it, although, if I say " I am
hunting a lion," I am saying both that there is a
lion, and that I am hunting it.   In the former case,
I am *not* asserting that the two properties of being
a unicorn and of being thought of by me both

belong to one and the same thing ; whereas, in the latter case, I am asserting that the two properties of being a lion and of being hunted by me *do* belong to one and the same thing. It is quite clear that there is *in fact*, this difference between the two propositions ; although no trace of it appears in their verbal expression. And why we should use the same form of verbal expression to convey such different meanings is more than I can say. It seems to me very curious that language, in this, as in the other instance which we have just considered of " Lions are real " and " Lions are mammalian," should have grown up just as if it were expressly designed to mislead philosophers ; and I do not know why it should have. Yet, it seems to me there is no doubt that in ever so many instances it has. Moreover, *exactly* what *is* meant by saying " I am thinking of a unicorn" is not by any means clear to me. I think we can assert at least this : In order that this proposition should be true, it is necessary (1) that I should be conceiving, with regard to a certain property, the hypothesis that there is something which possesses it, and (2) that the property in question should be such that, if anything did possess it there would be a unicorn. Although this is plainly true, it does not give us completely what is *meant* by the statement, " I am thinking of a unicorn " ; and I do not know what the complete meaning is. It is certainly *not* that I am conceiving with regard to the property of " being a unicorn," that there is something which possesses it ; since I may be thinking of a unicorn, without ever having conceived the property of " being a unicorn " at all. Whatever it does mean, the point which concerns us is that it is certainly *not* necessary for its truth, that the property of being a unicorn should, in fact, belong to anything what-ever, or, therefore, that there should in any sense whatever *be* a unicorn. And the fallacy I am attributing to Mr. Bradley is that of supposing that, *in some sense*, it must imply this latter.

This, then, is what I imagine to be at least one of the reasons which have led Mr. Bradley to suppose that the proposition " Time is unreal," *must* be consistent with the proposition " There *is* such a thing as Time." Put shortly, it is that he sees (what is perfectly true) that " Time is unreal " *must* be consistent with " We do think of Time ; " he thinks (falsely) that " We *do* think of Time " must imply, in some sense, " There *is* such a thing as Time ; " and finally, infers (correctly) from this true and this false premiss, that there *must* be some sense of the proposition " There is such a thing as Time " which is consistent with " Time is unreal."

It follows, then, that if Mr. Bradley means what he ought mean *both* by " Time is unreal " *and* by " Time exists," he is contradicting himself when he combines these two propositions. And I have said I feel convinced that he *does* mean what he ought to mean by the former. But I feel a good deal of doubt as to whether, all the same, he is contradicting himself, because it does seem to me doubtful whether he means what he ought to mean by the latter. The kind of thing which I imagine may be happening to him when he insists so strougly that Time *does* exist, *is a fact*, and *is*, is that, properly speaking, he is not attaching to these phrases any meaning whatever—*not*, therefore, that which they properly bear. It seems to me very possible that he has so strongly convinced himself of the false proposition that there *must* be *some* sense in which, if I think of a unicorn, there must *be* a unicorn, that wherever he knows the former proposition holds, he allows himself to use the latter *form of words*, without attaching any meaning to them. What he is really asserting so emphatically may, I think, be not anything which his words stand for, but simply this verbal proposition that there *must* be *some* sense in which they are true.

SOME JUDGMENTS OF PERCEPTION

I WANT to raise some childishly simple questions as to what we are doing when we make judgments of a certain kind, which we all do in fact exceedingly commonly make. The kind of judgments I mean are those which we make when, with regard to something which we are seeing, we judge such things as "That is an inkstand," "That is a table-cloth," "That is a door," etc., etc. ; or when, with regard to something which we are feeling with our hands, we judge such things as "This is cloth," "This is a finger," "This is a coin," etc., etc.

It is scarcely possible, I think, to exaggerate the frequency with which we make such judgments as these, nor yet the certainty with which we are able to make vast numbers of them. Any man, who is not blind, can, at almost any moment of his waking life, except when he is in the dark, make a large number of judgments of the first kind, with the greatest certainty. He has only to look about him, if he is indoors, to judge with regard to various things which he is seeing, such things as "That is a window," "That is a chair," "This is a book"; or, if he is out-of-doors, such things as "That is a house," "That is a motor-car," "That is a man," or "That is a stone," "That is a tree," "That is a cloud." And all of us, who are not blind, do in fact constantly make such judgments, even if, as a rule, we only make them as parts of more complicated judgments. What I mean is that, when we make such judgments as "Hullo! that clock has stopped," or "This chair is more comfortable than that one," or "That man looks like a foreigner," judgments of the simpler kind with which I am concerned are, so far as I can see, actually a part of what we are judging. In judging "That clock has stopped," part of what I am actually judging is, so far as I can see, "That is a clock;" and similarly if I judge "That tree is taller than this one," my judgment actually contains the two simpler judgments "That is a tree," and "This is a tree." Perhaps most judgments which we make, of the kind I mean, are, in this way, only parts of more complicated judgments : I do not know whether this is so or not. But in any case there can be no doubt that we make them exceedingly commonly. And even a blind man, or a man in the dark, can and does, very frequently, make judgments of the second kind— judgments about things which he is feeling with his hands. All of us, for instance, at almost any moment of our waking life, whether we are in the dark or not, have only to feel certain parts of our own bodies or of our clothes, in order to make, with great certainty, such judgments as "This is a finger," "This is a nose," "This is cloth." And similarly I have only to feel in my pockets to judge, with regard to objects which I meet with there, such things as "This is a coin," "This is a pencil," "This is a pipe."

Judgments of this kind would, I think, commonly, and rightly, be taken to be judgments, the truth of which involves the existence of material things or physical objects. If I am right in judging that this is an inkstand, it follows that there is at least one inkstand in the Universe ; and if there is an inkstand in the Universe, it follows that there is in it at least one material thing or physical object. This

may, of course, be disputed. Berkeley, if I understand him rightly, was clearly of opinion that there
was no inconsistency in maintaining that there were
in the Universe thousands of inkstands and trees
and stones and stars, and that yet there was in it
no such thing as matter. And perhaps the definition of matter, which he adopted, was such that
there really was no inconsistency in maintaining this.
Perhaps, similarly, other philosophers have sometimes adopted definitions of the expressions
"material things" and "physical objects," which
were such that all the judgments of this kind that
we make might quite well be true, without its being
true that there are in the Universe any material
things whatever. Perhaps, even, there may be
some justification for adopting definitions of those
terms which would yield the surprising result that
we may, with perfect consistency, maintain that the
world is full of minerals and vegetables and animals,
of all sorts of different kinds, and that yet there is
not to be found in it a single material thing. I do
not know whether there is or is not any utility in
using the terms "material thing" or "physical
object" in such a sense as this. But, whether there
is or not, I cannot help thinking that there is ample
justification for using them in another sense—a
sense in which from the proposition that there are
in the Universe such things as inkstands or fingers
or clouds, it strictly follows that there are in it at
least as many material things, and in which, therefore, we can *not* consistently maintain the existence
of inkstands, fingers, and clouds, while denying
that of material things. The kinds of judgment
which I have mentioned, and thousands of others
which might easily be mentioned, are obviously all
of the same sort in one very important respect—a
respect in which, for instance, such judgments as
"This is an emotion," "This is a judgment," "This

is a colour," are *not* of the same sort as they are. And it seems to me that we are certainly using the term "material thing" in *a* correct and useful way, if we express this important common property which they have, by saying that of each of them the same can truly be said as was said of the judgment "That is an inkstand": that, just as from the proposition "There is an inkstand" it follows that there is at least one material thing, so from the proposition "There is a tablecloth," it follows that there is at least one material thing; and similarly in all the other cases. We can certainly use the expression "Things *such as* inkstands, tablecloths, fingers, clouds, stars, etc.," to mean things such as these in a certain very important respect, which we all understand, though we may not be able to define it. And the term "material thing" certainly is and can be correctly used to mean simply things such as these in that respect—whatever it may be. Some term is certainly required to mean merely things such as these in that important respect; and, so far as I can see, there is no term which can be naturally used in this sense except the term "material things" and its equivalents. Thus understood, the term "material thing" certainly does stand for an important notion, which requires a name.

And, if we agree to use the term in this sense, then it is obvious that no more can be necessary for the truth of the assertion that there are material things, than is necessary for the truth of judgments of the kind with which I propose to deal. But no more can be necessary for the truth of these judgments than is actually asserted in or logically implied by them. And if we approach the question what is necessary for the truth of the assertion that there are material things, by asking what it is that we actually assert when we make such judgments as these, certain reasons for doubting how much is necessary are, I think, brought out much more clearly, than if we approach the question in any other way.   Many philosophers have told us a very great deal as to what they suppose to be involved in the existence of material things ; and some, at least, among them seem to have meant by "material things" such things as inkstands, fingers and clouds.   But I can think of only one type of view as to the constitution of material things, which is such that it is tolerably clear what answer those who hold it would give to the simple question ; What is it that I am judging, when I judge, as I now do, that that is an ink-stand?   The type of view I mean is that to which the view that Mill suggests, when he explains what he means by saying that Matter is a Permanent Possibility of Sensation, and also the view or views which Mr. Russell seems to suggest in his "Our Knowledge of the External World," seem to belong.   In the case of views of this kind, it is, I think, tolerably clear what answer those who hold them would give to *all* the questions I want to raise about judgments of the kind I have described.   But it does not seem to me at all certain that any view of this type is true ; and certainly many philosophers have held and do hold that all views of this type are false.   But in the case of those who do hold them to be false, I do not know, in any single case, what answer would be given to *all* the questions which I want to raise.   In the case of philosophers, who do not accept any view of the Mill-Russell type, none, so far as I know, has made it clear what answer he would give to *all* my questions : some have made it clear what answer they would give to *some* of them ; but many, I think, have not even made it clear what answer they would give to any.   Perhaps there is some simple and satisfactory answer, which has escaped me, that such philosophers could give to all my questions; but I cannot help thinking that assumptions as to the nature of material things have too often been made, without its even occurring to those who made them to ask, what, if they were true, we could be judging when we make such judgments as these; and that, if this question had been asked, it would have become evident that those assumptions were far less certain than they appeared to be.

I do not know that there is any excuse whatever for calling *all* judgments of the kind I mean "judgments of perception." All of them are, of course, judgments *about* things which we are at the moment perceiving, since, by definition, they are judgments about things which we are seeing or feeling with our hands; and all of them are, no doubt, also *based upon* something which we perceive about the thing in question. But the mere fact that a judgment is both about a thing which I am perceiving, and also based upon something which I perceive about that thing, does not seem to be a sufficient reason for calling it a judgment of perception; and I do not know that there is any other reason than this for calling *all* judgments of the kind I mean judgments of perception. I do not want therefore, to assert that *all* of them are so. But it seems to me quite plain that enormous numbers of them are so, in a perfectly legitimate sense. This judgment, which I now make, to the effect that *that* is a door, seems to me quite plainly to be a judgment of perception, in the simple sense that I make it because I do, in fact, see that that *is* a door, and assert in it no more than what I see; and what I see I, of course, perceive. In every case in which I judge, with regard to something which I am seeing or feeling with my hands, that it is a so-and-so, simply because I do perceive, by sight or touch, that it is in fact a thing of that kind, we can, I think, fairly say that the judgment in question is a judgment of perception. And enormous numbers of judgments of the kind I mean are, quite plainly, judgments of perception in this sense. They are not *all*, for the simple reason that some of them are mistaken. I may, for instance, judge, with regard to an animal which I see at a distance, that it is a sheep, when in fact it is a pig. And here my judgment is certainly not due to the fact that I see it to be a sheep; since I cannot possibly see a thing to be a sheep, unless it is one. It, therefore, is *not* a judgment of perception in this sense. And moreover, even where such a judgment is true, it may not always be a judgment of perception, for the reason that, whereas I only see the thing in question, the kind of thing which I judge it to be is of such a nature, that it is impossible for any one, by sight alone, to perceive anything to be of that kind. How to draw the line between judgments of this kind, which are judgments of perception, and those which are not, I do not know. That is to say, I do not know what conditions must be fulfilled in order that I may be truly said to be *perceiving*, by sight or touch, such things as that that is a door, this is a finger, and not *merely* inferring them. Some people may no doubt think that it is very unphilosophical in me to say that we *ever* can perceive such things as these. But it seems to me that we do, in ordinary life, constantly talk of *seeing* such things, and that, when we do so, we are neither using language incorrectly, nor making any mistake about the facts—supposing something to occur which never does in fact occur. The truth seems to me to be that we are using the term "perceive" in a way which is both perfectly correct and expresses a kind of thing which constantly does occur, only that some philosophers have not recognised that this is a correct usage of the term and have not been able to define it. I am not, therefore, afraid to say that I do now perceive that that is a door, and that that is a finger. Only, of course, when I say that I do, I do not mean to assert that part of what I "perceive," when I "perceive" these things, may not be something which, in an important sense, is known to me only by inference. It would be very rash to assert that "perception," in this sense of the word, entirely excludes inference. All that seems to me certain is that there is an important and useful sense of the word "perception," which is such that the amount and kind of inference, if inference there be, which is involved in my present perception that that is a door, is no bar to the truth of the assertion that I do perceive that it is one. Vast numbers, then, of the kind of judgments with which I propose to deal seem to me to be, in an important and legitimate sense, judgments of perception; although I am not prepared to define, any further than I have done, what that sense is. And though it is true that the questions which I shall raise apply just as much to those of them which are not judgments of perception as to those which are, it is, of course, also true that they apply just as much to those which are as to those which are not; so that I shall be really dealing with a large and important class among judgments of perception.

It is true that, if certain views which, if I understand them rightly, some Philosophers have seriously entertained, were true ones, it would be quite impossible that any of them should be judgments of perception. For some philosophers seem to me to have denied that we ever do in fact know such things as these, and others not only that we ever know them but also that they are ever true. And, if, in fact, I never do know such a thing, or if it is never true, it will of course, follow that I never perceive such a thing; since I certainly cannot, in this sense, perceive anything whatever, unless I both know it and it is true. But it seems to me a sufficient refutation of such views as these, simply to point to cases in which we do know such things. This, after all, you know, really is a finger : there is no doubt about it : I know it, and you all know it. And I think we may safely challenge any philosopher to bring forward any argument in favour either of the proposition that we do not know it, or of the proposition that it is not true, which does not at some point, rest upon some premiss which is, beyond comparison, less certain than is the proposition which it is designed to attack. The questions whether we do ever know such things as these, and whether there are any material things, seem to me, therefore, to be questions which there is no need to take seriously : they are questions which it is quite easy to answer, with certainty, in the affirmative. What does, I think, need to be taken seriously, and what is really dubious, is not the question, whether this is a finger, or whether I know that it is, but the question *what*, in certain respects, I am knowing, when I know that it is. And this is the question to which I will now address myself.

To begin with there is one thing which seems to me to be very certain indeed about such judgments. It is unfortunately a thing which I do not know how properly to express. There seem to me to be objections to every way of expressing it which I can think of. But I hope I may be able to make my meaning clear, in spite of the inadequacy of my expression. The thing I mean is a thing which may to some people seem so obvious as to be scarcely worth saying. But I cannot help thinking that it is not always clearly recognised, and even that some philosophers, to judge from what they say, might perhaps dispute it. It seems to me to be an assumption which is silently made in many treatments of the subject, and, as I say, it seems to me to be very certain indeed. But I think it is at all events worth while to try to make the assumption explicit, in case it should be disputed. If it really is not true, then the other questions to which I shall go on, and which seem to me really dubious and difficult, do not, I think, arise at all.

I will try to express this fundamental assumption, which seems to me so very certain, by saying it is the assumption that, in all cases in which I make a judgment of this sort, I have no difficulty whatever in picking out a thing, which is, quite plainly, in a sense in which nothing else is, *the* thing about which I am making my judgment; and that yet, though this thing is *the* thing about which I am judging, I am, quite certainly, *not*, in general, judging with regard to it, that *it* is a thing of that kind for which the term, which seems to express the predicate of my judgment, is a name. Thus, when I judge, as now, that That is an inkstand, I have no difficulty whatever in picking out, from what, if you like, you can call my total field of presentation at the moment, an object, which is undoubtedly, in a sense in which nothing else is, *the* object about which I am making this judgment; and yet it seems to me quite certain that of *this* object I am not judging that it is a whole inkstand. And similarly when I judge, with regard to something which I am feeling in my pocket, "This is a coin," I have no difficulty in picking out, from my field of presentation, an object, which is undoubtedly *the* object with which my judgment is concerned; and yet I am certainly not judging with regard to this object that it is a whole coin. I say that *always*, when I make such a judgment, I can pick out *the* one, among the objects presented to me at the time, about which I am making it; but I have only said that *in general* I am not judging with regard to this object that it is a thing of the kind, for which the term, which seems to express the predicate of my judgment, is a name. And I have limited my second proposition in this way, because there are cases, in which it does not, at first sight, seem quite so certain that I am not doing this, as in the two instances I have just given. When, for instance, I judge with regard to something, which I am seeing, "This is a soap-bubble," or "This is a drop of water," or even when I judge "This is a spot of ink," it may not seem quite so plain, that I may not be judging, with regard to the very object presented to me, that it is, itself, a whole soap-bubble, a whole drop of water, or a whole spot of ink, as it always is, in the case of an inkstand, or a coin, that I never take the presented object, about which I am judging, to be a whole inkstand, or a whole coin. The sort of reason why I say this will, of course, be obvious to any one, and it is obviously of a childish order. But I cannot say that it seems to me quite obvious that in such a case I am not judging of the presented object that it is a whole drop of water, in the way in which it does seem to be obvious that I am not judging of *this* presented object that it is an inkstand. That is why I limit myself to saying that, *in general*, when I judge "That is a so-and-so" I am not judging with regard to the presented object, about which my judgment is that *it* is a thing of the kind in question. As much as this seems to me to be a thing which any child can see. Nobody will suppose, for a moment, that when he judges such things as "This is a sofa," or "This is a tree," he is judging, with regard to the presented object about which his judgment plainly is, that it is a whole sofa or a whole tree : he can, at most, suppose that he is judging it to be a part of the surface of a sofa or a part of the surface of a tree. And certainly in the case of most judgments of this kind which we make, whether in the case of all or not, this is plainly the case : we are not judging, with regard to the presented object about which our judgment plainly is, that it is a thing of the kind, for which the term which appears to express the predicate of our judgment, is a name. And that this should be true of *most* judgments of this kind, whether of all or not, is quite sufficient for my purpose.

This much, then, seems to me to be very certain indeed. But I will try to make clearer exactly what I mean by it, by mentioning a ground on which I imagine it might perhaps be disputed.

The object of which I have spoken as *the* object, about which, in each particular case, such a judgment as this always is a judgment, is, of course, always an object of the kind which some philosophers would call a sensation, and others would call a sense-datum. Whether all philosophers, when they talk of sensations, mean to include among them such objects as these, I do not know. Some, who have given a great deal of attention to the subject, and for whom I have a great respect, talk of sensations in such a way, that I cannot be sure what they are talking about at all or whether there are such things. But many, I think, undoubtedly do mean to include such subjects as these. No doubt, in general, when they call them sensations, they mean to attribute to them properties, which it seems to me extremely doubtful whether they possess. And perhaps even those who call them sense-data, may, in part, be attributing to them properties which it may be doubtful whether they possess. If we want to define a sensation or a sense-datum, in a manner which will leave it not open to doubt what sort of things we are talking of, and that there are such things, I do not know that we can do it better than by saying that sense-data are the sort of things, *about* which such judgments as these always seem to be made—the sort of things which seem to be the real or ultimate subjects of all such judgments. Such a way of defining how the term "sense-datum" is used, may not seem very satisfactory; but I am inclined to think it may be as satisfactory as any which can be found. And it is certainly calculated to obviate some misunderstandings which may arise; since everybody can see, I think, what the thing is which I am describing as *the* thing about which he is making his judgment, when he judges "That is an inkstand," and that there is such a thing, even if he does not agree that this description applies to it.

I can, in fact, imagine that some of those who would call this thing a sensation would deny that my judgment is *about* it at all. It would sometimes be spoken of as the sensation which mediates my perception of this inkstand in this instance. And I can imagine that some of those who would so speak of it might be inclined to say that when I judge "This is an inkstand," my judgment is about this inkstand which I perceive, and not, in any sense at all, about the sensation which mediates my perception of it. They may perhaps imagine that the sensation mediates my perception of the inkstand only in the sense that it brings the inkstand before my mind in such a way that, once it is before my mind, I can make a judgment about it, which is *not* a judgment about the mediating sensation at all; and that such a judgment is the one I am actually expressing when I say "This is an inkstand." Such a view, if it is held, seems to me to be quite certainly false, and is what I have intended to deny. And perhaps I can put most clearly the reason why it seems to me false, by saying that, if (which may be doubted) there is anything which is this inkstand, that thing is certainly not given to me independently of this sense-datum, in such a sense that I can possibly make a judgment about it which is *not* a judgment about this sense-datum. I am not, of course, denying that I do perceive this inkstand, and that my judgment is, in a sense, a judgment about it. Both these things seem to me to be quite obviously true. I am only maintaining that my judgment is *also*, in another sense, a judgment about this sense-datum which mediates my perception of the inkstand. Those who say that this sense-datum does mediate my perception of the inkstand, would, of course, admit that my perception of the inkstand is, in a sense, dependent upon the sense-datum ; that it is dependent is implied in the mere statement that it is mediated by it. But it might be maintained that it is dependent on it only in the sense in which, when the idea of one object is called up in my mind, through association, by the idea of another, the idea which is called up is dependent on the idea which calls it up. What I wish to maintain, and what seems to me to be quite certainly true, is that my perception of this inkstand is dependent on this sense-datum, in a quite different and far more intimate sense than this. It is dependent on it in the sense that, if there is anything which is this inkstand, then, in perceiving that thing, I am knowing it *only* as *the* thing which stands in a certain relation to this sense-datum. When the idea of one object is called up in my mind by the idea of another, I do not know the second object *only* as *the* thing which has a certain relation to the first : on the contrary, I can make a judgment about the second object, which is not a judgment about the first. And similarly in the case of two sense-data which are presented to me simultaneously, I do not know the one *only* as a thing which has a certain relation to the other. But in the case of this sense-datum and this inkstand the case seems to me to be plainly quite different. If there be a thing which is this inkstand at all, it is certainly *only* known to me as *the* thing which stands in a certain relation to this sense-datum. It is not given to me, in the sense in which this sense-datum is given. If there be such a thing at all, it is quite certainly only known to me by description, in the sense in which Mr. Russell uses that phrase; and the description by which it is known is that of being *the* thing which stands to this sense-datum in a certain relation. That is to say, when I make such a judgment as " This inkstand is a good big one"; what I am really judging is : " There is a thing which stands to *this* in a certain relation, and which is an inkstand, and that thing is a good big one"—where "*this*" stands for this presented object. I am referring to or identifying the thing which is this inkstand, if there be such a thing at all, only as the thing which stands to this sense-datum in a certair relation ; and hence my judgment, though in one sense it may be said to be a judgment about the inkstand, is quite certainly also, in another sense, a judgment about this sense-datum. This seems to me so clear, that I wonder how anyone can deny it ; and perhaps nobody would. But I cannot help thinking that it is not clear to everybody ; partly because, so far as I can make out, nobody before Mr. Russell had pointed out the extreme difference there is between a judgment about a thing known only by description to the individual who makes the judgment, and a judgment about a thing not known to him only in this way ; and partly because so many people seem still utterly to have failed to understand what the distinction is which he expresses in this way. I will try to make the point clear, in a slightly different way. Suppose I am seeing two coins, lying side by side, and am not perceiving them in any other way except by sight.

It will be plain to everybody, I think, that, when I identify the one as "This one" and the other as "That one," I identify them only by reference to the two visual presented objects, which correspond respectively to the one and to the other. But what may not, I think, be realised, is that the sense in which I identify them by reference to the corresponding sense-data, is one which involves that every judgment which I make about the one is a judgment about the sense-datum which corresponds to it, and every judgment I make about the other, a judgment about the sense-datum which corresponds to *it* : I simply cannot make a judgment about either, which is not a judgment about the corresponding sense-datum. But if the two coins were given to me, in the sense in which the two sense-data are, this would certainly not be the case. I can identify and distinguish the two sense-data *directly*, this as this one, and that as that one : I do not need to identify either as *the* thing which has this relation to this other thing. But I certainly cannot thus directly identify the two coins. I have not four things presented to me (1) *this* sense-datum, (2) *that* sense-datum, (3) *this* coin, and (4) *that* coin, but two only—*this* sense-datum and *that* sense-datum. When, therefore, I judge " *This* is a coin," my judgment is certainly a judgment about the one sense-datum, and when I judge "And *that* is also a coin," it is certainly a judgment about the other. Only, in spite of what my language might seem to imply, I am certainly not judging either of the one sense-datum that it is a whole coin, nor yet of the other that it is one.

This, then, seems to me. fundamentally certain about judgments of this kind. Whenever we make such a judgment we can easily pick out an object (whether we call it a sensation or a sense-datum, or not), which is, in an easily intelligible sense, *the* object which is the real or ultimate subject of our judgment ; and yet, in many cases at all events, what we are judging with regard to this object is certainly not that it is an object of the kind, for which the term which appears to express the predicate of our judgment is a name.

But if this be so, what is it that I am judging, in all such cases, about the presented object, which is the real or ultimate subject of my judgment? It is at this point that we come to questions which seem to me to be really uncertain and difficult to answer.

To begin with, there is one answer which is naturally suggested by the reason I have given for saying that, in this case, it is quite obvious that I am not judging, with regard to this presented object, that *it* is an inkstand, whereas it is not in the same way, quite obvious that, in making such a judgment as " This is a soap-bubble " or "This is a drop of water," I may not be judging, of the object about which my judgment is, that that very object really is a soap-bubble or a drop of water. The reason I gave is that it is quite obvious that I do not take this presented object to be a *whole* inkstand : that, at most, I only take it to be part of the surface of an inkstand. And this reason naturally suggests that the true answer to our question may be that what I am judging of the presented object is just that it is a part of the surface of an inkstand. This answer seems to me to be obviously on quite a different level from the suggestion that I am judging it really to be an inkstand. It is not childishly obvious that I am not judging it to be part of the surface of an inkstand, as it is that I am not judging it to be an inkstand—a whole one.

On this view, when I say such things as " That is an inkstand," " That is a door," " This is a coin," these expressions would really only be a loose way of saying " That is part of the surface of an inkstand," "That is part of the surface of a door," "This is part of the surface of a coin." And there would, I think, plainly be nothing surprising in the fact that we should use language thus loosely. What, at first sight, appears to be a paradox, namely that, whereas I appear to be asserting of a given thing that it is of a certain kind, I am not really asserting of the thing in question that it is of that kind at all, would be susceptible of an easy explanation. And moreover, if this view were true, it would offer an excellent illustration of the difference between a thing known only by description and a thing not so known, and would show how entirely free from mystery that distinction is. On this view, when I judge "That inkstand is a good big one" I shall in effect be judging : "There is one and only one inkstand of which *this* is part of the surface, and the inkstand of which this is true is a good big one." It would be quite clear that the part of the surface of the inkstand was given to me in a sense in which the whole was not, just as it is in fact clear that I do now "*see*" this part of the surface of this inkstand, in a sense in which I do *not* "see" the whole ; and that my judgment, while it is, in fact, *about* both the whole inkstand, and also *about* one particular part of its surface, is *about* them in two entirely different senses.

This view is one, which it is at first sight, I think, very natural to suppose to be true. But before giving the reasons, why, nevertheless, it seems to me extremely doubtful, I think it is desirable to try to explain more precisely what I mean by it. The word "part" is one which is often used extremely vaguely in philosophy ; and I can imagine that some people would be willing to assent to the proposition that this sense-datum really is, in some sense or other, a "part" of this ink-stand, and that what I am judging with regard to

it, when I judge " This is an inkstand," is, in effect,
" There is an inkstand, of which *this* is a part," who
would be far from allowing that this can possibly be
what I am judging, when once they understand
what the sense is in which I am here using the word
" part." What this sense is, I am quite unable to
define ; but I hope I may be able to make my
meaning sufficiently clear, by giving instances of
things which are undoubtedly " parts " of other
things in the sense in question. There is, it seems
to me, a sense of the word " part," in which we all
constantly use the word with perfect precision, and,
which, therefore, we all understand very well, however little we may be able to define it. It is the
sense in which the trunk of any tree is undoubtedly
a part of that tree ; in which this finger of mine is
undoubtedly a part of my hand, and my hand a part
of my body. This is a sense in which every part of
a material thing or physical object is itself a material
thing or physical object ; and it is, so far as I can
see, the only proper sense in which a material thing
can be said to have parts. The view which I wish
to discuss is the view that I am judging this
presented object to be a part of an inkstand, in this
sense. And the nature of the view can perhaps be
brought out more clearly, by mentioning one
important corollary which would follow from it. I
am, of course, at this moment, seeing many parts of
the surface of this inkstand. But all these parts,
except one, are, in fact, themselves parts of that
one. That one is the one of which we should
naturally speak as " *the* part of the surface that I
am now seeing " or as " *this* part of the surface of
this inkstand." There is only one part of the
surface of this inkstand, which does thus contain, as
parts, all the other parts that I am now seeing.
And, if it were true that I am judging this presented
object to be a part of the surface of an inkstand at

all, in the sense I mean, it would follow that this presented object must, if my judgment "This is an inkstand" be true (as it certainly is), be identical with this part, which contains all the other parts which I am seeing; since there is plainly no other part with which it could possibly be identified. That is to say, if I am really judging of this presented object that it is part of the surface of an inkstand, in the sense I mean, it must be the case that everything which is true of what I should call "this part of the surface of this inkstand" is, in fact, true of this presented object.

This view, therefore, that what we are judging of the ultimate subject of our judgment, when we judge "This is a so-and-so," is, in general, merely that the subject in question is a *part* of a thing of the kind in question, can, I think, be most clearly discussed, by asking whether, in this case, this presented object can really be identical with this part of the surface of this inkstand. If it can't, then most certainly I am not judging of it that it is a part of the surface of an inkstand at all. For my judgment, whatever it is, is true. And yet, if this presented object is not identical with this part of the surface of this inkstand, it certainly is not a part of an inkstand at all; since there is no other part, either of this inkstand or of any other, with which it could possibly be supposed to be identical.

Can we, then, hold that this sense-datum really is identical with this part of the surface of this inkstand? That everything which is true of the one is true of the other?

An enormous number of very familiar arguments have been used by various philosophers, which, if they were sound, would show that we can not. Some of these arguments seem to me to be quite clearly not sound—all, for instance, which rest either on the assumption that this sense-datum can only exist so long as it is perceived, or on the assumption that it can only exist so long as it is perceived *by me*. Of others I suspect that they may have some force, though I am quite unable to see that they have any. Such, for instance, are all those which assume either that this sense-datum is a sensation or feeling of mine, in a sense which includes the assertion that it is dependent on my mind in the very same sense in which my perception of it obviously is so ; or that it is causally dependent on my body in the sense in which my perception of it admittedly is so. But others do seem to me to have great force. I will, however, confine myself to trying to state one, which seems to me to have as much as any. It will be found that this one involves an assumption, which does seem to me to have great force, but which yet seems to me to be doubtful. So far as I know, all good arguments against the view that this sense-datum really is identical with this part of the surface of the inkstand, do involve this same assumption, and have no more force than it has. But in this, of course, I may be wrong. Perhaps some one will be able to point out an argument, which is obviously quite independent of it, and which yet has force.

The argument I mean involves considerations which are exceedingly familiar, so familiar that I am afraid every one may be sick of hearing them alluded to. But, in spite of this fact, it seems to me not quite easy to put it quite precisely, in a way which will distinguish it clearly from other arguments involving the same familiar considerations, but which do not seem to me to be equally cogent. I want, therefore, to try to put it with a degree of precision, which will prevent irrelevant objections from being made to it—objections which would, I think, be relevant against some of these other arguments, but are not, I think, relevant against it.

The fact is that we all, exceedingly commonly, when, at each of two times, separated by a longer or shorter interval, we see a part of the surface of a material thing, in the sense in which I am now seeing this part of the surface of this inkstand, or when at one time we see such a surface and at another perceive one by touch, make, on the second occasion, the judgment " *This* part of a surface is the *same* part of the surface of the same thing, as that which I was seeing (or perceiving by touch) just now." How commonly we all do this can scarcely be exaggerated. I look at this inkstand, and then I look again, and on the second occasion I judge " This part of the surface of this inkstand is the same as, or at least contains a part which is the same as a part of, the part of its surface which I was seeing just now." Or I look at this finger and then I touch it, and I judge, on the second occasion, " This part of the surface of this finger is the same as one of those I was seeing just now." We all thus constantly identify a part of a surface of a material thing which we are perceiving at one time with a part which we *were* perceiving at another.

Now, when we do this—when we judge " This is the *same* part of the same thing as I was seeing or touching just now," we, of course, do not mean to exclude the possibility that the part in question may have changed during the interval; that it is really different, on the second occasion, either in shape or size or quality, or in all three, from what it was on the first. That is to say, the sense of sameness which we are here concerned with is one which clearly does not exclude change. We may even be prepared to assert, on general grounds, in all such cases, that the surface in question certainly must have changed. But nevertheless there is a great difference in one respect, between two kinds of such cases, both of which occur exceedingly commonly. If I watch somebody blowing air into a child's balloon, it constantly happens, at certain stages in the process, that I judge with regard to the part of the surface which I am seeing at that stage, not only that it *is* larger than it was at an earlier stage, but that it is *perceptibly* larger. Or, if I pull the face of an india-rubber doll, I may judge at a certain stage in the process that the patch of red colour on its cheek not only is different in shape from what it was at the beginning, but is *perceptibly* so ; it may, for instance, be a perceptibly flatter ellipse than it was to start with. Or, if I watch a person blushing, I may judge at a certain stage that a certain part of the surface of his face not only is different in colour from what it was, when I saw it before he began to blush, but is *perceptibly* so—perceptibly redder. In enormous numbers of cases we do thus judge of a surface seen at a given time that it is thus *perceptibly* different in size, or in shape, or in colour, from what it was when we saw it before. But cases are at least equally numerous in which, though we might, on general grounds be prepared to assert that it *must* have changed in some respect, we should not be prepared to assert that it had, in any respect whatever, changed *perceptibly*. Of this part of this surface of this inkstand, for instance, I am certainly not prepared to assert that it is now perceptibly different in any respect from what it was when I saw it just now. And similar cases are so numerous that I need not give further instances. We can, therefore, divide cases, in which we judge, of a part of a surface which we are seeing, "This is the same part of the surface of the same material thing as the one I saw just now," into cases where we should also judge "But it is perceptibly different from what it was then," and cases in which, even though we might assert "It *must* be different," we are certainly not prepared to assert that it is *perceptibly* so.

But now let us consider the cases in which we are not prepared to assert that the surface in question has changed perceptibly. The strange fact, from which the argument I mean is drawn, is that, in a very large number of such cases, it seems as if it were unmistakably true that the presented object, about which we are making our judgment when we talk of "This surface" at the later time, *is* perceptibly different, from that about which we are making it when we talk of the surface I saw just now. If, at the later time, I am at a sufficiently greater distance from the surface, the presented object which corresponds to it at the time seems to be perceptibly smaller, than the one which corresponded to it before. If I am looking at it from a sufficiently oblique angle, the later presented object often seems to be perceptibly different in shape—a perceptibly flatter ellipse, for instance. If I am looking at it, with blue spectacles on, when formerly I had none, the later presented object seems to be perceptibly different in colour from the earlier one. If I am perceiving it by touch alone, whereas formerly I was perceiving it by sight alone, the later presented object seems to be perceptibly different from the earlier, in respect of the fact that it is not coloured at all, whereas the earlier was, and that, on the other hand, it has certain tactual qualities, which the earlier had not got. All this seems to be as plain as it can be, and yet it makes absolutely no difference to the fact that of the surface in question we are *not* prepared to judge that it is perceptibly different from what it was. Sometimes, of course, where there seems to be no doubt that the later presented object is perceptibly different from the earlier, we may not notice that it is so. But even where we do notice the apparent difference, we do still continue to judge of the surface in question: This surface is not, so far as I can tell with certainty by perception, in any way different from what it was when I saw it or touched it just now ; I am *not* prepared to assert that it has changed perceptibly. It seems, therefore, to be absolutely impossible that the surface seen at the later time should be identical with the object presented then, and the surface seen at the earlier identical with the object presented then, for the simple reason that, whereas with regard to the later seen surface I am not prepared to judge that it is in any way perceptibly different from that seen earlier, it seems that with regard to the later sense-datum I cannot fail to judge that it *is* perceptibly different from the earlier one : the fact that they are perceptibly different simply stares me in the face. It seems, in short, that when, in such a case, I judge : " This surface is not, so far as I can tell, perceptibly different from the one I saw just now," I cannot possibly be judging of the presented object " *This* is not, so far as I can tell, perceptibly different from that object which was presented to me just now," for the simple reason that I *can* tell, as certainly, almost, as I can tell anything, that it is perceptibly different.

That is the argument, as well as I can put it, for saying that this presented object, is *not* identical with this part of the surface of this inkstand ; and that, therefore, when I judge " This is part of the surface of an inkstand," I am not judging of this presented object, which nevertheless is the ultimate subject of my judgment, that *it* is part of the surface of an inkstand. And this argument does seem to me to be a very powerful one.

But nevertheless it does not seem to me to be quite conclusive, because it rests on an assumption, which, though it seems to me to have great force, does not seem to me quite certain. The assumption

I mean is the assumption that, in such cases as those I have spoken of, the later presented object really is perceptibly different from the earlier. This assumption has, if I am not mistaken, seemed to many philosophers to be quite unquestionable ; they have never even thought of questioning it ; and I own that it used to be so with me. And I am still not sure that I may not be talking sheer nonsense in suggesting that it can be questioned. But, if I am, I am no longer able to see that I am. What now seems to me to be possible is that the sense-datum which corresponds to a tree, which I am seeing, when I am a mile off, may not really be perceived to *be* smaller than the one, which corresponds to the same tree, when I see it from a distance of only a hundred yards, but that it is only perceived to *seem* smaller ; that the sense-datum which corresponds to a penny, which I am seeing obliquely, is not really perceived to *be* different in shape from that which corresponded to the penny, when I was straight in front of it, but is only perceived to *seem* different—that all that is perceived is that the one *seems* elliptical and the other circular ; that the sense-datum presented to me when I have the blue spectacles on is not perceived to *be* different in colour from the one presented to me when I have not, but only to *seem* so ; and finally that the sense-datum presented when I touch this finger is not perceived to *be* different in any way from that presented to me when I see it, but only to *seem* so —that I do not perceive the one to be coloured and the other not to be so, but only that the one *seems* coloured and the other not. If such a view is to be possible, we shall have, of course, to maintain that the kind of experience which I have expressed by saying one *seems* different from the other—" *seems* circular," " *seems* blue," " *seems* coloured," and so on —involves an ultimate, not further analysable, kind of psychological relation, not to be identified either with that involved in being "perceived" to be so and so, or with that involved in being "judged" to be so and so ; since a presented object might, in this sense, *seem* to be elliptical, *seem* to be blue, etc., when it is neither perceived to be so, nor judged to be so. But there seems to me to be no reason why there should not be such an ultimate relation. The great objection to such a view seems to me to be the difficulty of believing that I don't actually perceive this sense-datum to *be* red, for instance, and that other to *be* elliptical ; that I only perceive, in many cases, that it *seems* so. I cannot, however, now persuade myself that it is quite clear that I do perceive it to *be* so. And, if I don't, then it seems really possible that this presented object really is identical with this part of the surface of this inkstand ; since, when I judge, as in the cases supposed, that the surface in question is *not*, so far as I can tell, perceptibly different from what it was, I might really be judging of the two sense-data that they also were not, so far as I can tell, perceptibly different, the only difference between the two that *is* perceptible, being that the one *seems* to be of a certain size, shape or colour, and the other to be of a different and incompatible size, shape or colour. Of course, in those cases, as in that of the balloon being blown up, where I "perceive" that the surface has changed, *e.g.* in size, it would have to be admitted that I do perceive of the two sense-data not merely that they *seem* different in size, but that they *are* so. But I think it would be possible to maintain that the sense in which, in these cases, I "perceive" them to *be* different, is a different one from that in which, both in these and in the others, I perceive them to *seem* so.

Possibly in making this suggestion that sense-data, in cases where most philosophers have assumed unhesitatingly that they are *perceived* to be different, are only really perceived to *seem* different, I am, as I said, talking sheer nonsense, though I cannot, at the moment, see that I am. And possibly, even if this suggestion itself is not nonsense, even if it is true, there may be other fatal objections to the view that this presented object really is identical with this part of the surface of this inkstand. But what seems to me certain is that, unless this suggestion is true, then this presented object is certainly *not* identical with this part of the surface of this inkstand. And since it is doubtful whether it is not nonsense, and still more doubtful whether it is true, it must, I think, be admitted to be highly doubtful whether the two *are* identical. But, if they are not identical, then what I am judging with regard to this presented object, when I judge " This is an inkstand," is certainly *not* that it is itself part of the surface of an inkstand ; and hence, it is worth while to inquire further, what, if I am not judging this, I *can* be judging with regard to it.

And here, I think, the first natural suggestion to make is that just as, when I talk of "this inkstand," what I seem really to mean is " *the* inkstand of which *this* is part of the surface," so that the inkstand is only known to me by description as the inkstand of which this material surface is part of the surface, so again when I talk of "this material surface," what I really mean is "*the* material surface to which *this* (presented object) has a certain relation," so that this surface is, in its turn, only known to me by description as *the* surface which has a certain relation to this presented object. If that were so, then what I should be judging of this presented object, when I judge " This is part of the surface of an inkstand," would be not that it is itself such a part, but that *the* thing which stands to it in a certain relation is such a part : in short, what I should be judging with regard to *it*, would be "There's one thing and one only which stands to *this* in *this* relation, and the thing which does so is part of the surface of an inkstand."

But if we are to adopt the view that something of this sort is what we are judging, there occurs at once the pressing question : What on earth can the relation be with regard to which we are judging, that one and only one thing stands in it to this presented object ? And this is a question to which, so far as I know, none of those philosophers, who *both* hold (as many do) that this presented object is *not* identical with this part of the surface of this inkstand, *and* also that there really is something of which it could be truly predicated that it is this part of the surface of this inkstand (that is to say, who reject all views of the Mill-Russell type), have given anything like a clear answer. It does not seem to have occurred to them that it requires an answer, chiefly, I think, because it has not occurred to them to ask what we can be judging when we make judgments of this sort. There are only two answers, that I can think of, which might be suggested with any plausibility.

Many philosophers, who take the view that the presented objects about which we make these judgments are sensations of ours, and some even who do not, are in the habit of talking of "*the* causes" of these objects as if we knew, in the case of each, that it had one and only one cause ; and many of them seem to think that this part of the surface of this inkstand could be correctly described as *the* cause of this presented object. They suggest, therefore, the view that what I am judging in this case might be : "This presented object has one and only one cause, and that cause is part of the surface of an inkstand." It seems to me quite obvious that *this* view, at all events, is utterly untenable. I do not believe for a moment, nor does any one, and certainly therefore do not judge, that this presented object has *only* one cause : I believe that it has a whole series of different causes. I do, in fact, believe that this part of the surface of this inkstand is *one* among the causes of my perception of this presented object : that seems to me to be a very well established scientific proposition. And I am prepared to admit that there *may* be good reasons for thinking that it is one among the causes of this presented object itself, though I cannot myself see that there are any. But that it is the *only* cause of this presented object I certainly do not believe, nor, I think, does anybody, and hence my judgment certainly cannot be " *The* cause of this is part of the surface of an inkstand." It might no doubt, be possible to define some *kind* of causal relation, such that it might be plausibly held that it and it alone causes this presented object *in that particular way*. But any such definition would, so far as I can see, be necessarily very complicated. And, even when we have got it, it seems to me it would be highly improbable we could truly say that what we are judging in these cases is : " This presented object has one and only one cause, of this special kind." Still, I do not wish to deny that some such view may *possibly* be true.

The only other suggestion I can make is that there may be some ultimate, not further definable relation, which we might for instance, call the relation of " being a manifestation of," such that we might conceivably be judging : " There is one and only one thing of which this presented object is a manifestation, and *that* thing is part of the surface of an inkstand." And here again, it seems to me just possible that this *may* be a true account of what we are judging ; only I cannot find the slightest sign that I am in fact aware of any such relation.

Possibly other suggestions could be made as to what the relation is, with regard to which it could be plausibly supposed that in all cases, where we make these judgments we are in fact judging of the presented object "There is one and only one thing which stands to this object in *this* relation." But it seems to me at least very doubtful whether there is any such relation at all ; whether, therefore, our judgment really is of this form, and whether therefore, this part of the surface of this inkstand really is known to me by description as *the* thing which stands in a certain relation to this presented object. But if it isn't, and if, also, we cannot take the view that what I am judging is that this presented object *itself* is a part of the surface of an inkstand, there would seem to be no possible alternative but that we must take some view of what I have called the Mill-Russell type. Views of this type, if I understand them rightly, are distinguished from those which I have hitherto considered, by the fact that, according to them, there is nothing whatever in the Universe of which it could truly be predicated that it is this part of the surface of this inkstand, or indeed that it is *a* part of the surface of an inkstand, or an inkstand, at all. They hold, in short, that though there are plenty of material things in the Universe, there is nothing in it of which it could truly be asserted that *it* is a material thing : that, though, when I assert "This is an inkstand," my assertion is true, and is such that it follows from it that there is in the Universe at least one inkstand, and, therefore, at least one material thing, yet it does not follow from it that there is anything which is a material thing. When I judge "This is an inkstand," I am judging this presented object to possess a certain property, which is such that, if there are things, which possess that property, there are inkstands and material things, but which is such that nothing which possesses it is itself a material thing ; so that in judging that there are material things, we are really always judging of some *other* property, which is not that of being a material thing, that there are things which possess *it*. It seems to me quite possible, of course, that some view of this type is the true one. Indeed, this paper may be regarded, if you like, as an argument in favour of the proposition that some such view *must* be true. Certainly one of my main objects in writing it was to put as plainly as I can some grave difficulties which seem to me to stand in the way of any other view ; in the hope that some of those, who reject all views of the Mill-Russell type, may explain clearly which of the alternatives I have suggested they would adopt, or whether, perhaps, some other which has not occurred to me. It does not seem to me to be always sufficiently realised how difficult it is to find *any* answer to my question "What are we judging in these cases?" to which there are not very grave objections, unless we adopt an answer of the Mill-Russell type. That an answer of this type *is* the true one, I am not myself, in spite of these objections, by any means convinced. The truth is I am completely puzzled as to what the true answer can be. At the present moment, I am rather inclined to favour the view that what I am judging of this presented object is that it is itself a part of the surface of an inkstand—that, therefore, it really is identical with this part of the surface of this inkstand, in spite of the fact that this involves the view that, where, hitherto, I have always supposed myself to be perceiving of two presented objects that they really were different, I was, in fact, only perceiving that they *seemed* to be different. But, as I have said, it seems to me quite possible that this

view is, as I have hitherto supposed, sheer nonsense ;
and, in any case, there are, no doubt, other serious
objections to the view that this presented object is
this part of the surface of this inkstand.

THE CONCEPTION OF INTRINSIC VALUE

MY main object in this paper is to try to define more precisely the most important question, which, so far as I can see, is really at issue when it is disputed with regard to any predicate of value, whether it is or is not a "subjective" predicate. There are three chief cases in which this controversy is apt to arise. It arises, first, with regard to the conceptions of "right" and "wrong," and the closely allied conception of "duty" or "what *ought* to be done." It arises, secondly, with regard to "good" and "evil," in some sense of those words in which the conceptions for which they stand are certainly quite distinct from the conceptions of "right" and "wrong," but in which nevertheless it is undeniable that ethics has to deal with them. And it arises, lastly, with regard to certain æsthetic conceptions, such as "beautiful" and "ugly;" or "good" and "bad," in the sense in which these words are applied to works of art, and in which, therefore, the question what is good and bad is a question not for ethics but for æsthetics.

.In all three cases there are people who maintain that the predicates in question are purely "subjective," in a sense which can, I think, be fairly easily defined. I am not here going to attempt a perfectly accurate definition of the sense in question; but, as the term "subjective" is so desperately ambiguous, I had better try to indicate roughly the sense I am thinking of. Take the word " beautiful " for example. There is a sense of the term " subjective," such that to say that " beautiful " stands for a subjective predicate, means, roughly, that any statement of the form " This is beautiful " merely expresses a psychological assertion to the effect that some particular individual or class of individuals either actually has, or would, under certain circumstances, have, a certain kind of mental attitude towards the thing in question. And what I mean by " having a mental attitude " towards a thing, can be best explained by saying that to desire a thing is to have one kind of mental attitude towards it, to be pleased with it is to have another, to will it is to have another ; and in short that to have any kind of feeling or emotion *towards* it is to have a certain mental attitude towards it—a different one in each case. Thus anyone who holds that when we say that a thing is beautiful, what we *mean* is merely that we ourselves or some particular class of people actually do, or would under certain circumstances, have, or permanently have, a certain feeling towards the thing in question, is taking a " subjective " view of beauty.

But in all three cases there are also a good many people who hold that the predicates in question are not, in this sense " subjective " ; and I think that those who hold this are apt to speak as if the view which they wish to maintain in opposition to it consisted simply and solely in holding its contra- dictory—in holding, that is, that the predicates in question are " objective," where " objective " simply means the same as " not subjective." But in fact I think this is hardly ever really the case. In the case of goodness and beauty, what such people are really anxious to maintain is by no means merely that these conceptions are " objective," but that, besides being " objective," they are also, in a sense which I shall try to explain, "intrinsic" kinds of value. It is this conviction—the conviction that goodness and beauty are *intrinsic* kinds of value, which is, I think, the strongest ground of their objection to any subjective view. And indeed, when they speak of the "objectivity" of these conceptions, what they have in mind is, I believe, always a conception which has no proper right to be called "objectivity," since it includes as an essential part this other characteristic which I propose to call that of being an "intrinsic" kind of value.

The truth is, I believe, that though, from the proposition that a particular kind of value is "intrinsic" it does follow that it must be "objective," the converse implication by no means holds, but on the contrary it is perfectly easy to conceive theories of *e.g.* "goodness," according to which goodness would, in the strictest sense, be "objective," and yet would not be "intrinsic." There is, therefore, a very important difference between the conception of "objectivity," and that which I will call "internality;" but yet, if I am not mistaken, when people talk about the "objectivity" of any kind of value, they almost always confuse the two, owing to the fact that most of those who deny the "internality" of a given kind of value, also assert its "subjectivity." How great the difference is, and that it is a fact that those who maintain the "objectivity" of goodness do, as a rule, mean by this not mere "objectivity," but "internality," as well, can, I think, be best brought out by considering an instance of a theory, according to which goodness would be objective but would not be intrinsic.

Let us suppose it to be held, for instance, that what is meant by saying that one type of human being A is "better" than another type B, is merely that the course of evolution tends to increase the numbers of type A and to decrease those of type

B.   Such a view has, in fact, been often suggested,
even if it has not been held in this exact form ; it
amounts merely to the familiar suggestion that
"better" means "better fitted to survive."   Obviously "better," on this interpretation of its meaning, is in no sense a "subjective" conception : the
conception of belonging to a type which tends to
be favoured by the struggle for existence more than
another is as "objective" as any conception can be.
But yet, if I am not mistaken, all those who object
to a subjective view of "goodness," and insist upon its
"objectivity," would object just as strongly to this
interpretation of its meaning as to any "subjective"
interpretation.   Obviously, therefore, what they
are really anxious to contend for is not merely
that goodness is "objective," since they are here
objecting to a theory which is "objective ;" but
something else.   And this something else is, I
think, certainly just that it is "intrinsic"—a
character which is just as incompatible with this
objective evolutionary interpretation as with any
and every subjective interpretation.   For if you
say that to call type A "better" than type B means
merely that it is more favoured in the struggle for
existence, it follows that the being "better" is a
predicate which does *not depend merely on the
intrinsic nature of A and B respectively.*   On the
contrary, although here and now A may be more
favoured than B, it is obvious that under other
circumstances or with different natural laws the
very same type B might be more favoured than A,
so that the very same type which, under one set of
circumstances, is better than B, would, under another
set, be worse.   Here, then, we have a case where
an interpretation of "goodness," which does make
it "objective," is incompatible with its being "intrinsic."   And it is just this same fact—the fact
that, on any "subjective" interpretation, the very

same kind of thing which, under some circumstances, is better than another, would, under others, be worse —which constitutes, so far as I can see, the fundamental objection to all "subjective" interpretations. Obviously, therefore, to express this objection by saying that goodness is "objective" is very incorrect; since goodness might quite well be "objective" and yet *not* possess the very characteristic which it is mainly wished to assert that it has.

In the case, therefore, of ethical and æsthetic "goodness," I think that what those who contend for the "objectivity" of these conceptions really wish to contend for is not mere "objectivity" at all, but principally and essentially that they are *intrinsic* kinds of value. But in the case of "right" and "wrong" and "duty," the same cannot be said, because many of those who object to the view that these conceptions are "subjective," nevertheless do not hold that they are "intrinsic." We cannot, therefore, say that what those who contend for the "objectivity" of right and wrong really mean is always chiefly that those conceptions are intrinsic, but we can, I think, say that what they do mean is certainly *not* "objectivity" in this case any more than the other; since here, just as there, it would be possible to find certain views, which are in every sense "objective," to which they would object just as strongly as to any subjective view. And though what is meant by "objectivity" in this case, is not that "right" and "wrong" are *themselves* "intrinsic," what is, I think, meant here too is that they have a fixed relation to a kind of value which *is* "intrinsic." It is this fixed relation to an intrinsic kind of value, so far as I can see, which gives to right and wrong that kind and degree of fixity and impartiality which they actually are felt to possess, and which is what people are thinking of when they talk of their "objectivity." Here, too, therefore,

to talk of the characteristic meant as "objectivity"
is just as great a misnomer as in the other cases;
since though it is a characteristic which is incompatible with any kind of "subjectivity," it is also
incompatible, for the same reason, with many kinds
of "objectivity."

For these reasons I think that what those who
contend for the "objectivity" of certain kinds of
value, or for the "objectivity" of judgments of
value, commonly have in mind is not really "objectivity" at all, but either that the kinds of value in
question are themselves "intrinsic," or else that they
have a fixed relation to some kind that is so. The
conception upon which they really wish to lay
stress is not that of "objective value," but that of
"intrinsic value," though they confuse the two.
And I think this is the case to a considerable extent
not only with the defenders of so-called "objectivity,"
but also with its opponents. Many of those who
hold strongly (as many do) that *all* kinds of value
are "subjective" certainly object to the so-called
"objective" view, not so much because it is
objective, as because it is not *naturalistic* or *positivistic*
—a characteristic which does naturally follow from
the contention that value is "intrinsic," but does
not follow from the mere contention that it is
"objective." To a view which is at the same time
both "naturalistic" or "positivistic" and also "objective," such as the Evolutionary view which I
sketched just now, they do not feel at all the same
kind or degree of objection as to any so-called "objective" view. With regard to so-called "objective"
views they are apt to feel not only that they are false,
but that they involve a particularly poisonous kind of
falsehood—the erecting into a "metaphysical" entity
of what is really susceptible of a simple naturalistic
explanation. They feel that to hold such a view is
not merely to make a mistake, but to make a super-

stitious mistake. They feel the same kind of contempt for those who hold it, which we are apt to feel towards those whom we regard as grossly superstitious, and which is felt by certain persons for what they call "metaphysics." Obviously, therefore, what they really object to is not simply the view that these predicates are "objective," but something else—something which does not at all follow from the contention that they are "objective," but which does follow from the contention that they are "intrinsic."

In disputes, therefore, as to whether particular kinds of value are or are not "subjective," I think that the issue which is really felt to be important, almost always by one side, and often by both, is not really the issue between "subjective" and "non-subjective," but between "intrinsic" and "non-intrinsic." And not only is this felt to be the more important issue; I think it really is so. For the difference that must be made to our view of the Universe, according as we hold that some kinds of value are "intrinsic" or that none are, is much greater than any which follows from a mere difference of opinion as to whether some are "non-subjective," or all without exception "subjective." To hold that any kinds of value are "intrinsic" entails the recognition of a kind of predicate extremely different from any we should otherwise have to recognise and perhaps unique; whereas it is in any case certain that there are "objective" predicates as well as "subjective."

But now what is this "internality" of which I have been speaking? What is meant by saying with regard to a kind of value that it is "intrinsic?" To express roughly what is meant is, I think, simple enough; and everybody will recognise it at once, as a notion which is constantly in people's heads; but I want to dwell upon it at some length, because I know of no place where it is expressly explained and defined, and because, though it seems very simple and fundamental, the task of defining it precisely is by no means easy and involves some difficulties which I must confess that I do not know how to solve.

I have already given incidentally the main idea in speaking of that evolutionary interpretation of "goodness," according to which, as I said, goodness would be "objective" but would not be "intrinsic." I there used as equivalent to the assertion that 'better,' on that definition, would not be 'intrinsic,' the assertion that the question whether one type of being A was better than another B would *not* depend *solely on the intrinsic natures of A and B*, but on circumstances and the laws of nature. And I think that this phrase will in fact suggest to everybody just what I do mean by "intrinsic" value. We can, in fact, set up the following definition. *To say that a kind of value is "intrinsic" means merely that the question whether a thing possesses it, and in what degree it possesses it, depends solely on the intrinsic nature of the thing in question.*

But though this definition does, I think, convey exactly what I mean, I want to dwell upon its meaning, partly because the conception of 'differing in intrinsic nature' which I believe to be of fundamental importance, is liable to be confused with other conceptions, and partly because the definition involves notions, which I do not know how to define exactly.

When I say, with regard to any particular kind of value, that the question whether and in what degree anything possesses it *depends solely on the intrinsic nature of the thing in question*, I mean to say two different things at the same time. I mean to say (1) that it is *impossible* for what is

strictly *one and the same* thing to possess that kind
of value at one time, or in one set of circumstances,
and *not* to possess it at another; and equally *impossible* for it to possess it in one degree at one
time, or in one set of circumstances, and to possess
it in a different degree at another, or in a different
set. This, I think, is obviously part of what is
naturally conveyed by saying that the question
whether and in what degree a thing possesses the
kind of value in question always depends *solely* on
the intrinsic nature of the thing. For if x and y
have different intrinsic natures, it follows that x
cannot be quite strictly one and the same thing as
y; and hence if x and y can have a different intrinsic value, only where their intrinsic natures are
different, it follows that one and the same thing
must always have the same intrinsic value. This,
then, is part of what is meant; and about this part
I think I need say no more, except to call attention
to the fact that it involves a conception, which as
we shall see is also involved in the other part, and
which involves the same difficulty in both cases—I
mean, the conception which is expressed by the
word 'impossible.' (2) The second part of what is
meant is that if a given thing possesses any kind of
intrinsic value in a certain degree, then not only
must that same thing possess it, under all circumstances, in the same degree, but also anything *exactly like* it, must, under all circumstances,
possess it in exactly the same degree. Or to put
it in the corresponding negative form : It is *impossible* that of two exactly similar things one should
possess it and the other not, or that one should
possess it in one degree, and the other in a different
one.

I think this second proposition also is naturally
conveyed by saying that the kind of value in
question depends solely on the intrinsic nature of

what possesses it. For we should naturally say of two things which were *exactly alike* intrinsically, in spite of their being *two*, that they possessed the *same* intrinsic nature. But it is important to call attention expressly to the fact that what I mean by the expression 'having a different intrinsic nature' is equivalent to 'not exactly alike' because here there is real risk of confusion between this conception and a different one. This comes about as follows. It is natural to suppose that the phrase 'having a different intrinsic nature' is equivalent to the phrase 'intrinsically different' or 'having different intrinsic properties.' But, if we do make this identification, there is a risk of confusion. For it is obvious that there is a sense in which, when things are exactly like, they must be 'intrinsically different' and have different intrinsic properties, merely because they are two. For instance, two patches of colour may be exactly alike, in spite of the fact that each possesses a constituent which the other does not possess, provided only that their two constituents are exactly alike.   And yet, in a certain sense, it is obvious that the fact that each has a constituent, which the other has not got, does constitute an intrinsic difference between them, and implies that each has an intrinsic property which the other has not got.   And even where the two things are simple the mere fact that they are *numerically* different does in a sense constitute an intrinsic difference between them, and each will have at least one intrinsic property which the other has not got —namely that of being identical with itself.   It is obvious therefore that the phrases 'intrinsically different' and 'having different intrinsic properties' are ambiguous. They may be used in such a sense that to say of two things that they are intrinsically different or have different intrinsic properties does *not* imply that they are not exactly alike, but only that they are *numerically* different. Or they may be used in a sense in which two things can be said to be intrinsically different, and to have different intrinsic properties *only* when they are not exactly alike. It is, therefore, extremely important to insist that when I say : Two things can differ in intrinsic value, only when they have different intrinsic natures, I am using the expression 'having different intrinsic natures' in the latter sense and not the former :— in a sense in which the mere fact that two things are two, or differ numerically, does *not* imply that they have different intrinsic natures, but in which they can be said to have different intrinsic natures, *only* where, besides differing numerically, they are also *not* exactly alike.

But as soon as this is explained, another risk of confusion arises owing to the fact that when people contrast mere numerical difference with a kind of intrinsic difference, which is *not* merely numerical, they are apt to identify the latter with *qualitative* difference. It might, therefore, easily be thought that by 'difference in intrinsic nature' I mean 'difference in quality.' But this identification of difference in quality with difference in intrinsic nature would also be a mistake. It is true that what is commonly meant by difference of quality, in the strict sense, always is a difference of intrinsic nature : two things cannot differ in quality without differing in intrinsic nature ; and that fact is one of the most important facts about qualitative difference. But the converse is by no means also true : although two things cannot differ in quality without differing in intrinsic nature, they can differ in intrinsic nature without differing in quality ; or, in other words, difference in quality is only *one* species of difference in intrinsic nature. That this is so follows from the fact that, as I explained, I am using the phrase 'different in intrinsic nature' as equivalent to 'not exactly like :' for it is quite plain that two things may not be exactly alike, in spite of the fact that they don't differ in quality, *e.g.* if the only difference between them were in respect of the *degree* in which they possess some quality they do possess. Nobody would say that a very loud sound was exactly like a very soft one, even if they were exactly like in quality ; and yet it is plain there is a sense in which their intrinsic nature is different. For this reason alone qualitative difference cannot be identified with difference in intrinsic nature. And there are still other reasons. Difference in size, for instance may be a difference in intrinsic nature, in the sense I mean, but it can hardly be called a difference in quality. Or take such a difference as the difference between two patterns consisting in the fact that the one is a yellow circle with a red spot in the middle, and the other a yellow circle with a blue spot in the middle. This difference would perhaps be loosely called a difference of quality ; but obviously it would be more accurate to call it a difference which consists in the fact that the one pattern has a *constituent* which is qualitatively different from any which the other has ; and the difference between being qualitatively different and having qualitatively different constituents is important both because the latter can only be defined in terms of the former, and because it is possible for simple things to differ from one another in the former way, whereas it is only possible for complex things to differ in the latter.

I hope this is sufficient to make clear exactly what the conception is which I am expressing by the phrase " different in intrinsic nature." The important points are (1) that it is a kind of difference which does *not* hold between two things, when they are *merely* numerically different, but only when, besides being numerically different, they are also *not* exactly alike and (2) that it is *not* identical with qualitative difference ; although qualitative difference is one particular species of it. The conception seems to me to be an extremely important and fundamental one, although, so far as I can see, it has no quite simple and unambiguous name : and this is the reason why I have dwelt on it at such length. " Not exactly like " is the least ambiguous way of expressing it ; but this has the disadvantage that it looks as if the idea of exact likeness were the fundamental one from which this was derived, whereas I believe the contrary to be the case. For this reason it is perhaps better to stick to the cumbrous phrase "different in intrinsic nature."

So much for the question what is meant by saying of two things that they " differ in intrinsic nature." We have now to turn to the more difficult question as to what is meant by the words " impossible " and " necessary " in the statement : A kind of value is intrinsic if and only if, it is *impossible* that x and y should have different values of the kind, unless they differ in intrinsic nature ; and in the equivalent statement : A kind of value is intrinsic if and only if, when anything possesses it, that same thing or anything exactly like it would *necessarily* or *must* always, under all circumstances, possess it in exactly the same degree.

As regards the meaning of this necessity and impossibility, we may begin by making two points clear.

(1) It is sometimes contended, and with some plausibility, that what we mean by saying that it is *possible* for a thing which possesses one predicate F to possess another G, is, sometimes at least, merely that some things which possess F do in fact also possess G. And if we give this meaning to "possible," the corresponding meaning of the statement it is *impossible* for a thing which

possesses F to possess G will be merely : Things which possess F never do in fact possess G.   If, then, we understood "impossible" in this sense, the condition for the "internality" of a kind of value, which I have stated by saying that if a kind of value is to be "intrinsic" it must be *impossible* for two things to possess it in different degrees, if they are exactly like one another, will amount merely to saying that no two things which are exactly like one another ever do, in fact, possess it in different degrees.   It follows, that, if this were all that were meant, this condition would be satisfied, if only it were true (as for all I know it may be) that, in the case of all things which possess any particular kind of intrinsic value, there happens to be nothing else in the Universe exactly like any one of them ; for if this were so, it would, of course, follow that no two things which are exactly alike did in fact possess the kind of value in question in different degrees, for the simple reason that everything which possessed it at all would be unique in the sense that there was nothing else exactly like it.   If this were all that were meant, therefore, we could prove any particular kind of value to satisfy this condition, by merely proving that there never has in fact and never will be anything exactly like any one of the things which possess it : and our assertion that it satisfied this condition would merely be an empirical generalisation.   Moreover if this were all that was meant it would obviously be by no means certain that purely subjective predicates could not satisfy the condition in question ; since it would be satisfied by any subjective predicate of which it happened to be true that everything which possessed it was, in fact, unique—that there was nothing exactly like it ; and for all I know there may be many subjective predicates of which this is true. It is, therefore, scarcely necessary to say that I am not using "impossible" in this sense. When I say that a kind of value, to be intrinsic, must satisfy the condition that it must be *impossible* for two things exactly alike to possess it in different degrees, I do not mean by this condition anything which a kind of value could be proved to satisfy, by the mere empirical fact that there was nothing else exactly like any of the things which possessed it. It is, of course, an essential part of my meaning that we must be able to say not merely that no two exactly similar things do *in fact* possess it in different degrees, but that, *if* there had been or were going to be anything exactly similar to a thing which does possess it, even though, in fact, there has not and won't be any such thing, that thing would have possessed or would possess the kind of value in question in exactly the same degree. It is essential to this meaning of "impossibility" that it should entitle us to assert what *would* have been the case, under conditions which never have been and never will be realised ; and it seems obvious that no mere empirical generalisation can entitle us to do this.

But (2) to say that I am not using ' necessity ' in this first sense, is by no means sufficient to explain what I do mean. For it certainly seems as if causal laws (though this is disputed) do entitle us to make assertions of the very kind that mere empirical generalisations do not entitle us to make. In virtue of a causal law we do seem to be entitled to assert such things as that, if a given thing had had a property or were to have a property F which it didn't have or won't have, it *would* have had or *would* have some other property G. And it might, therefore, be thought that the kind of ' necessity ' and ' impossibility ' I am talking of is this kind of causal ' necessity ' and ' impossibility.' It is, therefore, important to insist that I do *not* mean this kind either. If this were all I meant, it would again be by no means obvious, that purely subjective predicates might not satisfy our second condition. It may, for instance, for all I know, be true that there are causal laws which insure that in the case of everything that is 'beautiful,' anything exactly like any of these things would, in this Universe, excite a particular kind of feeling in everybody to whom it were presented in a particular way : and if that were so, we should have a subjective predicate which satisfied the condition that, when a given thing possesses that predicate, it is impossible (in the causal sense) that any exactly similar thing should not also possess it. The kind of necessity I am talking of is not, therefore, mere causal necessity either. When I say that if a given thing possesses a certain degree of intrinsic value, anything precisely similar to it *would* necessarily *have* possessed that value in exactly the same degree, I mean that it *would* have done so, even if it had existed in a Universe in which the causal laws were quite different from what they are in this one. I mean, in short, that it is *impossible* for any precisely similar thing to possess a different value, in precisely such a sense as that, in which it is, I think, generally admitted that it is *not* impossible that causal laws should have been different from what they are—a sense of impossibility, therefore, which certainly does not depend merely on causal laws.

That there is such a sense of necessity—a sense which entitles us to say that what has F *would* have G, even if causal laws were quite different from what they are—is, I think, quite clear from such instances as the following. Suppose you take a particular patch of colour, which is yellow. We can, I think, say with certainty that any patch exactly like that one, *would* be yellow, even if it existed in a Universe in which causal laws were quite different from what they are in this one. We can say that any such patch *must* be yellow, quite unconditionally, whatever the circumstances, and whatever the causal laws. And it is in a sense similar to this, in respect of the fact that it is neither empirical nor causal, that I mean the 'must' to be understood, when I say that if a kind of value is to be 'intrinsic,' then, supposing a given thing possesses it in a certain degree, anything exactly like that thing *must* possess it in exactly the same degree. To say, of 'beauty' or 'goodness' that they are 'intrinsic' is only, therefore, to say that this thing which is obviously true of 'yellowness' and 'blueness' and 'redness' is true of them. And if we give this sense to 'must' in our definition, then I think it is obvious that to say of a given kind of value that it is intrinsic *is* inconsistent with its being 'subjective.' For there is, I think, pretty clearly no subjective predicate of which we can say thus unconditionally, that, *if* a given thing possesses it, then anything exactly like that thing, *would*, under any circumstances, and under any causal laws, also possess it. For instance, whatever kind of feeling you take, it is plainly not true that supposing I have that feeling towards a given thing A, then *I* should necessarily under any circumstances have that feeling towards anything precisely similar to A: for the simple reason that a thing precisely similar to A *might* exist in a Universe in which I did not exist at all. And similarly it is not true of any feeling whatever, that if *somebody* has that feeling towards a given thing A, then, in any Universe, in which a thing precisely similar to A existed, *somebody* would have that feeling towards it. Nor finally is it even true, that if it is true of a given thing A, that, under actual causal laws, any one to whom A were presented in a certain way *would* have a certain feeling towards it, then the same hypothetical predicate would, in any Universe, belong to anything precisely similar to A : in every case it seems to be possible that there *might* be a Universe, in which the causal laws were such that the proposition would not be true.

It is, then, because in my definition of 'intrinsic' value the 'must' is to be understood in this unconditional sense, that I think that the proposition that a kind of value is 'intrinsic' is inconsistent with its being subjective. But it should be observed that in holding that there is this inconsistency, I am contradicting a doctrine which seems to be held by many philosophers. There are, as you probably know, some philosophers who insist strongly on a doctrine which they express by saying that no relations are purely external. And so far as I can make out one thing which they mean by this is just that, whenever x has any relation whatever which y has not got, x and y *cannot* be exactly alike : That any difference in relation necessarily entails a difference in intrinsic nature. There is, I think, no doubt that when these philosophers say this, they mean by their 'cannot' and 'necessarily' an unconditional 'cannot' and 'must.' And hence it follows they are holding that, if, for instance, a thing A pleases me now, then any other thing, B, precisely similar to A, must, under any circumstances, and in any Universe, please me also : since, if B did not please me, it would *not* possess a relation which A does possess, and therefore, by their principle, *could* not be precisely similar to A—*must* differ from it in intrinsic nature. But it seems to me to be obvious that this principle is false. If it were true, it would follow that I can know *a priori* such things as that no patch of colour which is seen by you and is not seen by me is ever exactly like any patch which is seen by me and is not seen by you ; or that no patch of colour which is surrounded by a red ring is ever exactly like one which is not so surrounded. But it is surely obvious, that, whether these things are true or not they are things which I cannot know *a priori*. It is simply *not* evident *a priori* that no patch of colour which is seen by A and not by B is ever exactly like one which is seen by B and not by A, and that no patch of colour which is surrounded by a red ring is ever exactly like one which is not. And this illustration serves to bring out very well both what is meant by saying of such a predicate as 'beautiful' that it is 'intrinsic,' and why, if it is, it cannot be subjective. What is meant is just that if A is beautiful and B is not, you could know *a priori* that A and B are *not* exactly alike ; whereas, with any such subjective predicate, as that of exciting a particular feeling in me, or that of being a thing which would excite such a feeling in any spectator, you cannot tell *a priori* that a thing A which did possess such a predicate and a thing B which did not, could not be exactly alike.

It seems to me, therefore, quite certain, in spite of the dogma that no relations are purely external, that there are many predicates, such for instance as most (if not all) subjective predicates or the objective one of being surrounded by a red ring, which do *not* depend solely on the intrinsic nature of what possesses them : or, in other words, of which it is *not* true that if x possesses them and y does not, x and y *must* differ in intrinsic nature. But what precisely is meant by this unconditional 'must,' I must confess I don't know. The obvious thing to suggest is that it is the logical 'must,' which certainly is unconditional in just this sense : the kind of necessity, which we assert to hold, for instance, when we say that whatever is a right-angled triangle *must* be a triangle, or that whatever is yellow *must* be. either yellow or blue. But I must say I cannot see that all unconditional necessity is of this nature. I do not see how it can be deduced from any logical law that, if a given patch of colour be yellow, then any patch which were exactly like the first would be yellow too. And similarly in our case of 'intrinsic' value, though I think it is true that beauty, for instance, is 'intrinsic,' I do not see how it can be deduced from any logical law, that if A is beautiful, anything that were exactly like A would be beautiful too, in exactly the same degree.

Moreover, though I do believe that both "yellow" (in the sense in which it applies to sense-data) and "beautiful" are predicates which, in this unconditional sense, depend only on the intrinsic nature of what possesses them, there seems to me to be an extremely important difference between them which constitutes a further difficulty in the way of getting quite clear as to what this unconditional sense of "must" is. The difference I mean is one which I am inclined to express by saying that though both yellowness and beauty are predicates which *depend* only on the intrinsic nature of what possesses them, yet while yellowness is itself an *intrinsic* predicate, *beauty* is not. Indeed it seems to me to be one of the most important truths about predicates of value, that though many of them *are* intrinsic kinds of value, in the sense I have defined, yet *none* of them are intrinsic properties, in the sense in which such properties as "yellow" or the property of "being a state of pleasure" or "being a state of things which contains a balance of pleasure" are intrinsic properties. It is obvious, for instance, that, if we are to reject *all* naturalistic theories of value, we must not only reject those theories, according to which no kind of value would be intrinsic, but must also reject such theories as those which assert, for instance, that to say that a state of mind is good

is to say that it is a state of being pleased ; or that
to say that a state of things is good is to say that it
contains a balance of pleasure over pain.   There
are, in short, two entirely different types of
naturalistic theory, the difference between which
may be illustrated by the difference between the
assertion, "A is good" *means* "A is pleasant" and
the assertion "A is good" *means* "A is a state of
pleasure."   Theories of the former type imply that
goodness is *not* an intrinsic kind of value, whereas
theories of the latter type imply equally emphatically that it is : since obviously such predicates as
that "of being a state of pleasure," or "containing a
balance of pleasure," *are* predicates like "yellow"
in respect of the fact that if a given thing possesses
them, anything exactly like the thing in question
must possess them.   It seems to me equally obvious
that *both* types of theory are false : but I do not
know how to exclude them both except by saying
that two different propositions are both true of
goodness, namely : (1) that it does depend *only* on
the intrinsic nature of what possesses it—which
excludes theories of the first type and (2) that,
though this is so, it is yet not itself an intrinsic
property—which excludes those of the second.   It
was for this reason that I said above that, if there
are any intrinsic kinds of value, they would
constitute a class of predicates which is, perhaps,
unique ; for I cannot think of any other predicate
which resembles them in respect of the fact, that
though *not* itself intrinsic, it yet shares with intrinsic
properties the characteristics of depending solely on
the intrinsic nature of what possesses it.   So far as
I know, certain predicates of value are the only
non-intrinsic properties which share with intrinsic
properties this characteristic of depending only on
the intrinsic nature of what possesses them.
     If, however, we are thus to say that predicates of

value, though *dependent* solely on intrinsic properties, are not themselves intrinsic properties, there must be some characteristic belonging to intrinsic properties which predicates of value never possess. And it seems to me quite obvious that there is ; only I can't see *what* it is. It seems to me quite obvious that if you assert of a given state of things that it contains a balance of pleasure over pain, you are asserting of it not only a *different* predicate, from what you would be asserting of it if you said it was "good"—but a predicate which is of quite a different *kind* ; and in the same way that when you assert of a patch of colour that it is "yellow," the predicate you assert is not only *different* from "beautiful," but of quite a different *kind*, in the same way as before. And of course the mere fact that many people have thought that goodness and beauty were subjective is evidence that there is *some* great difference of kind between them and such predicates as being yellow or containing a balance of pleasure. But *what* the difference is, if we suppose, as I suppose, that goodness and beauty are *not* subjective, and that they do share with "yellowness" and "containing pleasure," the property of depending *solely* on the intrinsic nature of what possesses them, I confess I cannot say. I can only vaguely express the kind of difference I feel there to be by saying that intrinsic properties seem to *describe* the intrinsic nature of what possesses them in a sense in which predicates of value never do. If you could enumerate *all* the intrinsic properties a given thing possessed, you would have given a *complete* description of it, and would not need to mention any predicates of value it possessed ; whereas no description of a given thing could be *complete* which omitted any intrinsic property. But, in any case, owing to the fact that predicates of intrinsic value are not themselves intrinsic properties, you cannot define "intrinsic property," in the way which at first sight seems obviously the right one. You cannot say that an intrinsic property is a property such that, if one thing possesses it and another does not, the intrinsic nature of the two things *must* be different. For this is the very thing which we are maintaining to be true of predicates of intrinsic value, while at the same time we say that they are *not* intrinsic properties. Such a definition of "intrinsic property" would therefore only be possible if, we could say that the necessity there is that, if x and y possess different intrinsic properties, their nature must be different, is a necessity of a *different kind* from the necessity there is that, if x and y are of different intrinsic values, their nature must be different, although both necessities are unconditional. And it seems to me possible that this is the true explanation. But, if so, it obviously adds to the difficulty of explaining the meaning of the unconditional "must," since, in this case, there would be two different meanings of "must," both unconditional, and yet neither, apparently, identical with the logical "must."

EXTERNAL AND INTERNAL RELATIONS

In the index to *Appearance and Reality* (First Edition) Mr. Bradley declares that *all* relations are "intrinsical"; and the following are some of the phrases by means of which he tries to explain what he means by this assertion. "A relation must at both ends *affect*, and pass into, the being of its terms" (p. 364). "Every relation essentially penetrates the being of its terms, and is, in this sense, intrinsical" (p. 392). "To stand in a relation and not to be relative, to support it and yet not to be infected and undermined by it, seems out of the question" (p. 142). And a good many other philosophers seem inclined to take the same view about relations which Mr. Bradley is here trying to express. Other phrases which seem to be sometimes used to express it, or a part of it, are these : "No relations are purely external"; "All relations qualify or modify or make a difference to the terms between which they hold"; "No terms are independent of any of the relations in which they stand to other terms." (See *e.g.*, Joachim, *The Nature of Truth*, pp. 11, 12, 46).

It is, I think, by no means easy to make out exactly what these philosophers mean by these assertions. And the main object of this paper is to try to define clearly one proposition, which, even if it does not give the whole of what they mean, seems to me to be always implied by what they mean, and to be certainly false. I shall try to make clear the exact meaning of this proposition, to point out some of its most important consequences, and to distinguish it clearly from certain other propositions which are, I think, more or less liable to be confused with it. And I shall maintain that, if we give to the assertion that a relation is "internal" the meaning which this proposition would give to it, then, though, in that sense, *some* relations are "internal," others, no less certainly, are not, but are "purely external."

To begin with, we may, I think, clear the ground, by putting on one side two propositions about relations, which, though they seem sometimes to be confused with the view we are discussing, do, I think, quite certainly not give the whole meaning of that view.

The first is a proposition which is quite certainly and obviously true of all relations, without exception, and which, though it raises points of great difficulty, can, I think, be clearly enough stated for its truth to be obvious. It is the proposition that, in the case of any relation whatever, the kind of fact which we express by saying that a given term A has that relation to another term B, or to a pair of terms B and C, or to three terms B, C, and D, and so on, in no case simply consists in the terms in question *together with* the relation. Thus the fact which we express by saying that Edward VII was father of George V, obviously does not simply consist in Edward, George, *and* the relation of fatherhood. In order that the fact may be, it is obviously not sufficient that there should merely be George and Edward and the relation of fatherhood ; it is further necessary that the relation should *relate* Edward to George, and not only so, but also that it should relate them in the particular way which we express by saying that Edward was

father of George, and not merely in the way which
we should express by saying that George was father
of Edward.   This proposition is, I think, obviously
true of all relations without exception : and the only
reason why I have mentioned it is because, in an
article in which Mr. Bradley criticises Mr. Russell
(*Mind*, 1910, p. 179), he seems to suggest that it is
inconsistent with the proposition that any relations
are merely external, and because, so far as I can
make out, some other people who maintain that all
relations are internal seem sometimes to think that
their contention follows from this proposition.   The
way in which Mr. Bradley puts it is that such facts
are unities which are not *completely analysable* ; and
this is, of course, true, if it means merely that in
the case of no such fact is there any set of
constituents of which we can truly say : This fact
is *identical with* these constituents.   But whether
from this it follows that all relations are internal
must of course depend upon what is meant by the
latter statement.   If it be merely used to express
this proposition itself, or anything which follows
from it, then, of course, there can be no doubt that
all relations are internal.   But I think there is no
doubt that those who say this do not mean by their
words *merely* this obvious proposition itself ; and I
am going to point out something which I think they
always imply, and which certainly does *not* follow
from it.

   The second proposition which, I think, may be
put aside at once as certainly not giving the whole
of what is meant, is the proposition which is, I
think, the natural meaning of the phrases "All
relations modify or affect their terms" or "All
relations make a difference to their terms."   There
is one perfectly natural and intelligible sense in
which a given relation may be said to modify a term
which stands in that relation, namely, the sense in

which we should say that, if, by putting a stick of sealing-wax into a flame, we make the sealing-wax melt, its relationship to the flame has modified the sealing-wax. This is a sense of the word " modify " in which part of what is meant by saying of any term that it is modified, is that it has actually undergone a change : and I think it is clear that a sense in which this is part of its meaning is the only one in which the word " modify " can properly be used. If, however, those who say that all relations modify their terms were using the word in this, its proper, sense, part of what would be meant by this assertion would be that all terms which have relations at all actually undergo changes. Such an assertion would be obviously false, for the simple reason that there are terms which have relations and which yet never change at all. And I think it is quite clear that those who assert that all relations are internal, in the sense we are concerned with, mean by this something which could be consistently asserted to be true of all relations without exception, even if it were admitted that some terms which have relations do not change. When, therefore, they use the phrase that all relations " modify " their terms as equivalent to "all relations are internal," they must be using "modify" in some meta-phorical sense other than its natural one. I think, indeed, that most of them would be inclined to assert that in every case in which a term A comes to have to another term B a relation, which it did not have to B in some immediately preceding interval, its having of that relation to that term causes it to undergo some change, which it would not have undergone if it had not stood in precisely hat relation to B and I think perhaps they would hink that this proposition follows from some proposition which is true of all relations, without exception, and which is what they mean by saying that all relations are internal. The question whether the coming into a new relation does thus always cause some modification in the term which comes into it is one which is often discussed, as if it had something to do with the question whether all relations are internal ; as when, for instance, it is discussed whether knowledge of a thing alters the thing known.   And for my part I should maintain that this proposition is certainly not true.   But what I am concerned with now is not the question whether it is true, but simply to point out that, so far as I can see, it can have nothing to do with the question whether all relations are internal, for the simple reason that it cannot possibly follow from any proposition with regard to *all* relations without exception.   It asserts with regard to all relational properties of a certain kind, that they have a certain kind of *effect* ; and no proposition of this sort can, I think follow from any universal proposition with regard to *all* relations.

We have, therefore, rejected as certainly not giving the whole meaning of the dogma that all relations are internal : (1) the obviously true proposition that no relational facts are *completely* analysable, in the precise sense which I gave to that assertion ; and (2) the obviously false proposition that all relations modify their terms, in the natural sense of the term " modify," in which it always has as part of its meaning " cause to undergo a change."   And we have also seen that this false proposition that any relation which a term comes to have always causes it to undergo a change is wholly irrelevant to the question whether *all* relations are internal or not.   We have seen finally that if the assertion that all relations modify their terms is to be understood as equivalent to the assertion that all are internal, " modify " must be understood in some metaphorical sense. The question is: What is this metaphorical sense?

And one point is, I think, pretty clear to begin with. It is obvious that, in the case of some relations, a given term A may have the relation in question, not only to one other term, but to several different terms. If, for instance, we consider the relation of fatherhood, it is obvious that a man may be father, not only of one, but of several different children. And those who say that all relations modify their terms always mean, I think, not merely that every different relation which a term has modifies it; but also that, where the relation is one which the term has to several different other terms, then, in the case of *each* of these terms, it is modified by the fact that it has the relation in question to that particular term. If, for instance, A is father of three children, B, C, and D, they mean to assert that he is modified, not merely by being a father, but by being the father of B, also by being the father of C, and also by being the father of D. The mere assertion that all *relations* modify their terms does not, of course, make it quite clear that this is what is meant; but I think there is no doubt that it is always meant; and I think we can express it more clearly by using a term, which I have already introduced, and saying the doctrine is that all *relational properties* modify their terms, in a sense which remains to be defined. I think there is no difficulty in understanding what I mean by a *relational property*. If A is father of B, then what you assert of A when you say that he is so is a *relational property*—namely the property of being father of B; and it is quite clear that this property is not itself a *relation*, in the same fundamental sense in which the relation of fatherhood is so; and also that, if C is a different child from B, then the property of being father of C is a different relational property from that of being father of B, although there is only *one* relation, that of fatherhood, from which both are derived. So far as I can make out, those philosophers who talk of all *relations* being internal, often actually mean by "relations" "relational properties"; when they talk of all the "relations" of a given term, they mean all its relational properties, and not merely all the different relations, of each of which it is true that the term has that relation to something. It will, I think, conduce to clearness to use a different word for these two entirely different uses of the term "relation" to call "fatherhood" a relation, and "fatherhood of B" a "relational property." And the fundamental proposition, which is meant by the assertion that all relations are internal, is, I think, a proposition with regard to relational properties, and not with regard to relations properly so-called. There is no doubt that those who maintain this dogma mean to maintain that all relational properties are related in a peculiar way to the terms which possess them— that they modify or are internal to them, in some metaphorical sense. And once we have defined what this sense is in which a *relational property* can be said to be internal to a term which possesses it, we can easily derive from it a corresponding sense in which the *relations*, strictly so called, from which relational properties are derived, can be said to be internal.

Our question is then : What is the metaphorical sense of "modify" in which the proposition that all relations are internal is equivalent to the proposition that all relational properties "modify" the terms which possess them? I think it is clear that the term "modify" would never have been used at all to express the relation meant, unless there had been some analogy between this relation and that which we have seen is the proper sense of "modify," namely, *causes* to change. And I think we can see where the analogy comes in by considering the statement, with regard to any particular term A and any relational property P which belongs to it, that A *would have been different from what it is if it had not had* P : the statement, for instance, that Edward VII would have been different if he had not been father of George V. This is a thing which we can obviously truly say of A and P, in some sense, whenever it is true of P that it *modified* A in the proper sense of the word : if the being held in the flame causes the sealing-wax to melt, we can truly say (in some sense) that the sealing-wax would not have been in a melted state if it had not been in the flame. But it seems as if it were a thing which might also be true of A and P, where it is *not* true that the possession of P *caused* A to change ; since the mere assertion that A would have been different, if it had not had P, does not necessarily imply that the possession of P *caused* A to have any property which it would not have had otherwise. And those who say that all relations are internal do sometimes tend to speak as if what they meant could be put in the form : In the case of every relational property which a thing has, it is always true that the thing which has it would have been different if it had not had that property ; they sometimes say even : If P be a relational property and A a term which has it, then it is always true that A *would not have been A* if it had not had P. This is, I think, obviously a clumsy way of expressing anything which could possibly be true, since, taken strictly, it implies the self-contradictory proposition that if A had not had P, it would not have been true that A did not have P. But it is nevertheless a more or less natural way of expressing a proposition which might quite well be true, namely, that, supposing

A has P, then anything which had not had P would necessarily have been different from A. This is the proposition which I wish to suggest as giving the metaphorical meaning of " P *modifies* A," of which we are in search. It is a proposition to which I think a perfectly precise meaning can be given, and one which does not at all imply that the possession of P *caused* any change in A, but which might conceivably be true of all terms and all the relational properties they have, without exception. And it seems to me that it is not unnatural that the proposition that this is true of P and A, should have been expressed in the form, " P modifies A," since it can be more or less naturally expressed in the perverted form, " If A had not had P it would have been different,"—a form of words, which, as we saw, can also be used whenever P does, in the proper sense, modify A.

I want to suggest, then, that one thing which is always implied by the dogma that, "All relations are internal," is that, in the case of every relational property, it can always be truly asserted of any term A which has that property, that any term which had not had it would necessarily have been different from A.

This is the proposition to which I want to direct attention. And there are two phrases in it, which require some further explanation.

The first is the phrase "would necessarily have been." And the meaning of this can be explained, in a preliminary way, as follows :—To say of a pair of properties P and Q, that any term which had had P would necessarily have had Q, is equivalent to saying that, in every case, from the proposition with regard to any given term that it has P, it *follows* that that term has Q : *follows* being understood in the sense in which from the proposition with regard to any term, that it is a right angle, it *follows* that it is an angle, and in which from the proposition with regard to any term that it is red it *follows* that it is coloured. There is obviously some very important sense in which from the proposition that a thing is a right angle, it does follow that it is an angle, and from the proposition that a thing is red it does follow that it is coloured. And what I am maintaining is that the metaphorical sense of "modify," in which it is maintained that all relational properties modify the subjects which possess them, can be defined by reference to this sense of "follows." The definition is: To say of a given relational property P that it modifies or is internal to a given term A which possesses it, is to say that from the proposition that a thing has not got P it follows that that thing is different from A. In other words, it is to say that the property of *not* possessing P, and the property of being different from A are related to one another in the peculiar way in which the property of being a right-angled triangle is related to that of being a triangle, or that of being red to that of being coloured.

To complete the definition it is necessary, however, to define the sense in which "different from A" is to be understood. There are two different senses which the statement that A is different from B may bear. It may be meant merely that A is *numerically* different from B, *other* than B, not identical with B. Or it may be meant that not only is this the case, but also that A is related to B in a way which can be roughly expressed by saying that A is *qualitatively* different from B. And of these two meanings, those who say "All relations make a *difference* to their terms," always, I think, mean difference in the latter sense and not merely in the former. That is to say, they mean, that if P be a relational property which belongs to A, then the absence of P entails not only numerical difference from A, but qualitative difference. But, in fact, from the proposition that a thing is qualitatively different from A, it does follow that it is also numerically different. And hence they are maintaining that every relational property is "internal to" its terms in both of two different senses at the same time. They are maintaining that, if P be a relational property which belongs to A, then P is internal to A both in the sense (1) that the absence of P entails qualitative difference from A ; and (2) that the absence of P entails numerical difference from A. It seems to me that neither of these propositions is true ; and I will say something about each in turn.

As for the first, I said before that I think some relational properties really are "internal to" their terms, though by no means all are. But, if we understand "internal to" in this first sense, I am not really sure that any are. In order to get an example of one which was, we should have, I think, to say that any two different qualities are always *qualitatively* different from one another : that, for instance, it is not only the case that anything which is pure red is qualitatively different from anything which is pure blue, but that the quality "pure red" itself is qualitatively different from the quality "pure blue." I am not quite sure that we can say this, but I think we can ; and if so, it is easy to get an example of a relational property which is internal in our first sense. The quality "orange" is intermediate in shade between the qualities yellow and red. This is a relational property, and it is quite clear that, on our assumption, it is an internal one. Since it is quite clear that any quality which were *not* intermediate between yellow and red, would necessarily be *other* than orange ; and if any quality *other* than orange must be *qualitatively* different

from orange, then it follows that "intermediate between yellow and red" is internal to "orange." That
is to say, the absence of the relational property "intermediate between yellow and red," *entails* the
property "different in quality from orange."

There is then, I think, a difficulty in being sure
that *any* relational properties are internal in this
first sense. But, if what we want to do is to show
that some are *not*, and that therefore the dogma
that all relations are internal is false, I think the
most conclusive reason for saying this is that if *all*
were internal in this first sense, all would necessarily
be internal in the second, and that this is plainly
false. I think, in fact, the most important consequence of the dogma that all relations are internal,
is that it follows from it that all relational properties
are internal in this second sense. I propose, therefore, at once to consider this proposition, with a
view to bringing out quite clearly what it means
and involves, and what are the main reasons for
saying that it is false.

The proposition in question is that, if P be a
relational property and A a term to which it does in
fact belong, then, no matter what P and A may be,
it may always be truly asserted of them, that any
term which had *not* possessed P would necessarily
have been other than—numerically different from—
A : or in other words, that A would necessarily, in
all conceivable circumstances, have possessed P.
And with this sense of "internal," as distinguished
from that which says *qualitatively different*, it is
quite easy to point out some relational properties
which certainly are internal in this sense. Let us
take as an example the relational property which
we assert to belong to a visual sense-datum when
we say of it that it has another visual sense-datum
as a spatial part : the assertion, for instance, with
regard to a coloured patch half of which is red and

half yellow: "This whole patch contains this patch'
(where "this patch" is a proper name for the red
half). It is here, I think, quite plain that, in a
perfectly clear and intelligible sense, we can say
that any whole, which had not contained that red
patch, could not have been identical with the whole
in question : that from the proposition with regard
to any term whatever that it does not contain *that*
particular patch it *follows* that that term is *other*
than the whole in question—though *not* necessarily
that it is qualitatively different from it. *That* particular whole could not have existed without having
that particular patch for a part. But it seems no
less clear, at first sight, that there are many other
relational properties of which this is not true. In
order to get an example, we have only to consider
the relation which the red patch has to the whole
patch, instead of considering as before that which
the whole has to it. It seems quite clear that,
though the whole could not have existed without
having the red patch for a part, the red patch might
perfectly well have existed without being part of
that particular whole. In other words, though
every relational property of the form "having *this*
for a spatial part" is "internal" in our sense, it
seems equally clear that every property of the form
"is a spatial part of this whole" is *not* internal, but
purely external. Yet this last, according to me, is
one of the things which the dogma of internal
relations denies. It implies that it is just as
necessary that anything, which is in fact a part of a
particular whole, should be a part of that whole, as
that any whole, which has a particular thing for a
part, should have that thing for a part. It implies,
in fact, quite generally, that any term which does in
fact have a particular relational property, could not
have existed without having that property. And in
saying this it obviously flies in the face of common

sense. It seems quite obvious that in the case of many relational properties which things have, the fact that they have them is *a mere matter of fact :* that the things in question *might* have existed without having them. That this, which seems obvious, is true, seems to me to be the most important thing that can be meant by saying that some relations are purely external. And the difficulty is to see how any philosopher could have supposed that it was not true : that, for instance, the relation of part to whole is no more external than that of whole to part. I will give at once one main reason which seems to me to have led to the view, that *all* relational properties are internal in this sense.

What I am maintaining is the common-sense view, which seems obviously true, that it may be true that A has in fact got P and yet also true that A might have existed without having P. And I say that this is equivalent to saying that it may be true that A has P, and yet *not* true that from the proposition that a thing has *not* got P it *follows* that that thing is *other* than A—numerically different from it. And one reason why this is disputed is, I think, simply because it is in fact true that if A has P, and x has *not*, it *does* follow that x is other than A. These two propositions, the one which I admit to be true (1) that if A has P, and x has not, it *does* follow that x is other than A, and the one which I maintain to be false (2) that if A has P, then from the proposition with regard to any term x that it has not got P, it *follows* that x is other than A, are, I think, easily confused with one another. And it is in fact the case that if they are not different, or if (2) follows from (1), then no relational properties are external. For (1) is certainly true, and (2) is certainly equivalent to asserting that none are. It is therefore absolutely essential, if we are to maintain external relations, to maintain that (2) does *not* follow from (1). These two propositions (1) and (2), with regard to which I maintain that (1) is true, and (2) is false, can be put in another way, as follows : (1) asserts that if A has P, then any term which has not, *must* be other than A. (2) asserts that if A has P, then any term which had not, *would necessarily be* other than A. And when they are put in this form, it is, I think, easy to see why they should be confused : you have only to confuse "must" or "is necessarily" with "would necessarily be." And their connexion with the question of external relations can be brought out as follows : To maintain external relations you have to maintain such things as that, though Edward VII was in fact father of George V, he *might* have existed without being father of George V. But to maintain this, you have to maintain that it is *not* true that a person who was *not* father of George would necessarily have been other than Edward. Yet it is, in fact, the case, that any person who was not the father of George, *must* have been other than Edward. Unless, therefore, you can maintain that from this true proposition it does *not* follow that any person who was *not* father of George *would necessarily* have been other than Edward, you will have to give up the view that Edward might have existed without being father of George.

By far the most important point in connexion with the dogma of internal relations seems to me to be simply to see clearly the difference between these two propositions (1) and (2), and that (2) does *not* follow from (1). If this is not understood, nothing in connexion with the dogma, can, I think, be understood. And perhaps the difference may seem so clear, that no more need be said about it. But I cannot help thinking it is not clear to everybody, and that it does involve the rejection of certain views, which are sometimes held as to the meaning of "follows." So I will try to put the point again in a perfectly strict form.

Let P be a relational property, and A a term to which it does in fact belong. I propose to define what is meant by saying that P is internal to A (in the sense we are now concerned with) as meaning that from the proposition that a thing has not got P, it "follows" that it is *other* than A.

That is to say, this proposition asserts that between the two properties "not having P" and "other than A," there holds that relation which holds between the property "being a right angle" and the property "being an angle," or between the property "red" and the property "coloured," and which we express by saying that, in the case of any thing whatever, from the proposition that that thing is a right angle it follows, or is deducible, that it is an angle.

Let us now adopt certain conventions for expressing this proposition.

We require, first of all, some term to express the *converse* of that relation which we assert to hold between a particular proposition q and a particular proposition p, when we assert that q *follows from* or *is deducible from p*. Let us use the term "entails" to express the converse of this relation. We shall then be able to say truly that "p entails q," when and only when we are able to say truly that "q follows from p" or "is deducible from p," in the sense in which the conclusion of a syllogism in Barbara follows from the two premisses, taken as one conjunctive proposition; or in which the proposition "This is coloured" follows from "This is red." "p entails q" will be related to "q follows from p" in the same way in which "A is greater than B" is related to "B is less than A."

We require, next, some short and clear method of expressing the proposition, with regard to two properties P and Q, that *any* proposition which asserts of a given thing that it has the property P *entails* the proposition that the thing in question also has the property Q. Let us express this proposition in the form

$$x\text{P entails } x\text{Q}$$

That is to say "xP entails xQ" is to mean the same as " Each one of all the various propositions, which are alike in respect of the fact that each asserts with regard to some given thing that that thing has P, entails *that one* among the various propositions, alike in respect of the fact that each asserts with regard to some given thing that that thing has Q, which makes this assertion with regard to the *same thing*, with regard to which the proposition of the first class asserts that it has P." In other words "xP entails xQ" is to be true, if and only if the proposition " AP entails AQ " is true, and if also all propositions which resemble this, in the way in which " BP entails BQ " resembles it, are true also ; where "AP" means the same as "A has P," "AQ" the same as "A has Q" etc., etc.

We require, next, some way of expressing the proposition, with regard to two properties P and Q, that any proposition which *denies* of a given thing that it has P *entails* the proposition, with regard to the thing in question, that it has Q.

Let us, in the case of any proposition, p, express the contradictory of that proposition by $\bar{p}$. The proposition " It is not the case that A has P " will then be expressed by $\overline{\text{AP}}$; and it will then be natural, in accordance with the last convention to express the proposition that any proposition which *denies* of a given thing that it has P *entails* the proposition, with regard to the thing in question, that it has Q, by

$$\overline{x\text{P}} \text{ entails } x\text{Q}.$$

And we require, finally, some short way of expressing the proposition, with regard to two things B and A, that B is *other* than (or not identical with) A. Let us express " B is identical with A " by " B = A "; and it will then be natural, according to the last convention, to express " B is not identical with A " by

$$\overline{B = A.}$$

We have now got everything which is required for expressing, in a short symbolic form, the proposition, with regard to a given thing A and a given relational property P, which A in fact possessess, that P is *internal* to A. The required expression is

$$\overline{x}P \text{ entails } \overline{(x = A)}$$

which is to mean the same as " Every proposition which asserts of any given thing that it has not got P *entails* the proposition, with regard to the thing in question, that it is other than A." And this proposition is, of course, logically equivalent to

$$(x = A) \text{ entails } x\, P$$

where we are using "logically equivalent," in such a sense that to say of any proposition p that it is logically equivalent to another proposition q is to say that both p entails q and q entails p. This last proposition again, is, so far as I can see, either identical with or logically equivalent to the propositions expressed by "anything which were identical with A would, in any conceivable universe, necessarily have P " or by "A could not have existed in any possible world without having P "; just as the proposition expressed by " In any possible world a right angle must be an angle " is, I take it, either identical with or logically equivalent to the proposition " (x is a right angle) entails (x is an angle)."

We have now, therefore, got a short means of symbolising, with regard to any particular thing A and any particular property P, the proposition that P is *internal* to A in the second of the two senses

distinguished on p. 286.   But we still require a means
of symbolising the general proposition that *every*
relational property is internal to any term which
possesses it—the proposition, namely, which was
referred to on p. 287, as the most important
consequence of the dogma of internal relations, and
which was called (2) on p. 289.

In order to get this, let us first get a means of
expressing with regard to some one particular
relational property P, the proposition that P is
internal to *any* term which possesses it.   This is a
proposition which takes the form of asserting with
regard to one particular property, namely P, that
any term which possesses that property also
possesses another—namely the one expressed by
saying that P is internal to it.   It is, that is to say,
an ordinary universal proposition, like "All men
are mortal."   But such a form of words is, as has
often been pointed out, ambiguous.   It may stand
for either of two different propositions.   It may
stand merely for the proposition "There is nothing,
which both is a man, and is not mortal"—a
proposition which may also be expressed by "If
anything is a man, that thing is mortal," and which
is distinguished by the fact that it makes no
assertion as to whether there are any men or not;
or it may stand for the conjunctive proposition "If
anything is a man, that thing is mortal, *and there
are men.*"   It will be sufficient for our purposes to
deal with propositions of the first kind—those
namely, which assert with regard to some two
properties, say Q and R, that there is nothing which
both does possess Q and does not possess R,
without asserting that anything does possess Q.
Such a proposition is obviously equivalent to the
assertion that *any* pair of propositions which
resembles the pair "AQ" and "AR," in respect
of the fact that one of them asserts of some particular

thing that it has Q and the other, of the same thing, that it has R, stand to one another in a certain relation : the relation, namely, which, in the case of "AQ" and "AR," can be expressed by saying that "It is not the case both that A has Q and that A has not got R." When we say "There is nothing which does possess Q and does not possess R" we are obviously saying something which is either identical with or logically equivalent to the proposition "In the case of every such pair of propositions it is not the case both that the one which asserts a particular thing to have Q is true, and that the one which asserts it to have R is false." We require, therefore, a short way of expressing the relation between two propositions p and q, which can be expressed by "It is not the case that p is true and q false." And I am going, quite arbitrarily to express this relation by writing

$$p * q$$

for "It is not the case that p is true and q false."

The relation in question is one which logicians have sometimes expressed by "p implies q." It is, for instance, the one which Mr. Russell in the *Principles of Mathematics* calls "material implication," and which he and Dr. Whitehead in *Principia Mathematica* call simply "implication." And if we do use "implication" to stand for this relation, we, of course, got the apparently paradoxical results that every false proposition implies every other proposition, both true and false, and that every true proposition implies every other true proposition : since it is quite clear that if p is false then, whatever q may be, "it is not the case that p is true and q false," and quite clear also, that if p and q are both true, then also "it is not the case that p is true and q false." And these results, it seems to me, appear to be paradoxical, solely because, if we use "implies" in any ordinary sense, they are quite certainly false.

Why logicians should have thus chosen to use the word "implies" as a name for a relation, for which it never is used by any one else, I do not know. It is partly, no doubt, because the relation for which they do use it—that expressed by saying "It is not the case that p is true and q false"—is one for which it is very important that they should have a short name, because it is a relation which is very fundamental and about which they need constantly to talk, while (so far as I can discover) it simply has no short name in ordinary life. And it is partly, perhaps, for a reason which leads us back to our present reason for giving some name to this relation. It is, in fact, natural to use "p implies q" to mean the same as "If p, then q." And though "If p then q" is hardly ever, if ever, used to mean the same as "It is not the case that p is true and q false"; yet the expression "If *anything* has Q, *it* has R" may, I think, be naturally used to express the proposition that, in the case of *every* pair of propositions which resembles the pair A Q and A R in respect of the fact that the first of the pair asserts of some particular thing that it has Q and the second, of the same thing, that it has R, it is not the case that the first is true and the second false. That is to say, if (as I propose to do) we express "It is not the case both that AQ is true and AR false" by

$$AQ * AR,$$

and if, further (on the analogy of the similar case with regard to "entails)," we express the proposition that of *every* pair of propositions which resemble A Q and A R in the respect just mentioned, it is true that the first has the relation * to the second by

$$xQ * xR$$

then, it *is* natural to express $xQ * xR$, by "If *anything* has Q, then *that thing* has R." And logicians may, I think, have falsely inferred that *since* it is natural to express "xQ $*$ xR" by "If *anything* has Q, then *that thing* has R," it *must* be natural to express "AQ $*$ AR" by "If AQ, then AR," and therefore also by "AQ implies AR." If this has been their reason for expressing "$p * q$" by "p implies q" then obviously their reason is a fallacy. And, whatever the reason may have been, it seems to me quite certain that "AQ $*$ AR" cannot be properly expressed either by "AQ implies AR" or by "If AQ, then AR," although "vQ $*$ xR" can be properly expressed by "If anything has Q, then that thing has R."

I am going, then, to express the universal pro-position, with regard to two particular properties Q and R, which asserts that "Whatever has Q, has R" or "If anything has Q, it has R," without asserting that anything has Q, by

$$x\text{Q} * x\text{R}$$

—a means of expressing it, which since we have adopted the convention that "$p * q$" is to mean the same as "It is not the case that p is true and q false," brings out the important fact that this proposition is either identical with or logically equivalent to the proposition that of *every* such pair of propositions as AQ and AR, it is true that it is not the case that the first is true and the second false. And having adopted this convention, we can now see how, in accordance with it, the proposition, with regard to a particular property P, that P is *internal* to *everything* which possesses it, is to be expressed. We saw that P is *internal* to A is to be expressed by

$$\overline{x\text{P}} \text{ entails } (\overline{x = \text{A}})$$

or by the logically equivalent proposition

$$(x = \text{A}) \text{ entails } x\text{P}$$

And we have now only to express the proposition that *anything* that has P, has also the property that P is *internal* to it. The required expression is

obviously as follows.   Just as "Anything that has
Q, has R " is to be expressed by

$$x\mathrm{Q} * x\mathrm{R}$$

so "Anything that has P, has also the property that
P is internal to it" will be expressed by

$$x\mathrm{P} * \{\overline{y\mathrm{P} \text{ entails } (\overline{y \quad x})}\}$$

or by

$$x\mathrm{P} * \{(\nu \quad x) \text{ entails } y\mathrm{P}\}.$$

We have thus got, in the case of any particular
property P, a means of expressing the proposition
that it is *internal* to *every* term that possesses it,
which is both short and brings out clearly the
notions that are involved in it.   And we do not
need, I think, any further special convention for
symbolising the proposition that *every* relational
property is internal to any term which possesses it
—the proposition, namely, which I called (2) above
(pp. 289, 290), and which on p. 287, I called the most
important consequence of the dogma of internal
relations.   We can express it simply enough as
follows :—

(2) = " What we assert of P when we say

$$x\mathrm{P} * \{\overline{y\mathrm{P} \text{ entails } (\overline{y=x})}\}$$

can be truly asserted of every relational property."

And now, for the purpose of comparing (2) with
(1), and seeing exactly what is involved in my
assertion that (2) does not follow from (1), let us try
to express (1) by means of the same conventions.

Let us first take the assertion with regard to a
particular thing A and a particular relational property
P that, from the proposition that A has P it *follows*
that nothing which has not got P is identical with
A.   This is an assertion which is quite certainly
true ; since, if anything which had not got P were
identical with A, it would follow that $\overline{\mathrm{AP}}$; and
from the proposition AP, it certainly *follows* that
$\overline{\mathrm{AP}}$ is false, and therefore also that " Something

which has not got P is identical with A " is false, or
that " Nothing which has not got P is identical with
A " is true. And this assertion, in accordance with
the conventions we have adopted, will be expressed
by

$$\text{AP entails } \{\overline{x\mathrm{P}} * \overline{(x = \mathrm{A})}\}$$

We want, next, in order to express (1), a means
of expressing with regard to a particular relational
property P, the assertion that, from the proposition,
with regard to *anything* whatever, that that thing
has got P, it *follows* that nothing which has not got
P is identical with the thing in question. This also
is an assertion which is quite certainly true ; since
it merely asserts (what is obviously true) that what

$$\text{AP entails } \{\overline{x\mathrm{P}} * \overline{(x = \mathrm{A})}\}$$

asserts of A, can be truly asserted of anything
whatever. And this assertion, in accordance with the
conventions we have adopted, will be expressed by

$$x\mathrm{P} \text{ entails } \{\overline{y\mathrm{P}} * \overline{(y = x)}\}.$$

The proposition, which I meant to call (1), but
which I expressed before rather clumsily, can now
be expressed by

(1) = " What we assert of P, when we say,

$$x\mathrm{P} \text{ entails } \{\overline{y\mathrm{P}} * \overline{(y = x)}\}$$

can be truly asserted of every relational property."

This is a proposition which is again quite certainly
true ; and, in order to compare it with (2), there is,
I think, no need to adopt any further convention for
expressing it, since the questions whether it is or
is not different from (2), and whether (2) does or
does not follow from it, will obviously depend on
the same questions with regard to the two propositions, with regard to the particular relational
property, P,

$$x\mathrm{P} \text{ entails } \{\overline{y\mathrm{P}} * \overline{(y = x)}\}$$

and

$$x\mathrm{P} * \{\overline{y\mathrm{P}} \text{ entails } \overline{(y = x)}\}$$

Now what I maintain with regard to (1) and (2) is that, whereas (1) is true, (2) is false. I maintain, that is to say, that the proposition "What we assert of P, when we say

$$xP * \{\overline{yP \text{ entails } (\overline{y=x})}\}.$$

is true of *every* relational property" is false, though I admit that what we here assert of P is true of *some* relational properties. Those of which it is true, I propose to call *internal* relational properties, those of which it is false *external* relational properties. The dogma of internal relations, on the other hand, implies that (2) is true; that is to say, that *every* relational property is *internal*, and that there are no *external* relational properties. And what I suggest is that the dogma of internal relations has been held only because (2) has been falsely thought to follow from (1).

And that (2) does not follow from (1), can, I think, be easily seen as follows. It can follow from (1) only if from any proposition of the form

$$p \text{ entails } (q * r)$$

there follows the corresponding proposition of the form

$$p * (q \text{ entails } r),$$

And that this is not the case can, I think, be easily seen by considering the following three propositions. Let p = "All the books on this shelf are blue," let q = "My copy of the *Principles of Mathematics* is a book on this shelf," and let r = "My copy of the *Principles of Mathematics* is blue." Now p here does absolutely *entail* $(q * r)$. That is to say, it absolutely follows from p that "My copy of the *Principles* is on this shelf," and "My copy of the *Principles* is *not* blue," are not, as a matter of fact, both true. But it by no means follows from this that $p * (q \text{ entails } r)$. For what this latter proposition means is "It is not the case both that p is true and that $(q \text{ entails } r)$ is false." And, as a matter of fact, (q entails r) is quite certainly false ; for from the proposition " My copy of the *Principles* is on this shelf " the proposition " My copy of the *Principles* is blue " does *not* follow. It is simply not the case that the second of these two propositions can be deduced from the first *by itself :* it is simply not the case that it stands to it in the relation in which it does stand to the conjunctive proposition " All the books on this shelf are blue *and* my copy of the *Principles* is on this shelf." This conjunctive proposition really does *entail* " My copy of the *Principles* is blue." But " My copy of the *Principles* is on this shelf," *by itself,* quite certainly does not entail " My copy of the Principles is blue." It is simply not the case that my copy of the Principles *couldn't* have been on this shelf without being blue. (q entails r) is, therefore, false. And hence "$p * (q$ entails r)," can only follow from "p entails ($q * r$)," if from this latter proposition $\bar{p}$ follows. But p quite certainly does not follow from this proposition : from the fact that ($q * r$) is deducible from p, it does not in the least follow that $\bar{p}$ is true. It is, therefore, clearly not the case that every proposition of the form

$$p \text{ entails } (q * r)$$

entails the corresponding proposition of the form

$$p * (q \text{ entails } r),$$

since we have found one particular proposition of the first form which does *not* entail the corresponding proposition of the second.

To maintain, therefore, that (2) follows from (1) is mere confusion. And one source of the confusion is, I think, pretty plain. (1) does allow you to assert that, if AP is true, then the proposition "$\overline{yP} * \{(y = A)\}$" *must* be true. What the "*must*" here expresses is merely that this proposition follows from AP, not that it is in itself a necessary proposition. But it is supposed, through

confusion, that what is asserted is that it is not
the case both that AP is true and that "$\overline{y\mathrm{P}}$ *
$(\overline{y=\mathrm{A}})$" is not, *in itself*, a necessary proposition ;
that is to say, it is supposed that what is asserted
is "AP * $\{\overline{y\mathrm{P}}$ entails $(\overline{y=\mathrm{A}})\}$"; since to say that
"$\overline{y\mathrm{P}}$ * $(\overline{y=\mathrm{A}})$" is, *in itself*, a necessary proposition
is the same thing as to say that "$\overline{y\mathrm{P}}$ entails
$(\overline{y=\mathrm{A}})$" is also true. In fact it seems to me
pretty plain that what is meant by saying of
propositions of the form "$x\mathrm{P}$ * $x\mathrm{Q}$" that they
are *necessary* (or "apodeictic") propositions, is
merely that the corresponding proposition of the
form "$x\mathrm{P}$ entails $x\mathrm{Q}$" is also true. "$x\mathrm{Q}$ *entails*
$x\mathrm{Q}$" is not *itself* a necessary proposition ; but, if
"$x\mathrm{P}$ entails $x\mathrm{Q}$" is *true*, then "$x\mathrm{P}$ * $x\mathrm{Q}$" is a
necessary proposition—and a necessary truth, since
no false propositions are necessary in themselves.
Thus what is meant by saying that " Whatever is
a right angle, is also an angle" is a necessary trnth,
is, so far as I can see, simply that the proposition
"(x is a right angle) entails (x is an angle)" is also
true. This seems to me to give what has, in fact,
been generally meant in philosophy by "necessary
truths," *e.g.* by Leibniz ; and to point out the
distinction between them and those true universal
propositions which are "mere matters of fact."
And if we want to extènd the meaning of the
name "necessary truth" in such a way that some
singular propositions may also be said to be
"necessary truths," we can, I think, easily do it
as follows. We can say that AP is itself a
necessary truth, if and only if the universal proposition" $(x=\mathrm{A})$ * $x\mathrm{P}$" (which, as we have seen,
follows from AP) is a necessary truth: that is to
say, if and only if $(x=\mathrm{A})$ entails $x\mathrm{P}$. With this
definition, what the dogma of internal relations
asserts is that in every case in which a given thing
actually has a given relational property, the fact

that it has that property is a necessary truth ; whereas what I am asserting is that, if the property in question is an " internal " property, then the fact in question will be a necessary truth, whereas if the property in question is "external," then the fact in question will be a mere " matter of fact."

So much for the distinction between (1) which is true, and (2), or the dogma of internal relations, which I hold to be false. But I said above, in passing, that my contention that (2) does not follow from (1), involves the rejection of certain views that have sometimes been held as to the meaning of "follows"; and I think it is worth while to say something about this.

It is obvious that the possibility of maintaining that (2) does not follow from (1), depends upon its being true that from "xP $*$ xQ" the proposition "xP entails xQ" does not follow. And this has sometimes been disputed, and is, I think, often not clearly seen.

To begin with, Mr. Russell, in the *Principles of Mathematics* (p. 34), treats the phrase "q can be deduced from p" as if it meant exactly the same thing as "$p * q$" or "p materially implies q"; and has repeated the same error elsewhere, *e.g.*, in *Philosophical Essays* (p. 166), where he is discussing what *he* calls the axiom of internal relations. And I am afraid a good many people have heen led to suppose that, since Mr. Russell has said this, it must be true. If it were true, then, of course, it would be impossible to distinguish between (1) and (2), and it would follow that, since (1) certainly is true, what I am calling the dogma of internal relations is true too. But I imagine that Mr. Russell himself would now be willing to admit that, so far from being true, the statement that "q can be deduced from p" means the same as "$p * q$" is simply an enormous

" howler " ; and I do not think I need spend any time in trying to show that it is so.

But it may be held that, though "p entails q" does not mean the same as "$p * q$," yet nevertheless from "$xP * xQ$" the proposition "xP entails xQ" does follow, for a somewhat more subtle reason ; and, if this were so, it would again follow that what I am calling the dogma of internal relations must be true. It may be held, namely, that though "AP entails AQ" does not mean simply "AP $*$ AQ" yet what it does mean is simply the conjunction "AP $*$ AQ *and* this proposition is an instance of a true formal implication" (the phrase "formal implication" being understood in Mr. Russell's sense, in which "$xP * xQ$" asserts a formal implication). This view as to what "AP entails AQ" means, has, for instance, if I understand him rightly, been asserted by Mr. O. Strachey in *Mind*, N.S., 93. And the same view has been frequently suggested (though I do not know that he has actually asserted it) by Mr. Russell himself (*e.g.*, *Principia Mathematica*, p. 21). If this view were true, then, though "xP entails xQ" would not be identical in meaning with "$xP * xQ$," yet it would follow from it ; since, if

$$xP * xQ$$

were true, then every particular assertion of the form AP $*$ AQ, would not only be true, but would be an instance of a true formal implication (namely "$xP * xQ$") and this, according to the proposed definition, is all that "xP entails xQ" asserts. If, therefore, it were true, it would again follow that all relational properties must be internal. But that this view also is untrue appears to me perfectly obvious. The proposition that I am in this room does "materially imply" that I am more than five years old, since both are true ;

and the assertion that it does is also an instance
of a true formal implication, since it is in fact
true that all the persons in this room are more than
five years old; but nothing appears to me more
obvious than that the second of these two propositions can *not* be deduced from the first—that
the kind of relation which holds between the
premisses and conclusion of a syllogism in
Barbara does *not* hold between them. To put
it in another way: it seems to me quite obvious
that the properties "being a person in this room"
and "being more than five years old" are not
related in the kind of way in which "being a
right angle" *is* related to "being an angle," and
which we express by saying that, in the case of
every term, the proposition that that term is an
angle can be deduced from the proposition that
it is a right angle.

These are the only two suggestions as to the
meaning of "p entails q" known to me, which,
if true, would yield the result that (2) does follow
from (1), and that therefore all relational properties
are internal; and both of these, it seems to me,
are obviously false. All other suggested meanings,
so far as I know, would leave it true that (2) does
not follow from (1), and therefore that I may
possibly be right in maintaining that some relational properties are external. It might, for
instance, be suggested that the last proposed
definition should be amended as follows—that
we should say: "p entails q" means "$p * q$ *and*
this proposition is an instance of a formal implication, which is not merely true but *self-evident*, like
the laws of Formal Logic." This proposed
definition would avoid the paradoxes involved in
Mr. Strachey's definition, since such true formal
implications as "all the persons in this room are
more than five years old" are certainly not self-

evident; and, so far as I. can see, it may state
something which is in fact true of p and q,
whenever and only when p entails q. I do not
myself think that it gives the *meaning* of "p entails
q," since the kind of relation which I see to hold
between the premisses and conclusion of a
syllogism seems to me to be one which is purely
" objective " in the sense that no psychological
term, such as is involved in the meaning of "self-
evident," is involved in its definition (if it has one).
I am not, however, concerned to dispute that some
such definition of "p entails q" as this may be
true.   Since it is evident that, even if it were, my
proposition that "xP entails xQ" does *not* follow
from "xP $*$ xQ," would still be true; and hence
also my contention that (2) does not follow
from (1).

So much by way of arguing that we are not
bound to hold that all relational properties are
internal in the particular sense, with which we are
now concerned, in which to say that they are means
that in every case in which a thing A has a relational
property, it follows from the proposition that a term
has *not* got that property that the term in question
is *other* than A.   But I have gone further and
asserted that some relational properties certainly
are *not* internal.   And in defence of this proposition
I do not know that I have anything to say but that
it seems to me evident in many cases that a term
which *has* a certain relational property *might* quite
well not have had it : that, for instance, from the
mere proposition that this is this, it by no means
follows that this has to other things all the relations
which it in fact has.   Everybody, of course, must
admit that if all the propositions which assert of it
that it has these properties, do in fact follow from
the proposition that this is this, we cannot see that
they do.   And so far as I can see, there is no

reason of any kind for asserting that they do, except the confusion which I have exposed. But it seems to me further that we can see in many cases that the proposition that this has that relation does *not* follow from the fact that it is this : that, for instance, the proposition that Edward VII was father of George V *is* a *mere* matter of fact.

I want now to return for a moment to that other meaning of "internal," (p. 286) in which to say that P is internal to A means not merely that anything which had not P would necessarily be *other* than A, but that it would necessarily be *qualitatively* different. I said that this was the meaning of "internal" in which the dogma of internal relations holds that all relational properties are "internal"; and that one of the most important consequences which followed from it, was that all relational properties are "internal" in the less extreme sense that we have just been considering. But, if I am not mistaken, there is another important consequence which also follows from it, namely, the Identity of Indiscernibles. For if it be true, in the case of every relational property, that any term which had not that property would necessarily be qualitatively different from any which had, it follows of course that, in the case of two terms one of which has a relational property, which the other has not the two are qualitatively different. But, from the proposition that x is other than y, it *does* follow that x has some relational property which y has not ; and hence, if the dogma of internal relations be true, it will follow that if x is other than y, x is always also qualitatively different from y, which is the principle of Identity of Indiscernibles. This is, of course, a further objection to the dogma of internal relations, since I think it is obvious that the principle of Identity of Indiscernibles is not true. Indeed, so far as I can see, the dogma of internal relations essentially consists in the joint assertion of two indefensible propositions : (1) the proposition that in the case of no relational property is it true of any term which has got that property, that it *might* not have had it and (2) the Identity of Indiscernibles.

I want, finally, to say something about the phrase which Mr. Russell uses in the *Philosophical Essays* to express the dogma of internal relations. He says it may be expressed in the form " Every relation is grounded in the natures of the related terms " (p. 160). And it can be easily seen, if the account which I have given be true, in what precise sense it does hold this. Mr. Russell is uncertain as to whether by "the nature" of a term is to be understood the term itself or something else. For my part it seems to me that by a term's nature is meant, not the term itself, but what may roughly be called all its qualities as distinguished from its relational properties. But whichever meaning we take, it will follow from what I have said, that the dogma of internal relations does imply that every relational property which a term has is, in a perfectly precise sense, *grounded* in its nature. It will follow that every such property is *grounded* in *the term*, in the sense that, in the case of every such property, it *follows* from the mere proposition that that term is that term that it has the property in question. And it will also follow that any such property is grounded in the qualities which the term has, in the sense, that if you take *all* the qualities which the term has, it will again follow in the case of each relational property, from the proposition that the term has *all* those qualities that it has the relational property in question ; since this is implied by the proposition that in the case of any such property, any term which had not had it would necessarily have been different in quality from the term in question. In both of these two senses, then, the dogma of internal relations does, I think, imply that every relational property is grounded in the nature of every term which possesses it; and in this sense that proposition is false. Yet it is worth noting, I think, that there is another sense of "grounded" in which it may quite well be true that every relational property *is* grounded in the nature of any term which possesses it. Namely that, in the case of every such property, the term in question has some quality *without* which it could not have had the property. In other words that the relational property *entails* some quality in the term, though no quality in the term *entails* the relational property.

THE NATURE OF MORAL PHILOSOPHY

I SHOULD like, if I can, to interest you to-night in one particular question about Moral Philosophy. It is a question which resembles most philosophical questions, in respect of the fact that philosophers are by no means agreed as to what is the right answer to it : some seem to be very strongly convinced that one answer is correct, while others are equally strongly convinced of the opposite. For my own part I do feel some doubt as to which answer is the right one, although, as you will see, I incline rather strongly to one of the two alternatives. I should like very much, if I could, to find some considerations which seemed to me absolutely convincing on the one side or the other ; for the question seems to me in itself to be an exceedingly interesting one.

I have said that the question is a question *about* Moral Philosophy ; and it seems to me in fact to be a very large and general question which affects the whole of Moral Philosophy. In asking it, we are doing no less than asking what it is that people are doing when they study Moral Philosophy at all : we are asking what sort of questions it is which it is the business of Moral Philosophy to discuss and try to find the right answer to. But I intend, for the sake of simplicity, to confine myself to asking it in two particular instances. Moral Philosophy has, in fact, to discuss a good many different ideas ; and though I think this same question may be raised with regard to them all, I intend to pick out two, which seem to me particularly fundamental, and to ask it with regard to them only.

My first business must be to explain what these two ideas are.

The name Moral Philosophy naturally suggests that what is meant is a department of philosophy which has something to do with morality. And we all understand roughly what is meant by morality. We are accustomed to the distinction between moral good and evil, on the one hand, and what is sometimes called physical good and evil on the other. We all make the distinction between a man's moral character, on the one hand, and his agreeableness or intellectual endowments, on the other. We feel that to accuse a man of immoral conduct is quite a different thing from accusing him merely of bad taste or bad manners, or from accusing him merely of stupidity or ignorance. And no less clearly we distinguish between the idea of being under a moral obligation to do a thing, and the idea of being merely under a legal obligation to do it. It is a common-place that the sphere of morality is much wider than the sphere of law : that we are morally bound to do and avoid many things, which are not enjoined or forbidden by the laws of our country ; and it is also sometimes held that, if a particular law is unjust or immoral, it may even be a moral duty to disobey it—that is to say that there may be a positive conflict between moral and legal obligation ; and the mere fact that this is held, whether truly or falsely, shows, at all events, that the one idea is quite distinct from the other.

The name Moral Philosophy, then, naturally suggests that it is a department of philosophy concerned with morality in this common sense.

And it is, in fact, true that one large department of Moral Philosophy is so concerned. But it would be a mistake to think that the whole subject is *only* concerned with morality. Another important department of it is, as I shall try to show, concerned with ideas which are *not* moral ideas, in this ordinary sense, though, no doubt, they may have something to do with them. And of the two ideas which I propose to pick out for discussion, while one of them is a moral idea, the other belongs to that department of Moral Philosophy, which is not concerned solely with morality, and is not, I think, properly speaking, a moral idea at all.

Let us begin with the one of the two, which is a moral idea.

The particular moral idea which I propose to pick out for discussion is the one which I have called above the idea of moral obligation—the idea of being morally bound to act in a particular way on a particular occasion. But what is, so far as I can see, precisely the same idea is also called by several other names. To say that I am under a moral obligation to do a certain thing is, I think, clearly to say the same thing as what we commonly express by saying that I ought to do it, or that it is my duty to do it. That is to say, the idea of moral obligation is identical with the idea of the moral "ought" and with the idea of duty. And it also seems at first sight as if we might make yet another identification.

The assertion that I ought to do a certain thing seems as if it meant much the same as the assertion that it would be wrong of me *not* to do the thing in question : at all events it is quite clear that, whenever it is my duty to do anything, it would be wrong of me not to do it, and that whenever it would be wrong of me to do anything, then it is my duty to refrain from doing it. In the case of these two ideas, the idea of what is wrong, and the idea of what is my duty or what I ought to do, different views may be taken as to whether the one is more fundamental than the other, or whether both are equally so; and on the question: *If* one of the two is more fundamdntal than the other, which of the two is so? Thus some people would say, that the idea of " wrong" is the more fundamental, and that the idea of "duty" is to be defined in terms of it: that, in fact, the statement "It is my duty to keep that promise" merely means "It would be wrong of me not to keep it"; and the statement " It is my duty not to tell a lie" merely means "It would be wrong of me to tell one." Others again would apparently say just the opposite: that duty is the more fundamental notion, and "wrong" is to be defined in terms of it. While others perhaps would hold that neither is more fundamental than the other; that both are equally fundamental, and that the statement "it would be wrong to do so and so" is only equivalent to, not identical in meaning with, "I ought not to do it." But whichever of these three views be the true one, there is, I think, no doubt whatever about the equivalence notion of the two ideas; and no doubt, therefore, that whatever answer be given to the question I am going to raise about the one, the same answer must be given to the corresponding question about the other.

The moral idea, then, which I propose to discuss, is the idea of duty or moral obligation, or, what comes to the same thing, the idea of what is wrong—morally wrong. Everybody would agree that this idea—or, to speak more accurately, one or both of these two ideas—is among the most fundamental of our moral ideas, whether or not they would admit that all others, for example the ideas of moral goodness, involve a reference to this one in their definition, or would hold that we have some others which are independent of it, and equally fundamental with it.

But there is a good deal of difficulty in getting clear as to what this idea of moral obligation itself is. Is there in fact only one idea which we call by this name ? Or is it possible that on some occasions when we say that so and so is a duty, we mean something different by this expression from what we do on others ? And that similarly when we say that so and so is morally wrong, we sometimes use this name "morally wrong " for one idea and sometimes for another ; so that one and the same thing may be "morally wrong" in one sense of the word, and yet *not* morally wrong in another ? I think, in fact, there are two different senses in which we use these terms ; and to point out the difference between them, will help to bring out clearly more the nature of each. And I think perhaps the difference can be brought out most clearly by considering the sort of moral rules with which we are all of us familiar.

Everybody knows that moral teachers are largely concerned in laying down moral rules, and in disputing the truth of rules which have been previously accepted. And moral rules seem to consist, to a very large extent, in assertions to the effect that it is always wrong to do certain actions or to refrain from doing certain others ; or (what comes to the same thing) that it is always your duty to refrain from certain actions, and positively to do certain others. The Ten Commandments for example, are instances of moral rules ; and most of them are examples of what are called negative rules—that is to say rules which assert merely that it is wrong to do certain positive actions, and therefore our duty to refrain from these actions ; instead of rules which assert of certain positive actions, that it is our duty to do them and therefore wrong to refrain from doing them. The fifth commandment, which tells us to honour

our father and mother, is apparently an exception ; it seems to be a positive rule. It is not, like the others, expressed in the negative form " Thou shalt *not* do so and so," and it is apparently really meant to assert that we ought to do certain positive actions, not merely that there are some positive action from which we ought to refrain. The difference between this one and the rest will thus serve as an example of the difference between positive and negative moral rules, a difference which is sometimes treated as if it were of great importance. And I do not wish to deny that there may be some important difference between seeing only that certain positive actions are wrong, and seeing also that, in certain cases, to refrain from doing certain actions is just as wrong as positively to do certain others. But this distinction between positive and negative rules is certainly of much less importance than another which is, I think, liable to be confused with it. So far as this distinction goes it is only a distinction between an assertion that it is wrong to do a positive action and an assertion that it is wrong to refrain from doing one : and each of these assertions is equivalent to one which asserts a duty—the first with an assertion that it is a duty to refrain, the second with an assertion that a positive action is a duty. But there is another distinction between some moral rules and others, which is of much greater import- ance than this one, and which does, I think, give a reason for thinking that the term "moral obliga- tion " is actually used in different senses on different occasions.

I have said that moral rules seem to consist, *to a large extent*, in assertions to the effect that it is always wrong to do certain *actions* or to refrain from doing certain others, or the equivalent assertions in terms of duty. But there is a large class of moral rules, with which we are all of us very familiar, which do not come under this definition. They are rules which are concerned not with our *actions*, in the natural sense of the word, but with our feelings, thoughts and desires. An illustration of this kind of rule can again be given from the Ten Commandments. Most of the ten, as we all know, are concerned merely with actions; but the tenth at least is clearly an exception. The tenth says "Thou shalt not covet thy neighbour's house, nor his wife, nor his servant, nor his ox, nor his ass, nor anything that is his," and, unless "covet" is merely a mistranslation of a word which stands for some kind of action, we plainly have here a rule which is concerned with our *feelings* and not with our actions. And one reason which makes the distinction between rules of this kind and rules concerned with actions important, is that our feelings are not, as a·rule, directly within the control of our will in the sense in which many of our actions are. I cannot, for instance, by any single act of will directly prevent from arising in my mind a desire for something that belongs to some one else, even if, when once the desire has arrived, I can by my will prevent its continuance; and even this last I can hardly do *directly* but only by forcing myself to attend to other considerations which may extinguish the desire. But though I thus cannot prevent myself altogether from coveting my neighbour's possessions, I can altogether prevent myself from stealing them. The action of stealing, and the feeling of covetousness, are clearly on a very different level in this respect. The action is *directly* within the control of my will, whereas the feeling is not. *If* I will not to take the thing (though of course some people may find a great difficulty in willing this) it does in general follow directly that I do not take it;

whereas, if I will not to desire it, it emphatically does not, even in general, follow directly that no desire for it will be there.   This distinction between the way in which our feelings and our actions are under the control of our wills is, I think, a very real one indeed ; we cannot help constantly recognising that it exists.   And it has an important bearing on the distinction between those moral rules which deal with actions and those which deal with feelings, for the following reason.   The philosopher Kant laid down a well-known proposition to the effect that " ought " implies " can " : that is to say, that it cannot be true that you " ought " to do a thing, unless it is true that you *could* do it, *if* you chose.   And as regards one of the senses in which we commonly use the words " ought " and " duty," I think this rule is plainly true.   When we say absolutely of ourselves or others, " I ought to do so and so " or " you ought to," we imply, I think, very often that the thing in question is a thing which we *could* do, *if* we chose ; though of course it may often be a thing which it is very difficult to choose to do.   Thus it is clear that I cannot truly say of anyone that he ought to do a certain thing, if it is a thing which it is physically impossible for him to do, however desirable it may be that the thing should be done.   And in this sense it is clear that it cannot be truly said of me that I ought not to have a certain feeling, or that I ought not to have had it, if it is a feeling which I could not, by any effort of my will, prevent myself from having.   The having or the prevention of a certain feeling is not, of course, strictly ever a *physical* impossibility, but it is very often impossible, in exactly the same sense, in which actions are physically impossible— that is to say that I could not possibly get it or prevent it, even if I would.   But this being so, it is plain that such a moral rule as that I ought not to covet my neighbour's possessions is, if it means to assert that I ought not, in that sense in which "ought" implies "can," a rule which cannot possibly be true. What it appears to assert is, absolutely universally, of *every* feeling of covetousness, that the feeling in question is one which the person who felt it *ought* not to have felt. But in fact a very large proportion of such feelings (I am inclined to say the vast majority) are feelings which the person who felt them could not have prevented feeling, if he would : they were beyond the control of his will. And hence it is quite emphatically *not* true that none of these feelings *ought* to have been felt, if we are using "ought" in the sense which implies that the person who felt them *could* have avoided them. So far from its being true that absolutely *none* of them ought to have been felt, this is only true of those among them, probably a small minority, which the person who felt them *could* have avoided feeling. If, therefore, moral rules with regard to feelings are to have a chance of being *nearly* true, we must understand the "ought" which occurs in them in some other sense. But with moral rules that refer to actions the case is very different. Take stealing for example. Here again what the Eighth Commandment appears to imply is that absolutely every theft which has ever occurred was an act which the agent ought not to have done ; and, if the "ought" is the one which implies "can," it implies, therefore, that every theft was an act which the agent, if he had chosen, could have avoided. And this statement that every theft which has been committed was an act which the thief, *if* he had so willed, could have avoided, though it may be doubted if it is absolutely universally true, is not a statement which is clearly absurd, like the statement that every covetous desire could have been avoided by the will of the person who felt it. It is probable that the vast majority of acts of theft have been acts which it was in the power of the thief to avoid, if he had willed to do so; whereas this is clearly not true of the vast majority of covetous desires. It is, therefore, quite possible that those who believe we ought never to steal are using "ought" in a sense which implies that stealing always *could* have been avoided; whereas it is I think quite certain that many of those who believe that we ought to avoid all covetous desires, do not believe for a moment that every covetous desire that has ever been felt was a desire which the person who felt it could have avoided feeling, if he had chosen. And yet they certainly do believe, in some sense or other, that no covetous desire *ought* ever to have been felt. The conclusion is, therefore, it seems to me, unavoidable that we do use "ought," the moral "ought," in two different senses; the one a sense in which to say that I ought to have done so and so does really imply that I could have done it, if I had chosen, and the other a sense in which it carries with it no such implication. I think perhaps the difference between the two can be expressed in this way. If we express the meaning of the first "ought," the one which does imply "can," by saying that "I ought to have done so and so" means "It actually *was* my duty to do it"; we can express the meaning of the second by saying that *e.g.* "I ought not to have felt so and so" means *not* "it *was* my duty to avoid that feeling," but "it *would* have been my duty to avoid it, *if* I had been able." And corresponding to these two meanings of "ought" we should, I think, probably distinguish two different sorts of moral rules, which though expressed in the same language, do in fact mean very different things. The one is a set of rules which assert (whether truly or falsely) that it always actually *is* a duty to do or to refrain from certain actions, and assert therefore that it always is in the power of the agent's will to do or to refrain from them ; whereas the other sort only assert that so and so *would* be a duty, if it *were* within our power, without at all asserting that it always is within our power.

We may, perhaps, give a name to the distinction I mean, by calling the first kind of rules—those which do assert that something actually is a duty—"rules of duty," and by calling the second kind—those which recommend or condemn something not in the control of our wills—"ideal rules" : choosing this latter name because they can be said to inculcate a moral "ideal"—something the attainment of which is not directly within the power of our wills. As a further example of the difference between ideal rules and rules of duty we may take the famous passage from the New Testament (Luke 6, 27) "Love your enemies, do good to them that hate you, bless them that curse you, pray for them that despitefully use you." Of these four rules, the three last may be rules of duty, because they refer to things which are plainly, as a rule, at least, in the power of your will ; but the first, if "love" be understood in its natural sense as referring to your feelings, is plainly only an "ideal" rule, since such feelings are obviously not directly under our own control, in the same way in which such actions as doing good to, blessing or praying for a person are so. To love certain people, or to feel no anger against them, is a thing which it is quite impossible to attain directly by will, or perhaps ever to attain completely at all. Whereas your behaviour towards them is a matter within your own control : even if you hate a person, or feel angry with him, you can so control yourself as not to do him harm, and even to confer benefits upon him. To do good to your enemies may, then, really be your duty ; but it cannot, in the strict sense, be your duty not to have evil feelings towards them : all that can possibly be true is that it would be your duty if you were able. Yet I think there can be no doubt that what Christ meant to condemn was the occurrence of such feelings altogether; and since, if what he meant to assert about them in condemning them, would have been certainly false, if he had meant to say that you *could* avoid ever feeling them, I think it is clear that what he meant to assert was *not* this, or not this only, but something else, which may quite possibly be true. That is to say, he was asserting an ideal rule, not merely a rule of duty.

It will be seen that this distinction which I am making coincides, roughly at all events, with the distinction which is often expressed as the distinction between rules which tell you what you ought to *be* and rules which tell you merely what you ought to *do*; or as the distinction between rules which are concerned with your inner life—with your thoughts and feelings—and those which are concerned only with your external actions. The rules which are concerned with what you ought to *be* or with your inner life are, for the most part at all events, "ideal" rules; while those which are concerned with what you ought to do or your external actions are very often, at least, rules of duty. And it is often said that one great difference between the New Testament and the Old is its comparatively greater insistence on "ideal" rules—upon a change of heart—as opposed to mere rules of duty. And that there is a comparatively greater insistence on ideal rules I do not wish to deny. But that there are plenty of ideal rules in the Old Testament too must not be forgotten. I have already given an example from the Ten Commandments : namely the rule which says you ought not to covet anything which belongs to your neighbour. And another is supplied by the Old Testament commandment, "Love thy neighbour as thyself," if by "love" is here meant a feeling which is not within our own control, and not merely that the Jew is to *help* other Jews by his external actions. Indeed, however great may be the difference between the Old Testament and the New in respect of comparative insistence on ideal rules rather than rules of duty, I am inclined to think that there is at least as great a difference, illustrated by this very rule, in another, quite different, respect—namely in the kind of rules, *both ideal and of duty*, which are insisted on. For whereas by "thy neighbour" in the Old Testament there is plainly meant only other Jews, and it is not conceived either that it is the duty of a Jew to help foreigners in general, or an ideal for him to love them; in the New Testament, where the same words are used, "my neighbour" plainly is meant to include all mankind. And this distinction between the view that beneficent action and benevolent feelings should be confined to those of our own nation, and the view that both should be extended equally to all mankind,—a distinction which has nothing to do with the distinction between being and doing, between inner and outer, but affects both equally—is, I am inclined to think, at least as important a difference between New Testament and Old, as the comparatively greater insistence on "ideal" rules. However, the point upon which I want at present to insist is the distinction between ideal rules and rules of duty. Both kinds are commonly included among moral rules, and, as my examples have shown, are often mentioned together as if no great difference were seen between them. What I want to insist on is that there is a great difference between them : that whereas rules of duty do directly assert of the idea of duty, in the sense in which to say that something is your duty implies that you *can* do it, that certain things are duties, the "ideal" rules do *not* assert this, but something different. Yet the "ideal" rules certainly do, in a sense, assert a "moral obligation." And hence we have to recognise that the phrase "moral obligation" is not merely a name for one idea only, but for two very different ideas; and the same will, of course, be true of the corresponding phrase "morally wrong."

When, therefore, I say that the idea of "moral obligation" is one of the fundamental ideas with which Moral Philosophy is concerned, I think we must admit that this one name really stands for two different ideas. But it does not matter for my purpose which of the two you take. Each of them is undoubtedly a moral idea, and whatever answer be given to the question we are going to raise about the one, will also certainly apply to the other.

But it is now time to turn to the other idea, with which I said that Moral Philosophy has been largely concerned, though it is not, strictly speaking, a moral idea, at all.

And I think, perhaps, a good way of bringing out what this idea is, is to refer to the Ethics of Aristotle. Everybody would admit that the fundamental idea, with which Aristotle's Ethics is concerned, is an idea which it is the business of Moral Philosophy to discuss; and yet I think it is quite plain that this idea is not a moral idea at all. Aristotle does not set out from the idea of moral obligation or duty (indeed throughout his treatise he only mentions this idea quite incidentally); nor even from the idea of moral goodness or moral excellence, though he has a good deal more to say about that; but from the idea of what he calls "the human good," or "good for man." He starts by raising the question what the good for man *is*, and his whole book is arranged in the form of giving a detailed answer to that question. And I think we can gather pretty well what the idea is, which he calls by this name, by considering what he says about it. There are two points, in particular, which he insists upon from the outset : first, that nothing can be good, in the sense he means, unless it is something which is worth having for its own sake, and not merely for the sake of something else ; it must be good *in itself* ; it must not, like wealth (to use one example which he gives) be worth having merely for the sake of what you can do with it ; it must be a thing which is worth having even if nothing further comes of it. And secondly (what partly covers the former, but also, I think, says something more) it must, he says, be something that is "self-sufficient" : something which, even if you had nothing else would make your life worth having. And further light is thrown upon his meaning when he comes to tell you what he thinks the good for man is : the good, he says, is "mental activity—where such activity is of an excellent kind, or, if there are several different kinds of excellent mental activity, that which has the best and most perfect kind of excellence ; and also " (he significantly adds) "mental activity which lasts through a sufficiently long life." The word which I have here translated "excellence" is what is commonly translated "virtue" ; but it does not mean quite the same as we mean by "virtue," and that in a very important respect. "Virtue" has come to mean exclusively *moral* excellence ; and if that were all Aristotle meant, you might think that what he means by "good" came very near being a moral idea. But it turns out that he includes among "excellences," intellectual excellence, and even that he thinks that the best and most perfect excellence of which he speaks is a particular kind of intellectual excellence, which no one would think of calling a moral quality, namely, the sort of excellence which makes a man a good philosopher. And as for the word which I have translated "activity," the meaning of this can be best brought out by mentioning the reason which Aristotle himself gives for saying that mere excellence itself is not (as some of the Greeks had said) the good for man. He says, truly enough, that a man may possess the greatest excellence—he may be a very excellent man—even when he is asleep, or is doing nothing; and he points out that the possession of excellence when you are asleep is not a thing that is desirable *for its own sake*—obviously only for the sake of the effects it may produce when you wake up. It is not therefore, he thinks, mere mental excellence, but the *active exercise* of mental excellence—the state of a man's mind, when he not only possesses excellent faculties, moral or intellectual, but is actively engaged in using them, which really constitutes the human good.

Now, when Aristotle talks of "the good for man," there is, I think, as my quotation is sufficient to show, a certain confusion in his mind between what is *good* for man and what is *best* for man. What he really holds is that *any* mental activity which exhibits excellence and is pleasurable is *a* good; and when he adds that, if there are many excellences, *the* good must be mental activity which exhibits the *best* of them, and that it must last through a sufficiently long life, he only means that this is necessary if a man is to get the *best* he can get, not that this is the *only* good he can get. And the idea which I wish to insist on is not, therefore, the idea of "*the* human good," but the more fundamental idea of "good"; the idea, with regard to which he holds that the working of our minds in some excellent fashion is the only good thing that any of us can possess; and the idea of which "better" is the comparative, when he says that mental activity which exhibits some sorts of excellence is *better* than mental activity which exhibits others, though both are good, and that excellent mental activity continued over a longer time is *better* than the same continued for a shorter. This idea of what is "good," in the sense in which Aristotle uses it in these cases, is an idea which we all of us constantly use, and which is certainly an idea which it is the business of Moral Philosophy to discuss, though it is not a moral idea. The main difficulty with regard to it is to distinguish it clearly from other senses in which we use the same word. For, when we say that a thing is "good," or one thing "better" than another, we by no means always mean that it is better in this sense. Often, when we call a thing good we are not attributing to it any characteristic which it would possess *if it existed quite alone*, and if nothing further were to come of it ; but are merely saying of it that it is a sort of thing from which other good things do in fact come, or which is such that, when accompanied by other things, the whole thus formed is "good" in Aristotle's sense, although, by itself, it is not. Thus a man may be "good," and his character may be "good," and yet neither are "good" in this fundamental sense, in which goodness is a characteristic which a thing would possess, if it existed quite alone. For, as Aristotle says, a good man may exist, and may have a good character, even when he is fast asleep ; and yet if there were nothing in the Universe but good men, with good characters, all fast asleep, there would be nothing in it which was "good" in the fundamental sense with which we are concerned. Thus "moral goodness," in the sense of good character, as distinguished from the actual working of a good character in various forms of mental activity, is certainly not "good" in the sense in which good means "good for its own sake." And even with regard to the actual exercise of certain forms of moral excellence, it seems to me that in estimating the value of such exercise relatively to other things, we are apt to take into account, not merely its intrinsic value—the sort of value which it would possess, if it existed quite alone—but also its effects : we rate it higher than we should do if we were considering only its intrinsic value, because we take into account the other good things which we know are apt to flow from it. Certain things which have intrinsic value are distinguished from others, by the fact that more good consequences are apt to flow from them ; and where this is the case, we are apt, I think, quite unjustly, to think that their intrinsic value must be higher too. One thing, I think, is clear about intrinsic value—goodness in Aristotle's sense— namely that it is only actual occurrences, actual states of things over a certain period of time—not such things as men, or characters, or material things, that can have any intrinsic value at all. But even this is not sufficient to distinguish intrinsic value clearly from other sorts of goodness : since even in the case of actual occurrences, we often call them good or bad for the sake of their effects or their promise of effects. Thus we all hope that the state of things in England, as a whole, will really be better some day than it has been in the past—that there will be progress and improvement : we hope, for instance, that, if we consider the whole of the lives lived in England during some year in the next century, it may turn out that the state of things, as a whole, during that year will be really better than it ever has been in any past year. And when we use "better" in this way—in the sense in which progress or improvement means a change to a *better* state of things—we are certainly thinking partly of a state of things which has a greater intrinsic value. And we certainly do not mean by improvement merely *moral* improvement. An improvement in moral conditions, other things being equal, may no doubt be a gain in intrinsic value; but we should certainly hold that, moral conditions being equal, there is yet room for improvement in other ways—in the diminution of misery and purely physical evils, for example. But in considering the degree of a real change for the better in intrinsic value, there is certainly danger of confusion between the degree in which the actual lives lived are really intrinsically better, and the degree in which there is improvement merely in the *means* for living a good life. If we want to estimate rightly what would constitute an intrinsic improvement in the state of things in our imagined year next century, and whether it would on the whole be really "good" at all, we have to consider what value it would have if it were to be the last year of life upon this planet; if the world were going to come to an end, as soon as it was over; and therefore to discount entirely all the promises it might contain of future goods. This criterion for distinguishing whether the kind of goodness which we are attributing to anything is really intrinsic value or not, the criterion which consists in considering whether it is a characteristic which the thing would possess, if it were to have absolutely no further consequences or accompaniments, seems to me to be one which it is very necessary to apply if we wish to distinguish clearly between different meanings of the word "good." And it is only the idea of what is good, where by "good" is meant a characteristic which has this mark, that I want now to consider.

The two ideas, then, with regard to which I want to raise a question, are first the moral idea of "moral obligation" or "duty," and secondly the non-moral idea of "good" in this special sense.

And the question with regard to them, which I want to raise, is this. With regard to both ideas many philosophers have thought and still think— not only *think*, but seem to be absolutely convinced, that when we apply them to anything—when we assert of any action that it ought not to have been done, or of any state of things that it was or would be good or better than another, then it *must* be the case that *all* that we are asserting of the thing or things in question is simply and solely that some person or set of persons actually does have, or has a tendency to have a certain sort of feeling towards the thing or things in question : that there is absolutely no more in it than this. While others seem to be convinced, no less strongly, that there *is* more in it than this : that when we judge that an action is a duty or is really wrong, we are *not* merely making a judgment to the effect that some person or set of persons, have, or tend to have a certain sort of feeling, when they witness or think of such actions, and that similarly when we judge that a certain state of things was or would be better than another, we are *not* merely making a judgment about the feelings which some person or set of persons would have, in witnessing or thinking of the two states of things, or in comparing them together. The question at issue between these two views is often expressed in other less clear forms. It is often expressed as the question whether the ideas of duty and of good or value, are or are not, "objective" ideas : as the problem as to the "objectivity" of duty and intrinsic value. The first set of philosophers would maintain that the notion of the "objectivity" of duty and of value is a mere chimera ; while the second would maintain that these ideas really are "objective." And others express it as the question whether the ideas of duty and of good are "absolute" or purely "relative :', whether there is any such thing as an absolute duty or an absolute good, or whether good and duty are purely relative to human feelings and desires. But both these ways of expressing it are, I think, apt to lead to confusion. And another even less clear way in which it is put is by asking the question : Is the assertion that such and such a thing is a duty, or has intrinsic value, ever *a dictate of reason?* But so far as I can gather, the question really at issue, and expressed in these obscure ways, is the one which I have tried to state. It is the question whether when we judge (whether truly or falsely) that an action is a duty or a state of things good, *all* that we are thinking about the action or the state of things in question, is simply and solely that we ourselves or others have or tend to have a certain feeling towards it when we contemplate or think of it. And the question seems to me to be of great interest, because, if this is all, then it is evident that all the ideas with which Moral Philosophy is concerned are merely psychological ideas ; and all moral rules, and statements as to what is intrinsically valuable, merely true or false psychological statements ; so that the whole of Moral Philosophy and Ethics will be merely departments of Psychology. Whereas, if the contrary is the case, then these two ideas of moral obligation and intrinsic value, will be no more purely psychological ideas than are the ideas of shape or size or number ; and Moral Philosophy will be concerned with characteristics of actions and feelings and states of affairs, which these actions and feelings and states of affairs would or might have possessed, even if human psychology had been quite different from what it is.

Which, then, of these two views is the true one ? Are these two ideas merely psychological ideas in the sense which I have tried to explain, or are they not ?

As I have said, I feel some doubts myself whether they are or not : it does not seem to me to be a matter to dogmatize upon. But I am strongly inclined to think that they are not merely psychological ; that Moral Philosophy and Ethics are not mere departments of Psychology. In favour of the view that the two ideas in question are merely psychological, there is, so far as I am aware, nothing whatever to be said, except that so many philosophers have been absolutely convinced that they are. None of them seem to me to have succeeded in bringing forward a single argument in favour of their view. And against the view that they are, there seem to me to be some quite definite arguments, though I am not satisfied that any of these arguments are absolutely conclusive. I will try to state briefly and clearly what seem to me the main arguments against the view that these are merely psychological ideas ; although, in doing so, I am faced with a certain difficulty. For though, as I have said, many philosophers are absolutely convinced, that "duty" and "good" do merely stand for psychological ideas, they are by no means agreed *what* the psychological ideas are for which they stand. Different philosophers have hit on very different ideas as being the ideas for which they stand; and this very fact that, if they *are* psychological ideas at all, it is so difficult to agree as to *what* ideas they are, seems to me in itself to be an argument against the view that they are so.

Let me take each of the two ideas separately, and try to exhibit the sort of objection there seems to be to the view that it is merely a psychological idea.

Take first the idea of moral obligation. What purely psychological assertion can I be making about an action, when I assert that it was "wrong," that it ought not to have been done ?

In this case, one view, which is in some ways the most plausible that can be taken, is that in every case I am merely making an assertion about my own psychology. But what assertion about my own psychology can I be making? Let us take as an example, the view of Prof. Westermarck, which is as plausible a view of this type as any that I know of. He holds that what I am judging when I judge an action to be wrong, is merely that it is of a sort which *tends* to excite in me a peculiar kind of feeling—the feeling of moral indignation or disapproval. He does not say that what I am judging is that the action in question *is actually* exciting this feeling in me. For it is obviously not true that, when I judge an action to be much more wrong than another, I am always actually feeling much indignation at the thought of either, or much more indignation at the thought of the one than at that of the other ; and it is inconceivable that I should constantly be making so great a mistake as to my own psychology, as to think that I am actually feeling great indignation when I am not. But he thinks it is plausible to say that I am making a judgment as to the *tendency* of such actions to excite indignation in me ; that, for instance, when I judge that one is much more wrong than the other, I am merely asserting the fact, taught me by my past experience, that, if I were to witness the two actions, under similar circumstances, I should feel a much more intense indignation at the one than at the other. [1]

---

[1] E Westermarck, *The Origin and Development of Moral Ideas*, Vol. I, pp. 4, 13, 17-18, 100-101. On p. 105, however, Westermarck suggests a view inconsistent with this one : namely that, when I judge an action to be wrong, I am not *merely* asserting that it has a tendency to excite moral indignation in me, but am also asserting that other people *would be* convinced that it has a tendency to excite moral indignation in them, if they "knew the act and all its attendant circumstances as well as [I do], and if, at the same time their emotions were as refined as [mine]."

But there is one very serious objection to such a view, which I think that those who take it are apt not fully to realise. If this view be true, then when I judge an action to be wrong, I am merely making a judgment about my own feelings towards it; and when you judge it to be wrong, you are merely making a judgment about yours. And hence the word "wrong" in my mouth, means something entirely different from what it does in yours; just as the word "I" in my mouth stands for an entirely different person from what it does in yours—in mine it stands for me, in yours it stands for you. That is to say when I judge of a given action that it was wrong, and you perhaps of the very same action that it was not, we are not in fact differing in opinion about it at all; any more than we are differing in opinion if I make the judgment "I came from Cambridge to-day" and you make the judgment "I did not come from Cambridge to-day." When I say "That was wrong" I am merely saying "That sort of action excites indignation in me, when I see it"; and when you say "No; it was not wrong" you are merely saying "It does not excite indignation in me, when I see it." And obviously both judgments may perfectly well be true together; just as my judgment that I did come from Cambridge to-day and yours that you did not, may perfectly well be true together. In other words, and this is what I want to insist on, if this view be true, then there is absolutely no such thing as a difference of opinion upon moral questions. If two persons think they differ in opinion on a moral question (and it certainly seems as if they sometimes *think* so), they are always, on this view, making a mistake, and a mistake so gross that it seems hardly possible that they should make it : a mistake as gross as that which would be involved in thinking that when you say "I did not come from Cambridge to-day" you are denying what I say when I say "I did." And this seems to me to be a very serious objection to the view. Don't people, in fact, sometimes really differ in opinion on a moral question? Certainly all appearances are in favour of the view that they do : and yet, if they do, that can only be if when I think a thing to be wrong, and you think it not to be wrong, I mean by "wrong" the very *same* characteristic which you mean, and am thinking that the action possesses this characteristic while you are thinking it does not. It must be the very *same* characteristic which we both mean ; it cannot be, as this view says it is, merely that I am thinking that it has to my feelings the very same relation, which you are thinking that it has not got to yours ; since, if this were all, then there would be no difference of opinion between us.

And this view that when we talk of wrong or duty, we are not merely, each of us, making a statement about the relation of the thing in question to our own feelings, may be reinforced by another consideration. It is commonly believed that some moral rules exhibit a *higher* morality than others : that, for instance a person who believes that it is our duty to do good to our enemies, has a higher moral belief, than one who believes that he has no such duty, but only a duty to do good to his friends or fellow-countrymen. And Westermarck himself believes that, some moral beliefs, "mark a stage of higher refinement in the evolution of the moral consciousness."* But what, on his view can be meant by saying that one moral belief is higher than another? If A believes that it is his duty to do good to his enemies and B believes that it is not, in what sense can A's belief be higher than B's? Not, on this view, in the sense that what A believes is true, and what B believes is not ; for what A is believing is merely that the idea of not doing good

* Ibid. p. 89.

to your enemies tends to excite in him a feeling of moral indignation, and what B believes is merely that it does not tend to excite this feeling in *him* : and both beliefs may perfectly well be true ; it may really be true that the same actions do excite the feeling in A, and that they don't in B. What then, could Westermarck mean by saying that A's morality is higher than B's ? So far as I can see, what, on his own views, he would have to mean is merely that he himself, Westermarck, shares A's morality and does not share B's : that it is true of him, as of A, that neglecting to do good to enemies excites his feelings of moral indignation and not true of him as it is of B, that it does *not* excite such feelings in him. In short he would have to say that what he means by calling A's morality the higher is merely "A's morality is *my* morality, and B's is not." But it seems to me quite clear that when we say one morality is higher than another, we do not merely mean that it is our own. We are not merely asserting that it has a certain relation to our own feelings, but are asserting, if I may say so, that the person who has it has a better moral taste than the person who has not. And whether or not this means merely, as I think, that what the one believes is true, and what the other believes is false, it is at all events inconsistent with the view that in all cases we are merely making a statement about our own feelings.

For these reasons it seems to me extremely difficult to believe that when we judge things to be wrong, each of us is merely making a judgment about *his own* psychology. But if not about our own, then about whose ? I have already said that the view that, if the judgment is merely a psychological one at all, it is a judgment about our own psychology, is in some ways more plausible than any other view. And I think we can now see that any other view is *not* plausible. The alternatives are that I should be making a judgment about the psychology of all mankind, or about that of some particular section of it. And that the first alternative is not true, is, I think, evident from the fact that, when I judge an action to be wrong, I may emphatically *not* believe that it is true of all mankind that they would regard it with feelings of moral disapproval. I may know perfectly well that some would not. Most philosophers, therefore, have not ventured to say that this is the judgment I am making; they say, for instance, that I am making a judgment about the feelings of the particular society to which I belong—about, for instance, the feelings of an impartial spectator in that society. But, if this view be taken, it is open to the same objections as the view that I am merely making a judgment about my own feelings. If we could say that every man, when he judges a thing to be wrong, was making a statement about the feelings of all mankind, then when A says " This is wrong " and B says " No, it isn't," they would really be differing in opinion, since A would be saying that all mankind feel in a certain way towards the action, and B would be saying that they don't. But if A is referring merely to his society and B to his, and their societies are different, then obviously they are not differing in opinion at all : it may perfectly well be true both that an impartial spectator in A's society does have a certain sort of feeling towards actions of the sort in question, and that an impartial spectator in B's does not. This view, therefore, implies that it is impossible for two men belonging to different societies ever to differ in opinion on a moral question. And this is a view which I find it almost as hard to accept as the view that *no* two men ever differ in opinion on one.

For these reasons I think there are serious

objections to the view that the idea of moral obligation is merely a psychological idea.

But now let us briefly consider the idea of
"good," in Aristotle's sense, or intrinsic value.

As regards this idea, there is again a difference
of opinion among those who hold that it is a
psychological idea, as to *what* idea it is. The
majority seem to hold that it is to be defined,
somehow, in terms of desire ; while others have
held that what we are judging when we judge that
one state of things is or would be intrinsically
better than another, is rather that the belief that
the one was going to be realized would, under
certain circumstances, give more pleasure to some
man or set of men, than the belief that the other
was. But the same objections seem to me to apply
whichever of these two views be taken.

Let us take desire. About whose desires am I
making a judgment, when I judge that one state of
things would be better than another ?

Here again, it may be said, first of all, that I am
merely making a judgment about my own. But in
this case the view that my judgment is merely
about my own psychology is, I think, exposed to
an obvious objection to which Westermarck's view
that my judgments of moral obligation are about
my own psychology was not exposed. The obvious
objection is that it is evidently not true that I do
in fact always desire more, what I judge to be
better : I may judge one state of things to be better
than another, even when I know perfectly well not
only that I don't desire it more, but that I have no
tendency to do so. It is a notorious fact that men's
strongest desires are, as a rule, for things in which
they themselves have some personal concern ; and
yet the fact that this is so, and that they know it to
be so, does not prevent them from judging that
changes, which would not affect them personally,

would constitute a very much greater improvement in the world's condition, than changes which would. For this reason alone the view that when I judge one state of things to be better than another I am merely making a judgment about my own psychology, must, I think, be given up : it is incredible that we should all be making such mistakes about our feelings, as, on this view, we should constantly be doing. And there is, of course, besides, the same objection, as applied in the case of moral obligation : namely that, if this view were true, no two men could ever differ in opinion as to which of two states was the better, whereas it appears that they certainly sometimes do differ in opinion on such an issue.

My judgment, then, is not merely a judgment about my own psychology : but, if so, about whose psychology is it a judgment? It cannot be a judgment that all men desire the one state more than the other ; because that would include the judgment that I myself do so, which, as we have seen, I often know to be false, even while I judge that the one state really is better. And it cannot, I think, be a judgment merely about the feelings or desires of an impartial spectator in my own society ; since that would involve the paradox that men belonging to different societies could never differ in opinion as to what was better. But we have here to consider an alternative, which did not arise in the case of moral obligation. It is a notorious fact that the satisfaction of some of our desires is incompatible with the satisfaction of others, and the satisfaction of those of some men with the satisfaction of those of others. And this fact has suggested to some philosophers that what we mean by saying that one state of things would be better than another, is merely that it is a state in which more of the desires, of those who were in it, would be satisfied at once, than would be the case with the other. But to this view the fundamental objection seems to me to be that whether the one state was better than the other would depend not merely upon the number of desires that were simultaneously satisfied in it, but upon what the desires were desires for. I can imagine a state of things in which all desires were satisfied, and yet can judge of it that it would not be so good as another in which some were left unsatisfied. And for this reason I cannot assent to the view that my judgment, that one state of things is better than another is merely a judgment about the psychology of the people concerned in it.

This is why I find it hard to believe that either the idea of moral obligation or the idea of intrinsic value is merely a psychological idea. It seems to me that Moral Philosophy cannot be merely a department of Psychology. But no doubt there may be arguments on the other side to which I have not done justice.

THE END

INDEX

International Library of Philosophy & Scientific Method

Editor: Ted Honderich

List of titles, page two

International Library of Psychology Philosophy & Scientific Method

Editor: C K Ogden

List of titles, page six

ROUTLEDGE AND KEGAN PAUL LTD
68 Carter Lane London EC4

International Library of Philosophy and Scientific Method
(*Demy 8vo*)

Allen, R. E. (Ed.)
Studies in Plato's Metaphysics
Contributors: J. L. Ackrill, R. E. Allen, R. S. Bluck, H. F. Cherniss, F. M. Cornford, R. C. Cross, P. T. Geach, R. Hackforth, W. F. Hicken, A. C. Lloyd, G. R. Morrow, G. E. L. Owen, G. Ryle, W. G. Runciman, G. Vlastos
464 pp. 1965. (2nd Impression 1967.) 70s.

Armstrong, D. M.
Perception and the Physical World
208 pp. 1961. (3rd Impression 1966.) 25s.
A Materialist Theory of the Mind
376 pp. 1967. (2nd Impression 1969.) 50s.

Bambrough, Renford (Ed.)
New Essays on Plato and Aristotle
Contributors: J. L. Ackrill, G. E. M. Anscombe, Renford Bambrough, R. M. Hare, D. M. MacKinnon, G. E. L. Owen, G. Ryle, G. Vlastos
184 pp. 1965. (2nd Impression 1967.) 28s.

Barry, Brian
Political Argument
382 pp. 1965. (3rd Impression 1968.) 50s.

Bird, Graham
Kant's Theory of Knowledge:
An Outline of One Central Argument in the *Critique of Pure Reason*
220 pp. 1962. (2nd Impression 1965.) 28s.

Brentano, Franz
The True and the Evident
Edited and narrated by Professor R. Chisholm
218 pp. 1965. 40s.
The Origin of Our Knowledge of Right and Wrong
Edited by Oskar Kraus. English edition edited by Roderick M. Chisholm. Translated by Roderick M. Chisholm and Elizabeth H. Schneewind
174 pp. 1969. 40s.

Broad, C. D.
Lectures on Physical Research
Incorporating the Perrott Lectures given in Cambridge University in 1959 and 1960
461 pp. 1962. (2nd Impression 1966.) 56s.

Crombie, I. M.
An Examination of Plato's Doctrine
1. Plato on Man and Society
408 pp. 1962. (3rd Impression 1969.) 42s.
II. Plato on Knowledge and Reality
583 pp. 1963. (2nd Impression 1967.) 63s.

2

International Library of Philosophy and Scientific Method

(*Demy 8vo*)

Day, John Patrick
Inductive Probability
352 pp. 1961. 40s.

Dretske, Fred I.
Seeing and Knowing
270 pp. 1969. 35s.

Ducasse, C. J.
Truth, Knowledge and Causation
263 pp. 1969. 50s.

Edel, Abraham
Method in Ethical Theory
379 pp. 1963. 32s.

Fann, K. T. (Ed.)
Symposium on J. L. Austin
Contributors: A. J. Ayer, Jonathan Bennett, Max Black, Stanley Cavell,
Walter Cerf, Roderick M. Chisholm, L. Jonathan Cohen, Roderick Firth, L. W.
Forguson, Mats Furberg, Stuart Hampshire, R. J. Hirst, C. G. New, P. H.
Nowell-Smith, David Pears, John Searle, Peter Strawson, Irving Thalberg,
J. O. Urmson, G. J. Warnock, Jon Wheatly, Alan White
512 pp. 1969.

Flew, Anthony
Hume's Philosophy of Belief
A Study of his First "Inquiry"
269 pp. 1961. (2nd Impression 1966.) 30s.

Fogelin, Robert J.
Evidence and Meaning
Studies in Analytical Philosophy
200 pp. 1967. 25s.

Gale, Richard
The Language of Time
256 pp. 1968. 40s.

Goldman, Lucien
The Hidden God
A Study of Tragic Vision in the *Pensées* of Pascal and the Tragedies of Racine.
Translated from the French by Philip Thody
424 pp. 1964. 70s.

Hamlyn, D. W.
Sensation and Perception
A History of the Philosophy of Perception
222 pp. 1961. (3rd Impression 1967.) 25s.

International Library of Philosophy and Scientific Method
(*Demy 8vo*)

Kemp, J.
Reason, Action and Morality
216 pp. 1964. 30s.

Körner, Stephan
Experience and Theory
An Essay in the Philosophy of Science
272 pp. 1966. (2nd Impression 1969.) 45s.

Lazerowitz, Morris
Studies in Metaphilosophy
276 pp. 1964. 35s.

Linsky, Leonard
Referring
152 pp. 1968. 35s.

MacIntosh, J. J., and Coval, S. C. (Ed.)
The Business of Reason
280 pp. 1969. 42s.

Merleau-Ponty, M.
Phenomenology of Perception
Translated from the French by Colin Smith
487 pp. 1962. (4th Impression 1967.) 56s.

Perelman, Chaim
The Idea of Justice and the Problem of Argument
Introduction by H. L. A. Hart. Translated from the French by John Petrie
224 pp. 1963. 28s.

Ross, Alf
Directives, Norms and their Logic
192 pp. 1967. 35s.

Schlesinger, G.
Method in the Physical Sciences
148 pp. 1963. 21s.

Sellars, W. F.
Science, Perception and Reality
374 pp. 1963. (2nd Impression 1966.) 50s.

Shwayder, D. S.
The Stratification of Behaviour
A System of Definitions Propounded and Defended
428 pp. 1965. 56s.

Skolimowski, Henryk
Polish Analytical Philosophy
288 pp. 1967. 40s.

International Library of Philosophy and Scientific Method
(*Demy 8vo*)

Smart, J. J. C.
Philosophy and Scientific Realism
168 pp. 1963. (3rd Impression 1967.) 25s.

Smythies, J. R. (Ed.)
Brain and Mind
Contributors: Lord Brain, John Beloff, C. J. Ducasse, Antony Flew, Hartwig
Kuhlenbeck, D. M. MacKay, H. H. Price, Anthony Quinton and J. R. Smythies
288 pp. 1965. 40s.

Science and E.S.P.
Contributors: Gilbert Murray, H. H. Price, Rosalind Heywood, Cyril Burt,
C. D. Broad, Francis Huxley and John Beloff
320 pp. about 40s.

Taylor, Charles
The Explanation of Behaviour
288 pp. 1964. (2nd Impression 1965.) 40s.

Williams, Bernard, and Montefiore, Alan
British Analytical Philosophy
352 pp. 1965. (2nd Impression 1967.) 45s.

Winch, Peter (Ed.)
Studies in the Philosophy of Wittgenstein
Contributors: Hidé Ishiguro, Rush Rhees, D. S. Shwayder, John W. Cook,
L. R. Reinhardt and Anthony Manser
224 pp. 1969.

Wittgenstein, Ludwig
Tractatus Logico-Philosophicus
The German text of the *Logisch-Philosophische Abhandlung* with a new
translation by D. F. Pears and B. F. McGuinness. Introduction by
Bertrand Russell
188 pp. 1961. (3rd Impression 1966.) 21s.

Wright, Georg Henrik Von
Norm and Action
A Logical Enquiry. The Gifford Lectures
232 pp. 1963. (2nd Impression 1964.) 32s.

The Varieties of Goodness
The Gifford Lectures
236 pp. 1963. (3rd Impression 1966.) 28s.

Zinkernagel, Peter
Conditions for Description
Translated from the Danish by Olaf Lindum
272 pp. 1962. 37s. 6d.

International Library of Psychology, Philosophy, and Scientific Method
(*Demy 8vo*)

PHILOSOPHY

Anton, John Peter
Aristotle's Theory of Contrariety
276 pp. 1957. 25s.

Black, Max
The Nature of Mathematics
A Critical Survey
242 pp. 1933. (5th Impression 1965.) 28s.

Bluck, R. S.
Plato's Phaedo
A Translation with Introduction, Notes and Appendices
226 pp. 1955. 21s.

Broad, C. D.
Five Types of Ethical Theory
322 pp. 1930. (9th Impression 1967.) 30s.

The Mind and Its Place in Nature
694 pp. 1925. (7th Impression 1962.) 70s. See also Lean, Martin

Buchler, Justus (Ed.)
The Philosophy of Peirce
Selected Writings
412 pp. 1940. (3rd Impression 1956.) 35s.

Burtt, E. A.
The Metaphysical Foundations of Modern Physical Science
A Historical and Critical Essay
364 pp. 2nd (revised) edition 1932. (5th Impression 1964.) 35s.

Carnap, Rudolf
The Logical Syntax of Language
Translated from the German by Amethe Smeaton
376 pp. 1937. (7th Impression 1967.) 40s.

Chwistek, Leon
The Limits of Science
Outline of Logic and of the Methodology of the Exact Sciences
With Introduction and Appendix by Helen Charlotte Brodie
414 pp. 2nd edition 1949. 32s.

Cornford, F. M.
Plato's Theory of Knowledge
The Theaetetus and Sophist of Plato
Translated with a running commentary
358 pp. 1935. (7th Impression 1967.) 28s.

International Library of Psychology, Philosophy, and Scientific Method
(*Demy 8vo*)

Cornford, F. M. (*continued*)
Plato's Cosmology
The Timaeus of Plato
Translated with a running commentary
402 pp. Frontispiece. 1937. (5th Impression 1966.) 45s.

Plato and Parmenides
Parmenides' *Way of Truth* and Plato's *Parmenides*
Translated with a running commentary
280 pp. 1939. (5th Impression 1964.) 32s.

Crawshay-Williams, Rupert
Methods and Criteria of Reasoning
An Inquiry into the Structure of Controversy
312 pp. 1957. 32s.

Fritz, Charles A.
Bertrand Russell's Construction of the External World
252 pp. 1952. 30s.

Hulme, T. E.
Speculations
Essays on Humanism and the Philosophy of Art
Edited by Herbert Read. Foreword and Frontispiece by Jacob Epstein
296 pp. 2nd edition 1936. (6th Impression 1965.) 40s.

Lazerowitz, Morris
The Structure of Metaphysics
With a Foreword by John Wisdom
262 pp. 1955. (2nd Impression 1963.) 30s.

Lodge, Rupert C.
Plato's Theory of Art
332 pp. 1953. 25s.

Mannheim, Karl
Ideology and Utopia
An Introduction to the Sociology of Knowledge
With a Preface by Louis Wirth. Translated from the German by Louis Wirth and Edward Shils
360 pp. 1954. (2nd Impression 1966.) 30s.

Moore, G. E.
Philosophical Studies
360 pp. 1922. (6th Impression 1965.) 35s. See also Ramsey, F. P.

International Library of Psychology, Philosophy, and Scientific Method
(*Demy 8vo*)

Ogden, C. K., and Richards, I. A.
The Meaning of Meaning
A Study of the Influence of Language upon Thought and of the Science of Symbolism
With supplementary essays by B. Malinowski and F. G. Crookshank
394 pp. 10th Edition 1949. (6th Impression 1967.) 32s.
See also Bentham, J.

Peirce, Charles, *see* Buchler, J.

Ramsey, Frank Plumpton
The Foundations of Mathematics and other Logical Essays
Edited by R. B. Braithwaite. Preface by G. E. Moore
318 pp. 1931. (4th Impression 1965.) 35s.

Richards, I. A.
Principles of Literary Criticism
312 pp. 2nd Edition. 1926. (17th Impression 1966.) 30s.

Mencius on the Mind. Experiments in Multiple Definition
190 pp. 1932. (2nd Impression 1964.) 28s.

Russell, Bertrand, *see* Fritz, C. A.; Lange, F. A.; Wittgenstein, L.

Smart, Ninian
Reasons and Faiths
An Investigation of Religious Discourse, Christian and Non-Christian
230 pp. 1958. (2nd Impression 1965.) 28s.

Vaihinger, H.
The Philosophy of As If
A System of the Theoretical, Practical and Religious Fictions of Mankind
Translated by C. K. Ogden
428 pp. 2nd edition 1935. (4th Impression 1965.) 45s.

Wittgenstein, Ludwig
Tractatus Logico-Philosophicus
With an Introduction by Bertrand Russell, F.R.S., German text with an English translation en regard
216 pp. 1922. (9th Impression 1962.) 21s.
For the Pears-McGuinness translation—*see page 5*

Wright, Georg Henrik von
Logical Studies
214 pp. 1957. (2nd Impression 1967.) 28s.

International Library of Psychology, Philosophy, and Scientific Method
(*Demy 8vo*)

Zeller, Eduard
Outlines of the History of Greek Philosophy
Revised by Dr. Wilhelm Nestle. Translated from the German by L. R. Palmer
248 pp. 13th (revised) edition 1931. (5th Impression 1963.) 28s.

PSYCHOLOGY

Adler, Alfred
The Practice and Theory of Individual Psychology
Translated by P. Radin
368 pp. 2nd (revised) edition 1929. (8th Impression 1964.) 30s.

Eng, Helga
The Psychology of Children's Drawings
From the First Stroke to the Coloured Drawing
240 pp. 8 colour plates. 139 figures. 2nd edition 1954. (3rd Impression 1966.) 40s.

Koffka, Kurt
The Growth of the Mind
An Introduction to Child-Psychology
Translated from the German by Robert Morris Ogden
456 pp 16 figures. 2nd edition (revised) 1928. (6th Impression 1965.) 45s.

Principles of Gestalt Psychology
740 pp. 112 figures. 39 tables. 1935. (5th Impression 1962.) 60s.

Malinowski, Bronislaw
Crime and Custom in Savage Society
152 pp. 6 plates. 1926. (8th Impression 1966.) 21s.

Sex and Repression in Savage Society
290 pp. 1927. (4th Impression 1953.) 30s.
See also Ogden, C. K.

Murphy, Gardner
An Historical Introduction to Modern Psychology
488 pp. 5th edition (revised) 1949. (6th Impression 1967.) 40s.

Paget, R.
Human Speech
Some Observations, Experiments, and Conclusions as to the Nature, Origin, Purpose and Possible Improvement of Human Speech
374 pp. 5 plates. 1930. (2nd Impression 1963.) 42s.

Petermann, Bruno
The Gestalt Theory and the Problem of Configuration
Translated from the German by Meyer Fortes
364 pp. 20 figures. 1932. (2nd Impression 1950.) 25s.

International Library of Psychology, Philosophy, and Scientific Method
(*Demy 8vo*)

Piaget, Jean
The Language and Thought of the Child
Preface by E. Claparède. Translated from the French by Marjorie Gabain
220 pp. 3rd edition (revised and enlarged) 1959. (3rd Impression 1966.) 30s.

Judgment and Reasoning in the Child
Translated from the French by Marjorie Warden
276 pp. 1928. (5th Impression 1969.) 30s.

The Child's Conception of the World
Translated from the French by Joan and Andrew Tomlinson
408 pp. 1929. (4th Impression 1964.) 40s.

The Child's Conception of Physical Causality
Translated from the French by Marjorie Gabain
(3rd Impression 1965.) 30s.

The Moral Judgment of the Child
Translated from the French by Marjorie Gabain
438 pp. 1932. (4th Impression 1965.) 35s.

The Psychology of Intelligence
Translated from the French by Malcolm Piercy and D. E. Berlyne
198 pp. 1950. (4th Impression 1964.) 18s.

The Child's Conception of Number
Translated from the French by C. Gattegno and F. M. Hodgson
266 pp. 1952. (3rd Impression 1964.) 25s.

The Origin of Intelligence in the Child
Translated from the French by Margaret Cook
448 pp. 1953. (2nd Impression 1966.) 42s.

The Child's Conception of Geometry
In collaboration with Bärbel Inhelder and Alina Szeminska. Translated from the French by E. A. Lunzer
428 pp. 1960. (2nd Impression 1966.) 45s.

Piaget, Jean, and Inhelder, Bärbel
The Child's Conception of Space
Translated from the French by F. J. Langdon and J. L. Lunzer
512 pp. 29 figures. 1956. (3rd Impression 1967.) 42s.

Roback, A. A.
The Psychology of Character
With a Survey of Personality in General
786 pp. 3rd edition (revised and enlarged 1952.) 50s.

Smythies, J. R.
Analysis of Perception
With a Preface by Sir Russell Brain, Bt.
162 pp. 1956. 21s.

International Library of Psychology, Philosophy, and Scientific Method
(*Demy 8vo*)

van der Hoop, J. H.
Character and the Unconscious
A Critical Exposition of the Psychology of Freud and Jung
Translated from the German by Elizabeth Trevelyan
240 pp. 1923. (2nd Impression 1950.) 20s.

Woodger, J. H.
Biological Principles
508 pp. 1929. (Re-issued with a new Introduction 1966.) 60s.

PRINTED BY HEADLEY BROTHERS LTD 109 KINGSWAY LONDON WC2 AND ASHFORD KENT